A GUIDE TO
Language Testing

DEVELOPMENT • EVALUATION • RESEARCH

Grant Henning

University of California, Los Angeles

HEINLE & HEINLE PUBLISHERS

A Division of Wadsworth, Inc.

Boston, Massachusetts 02116

Library of Congress Cataloging-in-Publication Data

Henning, Grant.
   A guide to language testing: development, evaluation, research.

Bibliography.
   1. English language—Study and teaching—Foreign speakers.   2. English language—Ability testing.
I. Title.
PE1128.A2H45   1987   428'.076   86-23446
ISBN 0-8384-2693-X

Production coordinator: Maeve A. Cullinane
Designer: Carson Design
Compositor: Publication Services, Inc.
Printer: McNaughton & Gunn, Inc.

Printed in the U.S.A.
63 22770

First printing: February 1987
8 10 9

Table of Contents

Dedication

To my students at UCLA and American University in Cairo, who inspired, criticized, and encouraged this work, and who proved to be the ultimate test.

Preface

The present volume began as a synthesis of class notes for an introductory course in testing offered to graduate students of Teaching English as a Second/ Foreign Language. Chapters one through seven formed the point of departure for a one-semester course, supplemented with popular tests, articles on current testing techniques, and student projects in item writing and item and test analysis. To address the advent of important new developments in measurement theory and practice, the work was expanded to include introductory information on item response theory, item banking, computer adaptive testing, and program evaluation. These current developments form the basis of the later material in the book, chapters eight through ten, and round out the volume to be a more complete guide to language test development, evaluation, and research.

The text is designed to meet the needs of teachers and teachers-in-training who are preparing to develop tests, maintain testing programs, or conduct research in the field of language pedagogy. In addition, many of the ideas presented here will generalize to a wider audience and a greater variety of applications. The reader should realize that, while few assumptions are made about prior exposure to measurement theory, the book progresses rapidly. The novice is cautioned against beginning in the middle of the text without comprehension of material presented in the earlier chapters. Familiarity with the rudiments of statistical concepts such as correlation, regression, frequency distributions, and hypothesis testing will be useful in several chapters treating statistical concepts. A working knowledge of elementary algebra is essential. Some rather technical material is introduced in the book, but bear in mind that mastery of these concepts and techniques is not required to become an effective practitioner in the field. Let each reader concentrate on those individually challenging matters that will be useful to him or her in application. While basic principles in measurement theory are discussed, this is essentially a "how-to" book, with focus on practical application.

This volume will be helpful for students, practitioners, and researchers. The exercises at the end of each chapter are meant to reinforce the concepts and techniques presented in the text. Answers to these exercises at the back of the book provide additional support for students. A glossary of technical terms is also provided. Instructors using this text will probably want to supplement it with sample tests, publications on current issues in testing, and computer printouts from existing test analysis software. These supplementary materials, readily available, will enhance the concrete, practical foundation of this text.

Grant Henning

A GUIDE TO
Language Testing

Chapter One

Language Measurement: Its Purposes, Its Types, Its Evaluation

There could be no science as we know it without measurement. Testing, including all forms of language testing, is one form of measurement. Just as we weigh potatoes, examine the length of a piece of cloth, count eggs in a carton, or check the volume of a container of milk, so we test reading comprehension or spelling to determine to what degree these abilities are present in the learner. There is potential for error when we weigh potatoes. For example, the scale might not work properly, or it may not be highly sensitive, so that we must settle for a rough estimate of the correct weight. Furthermore, the potatoes might be wet or dirty, or there might be a few yams mixed in. In either case our measurement may be inaccurate.

In the same way, tests of language abilities may be inaccurate or *unreliable* in the sense that repeated measures may give different results. These measures may also be *invalid* in the sense that other abilities are mixed in. Our test of reading comprehension on closer examination may turn out to be a test of grammar or vocabulary, or at least a few such items may be "mixed in." Tests, to be useful, must provide us with reliable and valid measurements for a variety of purposes.

1.1 Purposes of Language Tests

Diagnosis and Feedback

Perhaps the most common use of language tests, and educational tests in general, is to pinpoint strengths and weaknesses in the learned abilities of the student. We may discover through testing that a given student has excellent pronunciation and fluency of oral production in the language of interest, but that he or she has a low level of reading comprehension. On further testing, we might

1

find that a low or too highly specialized vocabulary is a major factor underlying low reading comprehension for this student. We might recommend suitable approaches for vocabulary expansion.

This use of tests, frequently termed *diagnostic testing*, is of value in that it provides critical information to the student, teacher, and administrator that should make the learning process more efficient. Without the specific information thus made available, the teacher might persist in teaching pronunciation to this student and fail entirely to address a weakness in the area of vocabulary.

Screening and Selection

Another important use of tests is to assist in the decision of who should be allowed to participate in a particular program of instruction. In every instructional program, teaching staff and facilities are limited in number and capacity. It becomes a matter of serious concern to find an equitable means of determining who should be allowed to participate when there are more applicants than spaces available. Such selection decisions are often made by determining who is most likely to benefit from instruction, to attain mastery of language or content area, or to become the most useful practitioner in the vocational domain represented.

Considerable controversy has arisen about the fairness of tests and the possibility that they may contain cultural or other biases against minority population groups when used for purposes of selection (Scheuneman, 1984). Some researchers seem to indicate that the effects of cultural bias, though present, may be small and actually in favor of minorities (Chen and Henning, 1985). However, most educators agree that some, though perhaps not entire, reliance must still be placed on test scores when screening or selection decisions are being made (Lennon, 1978). In order for such decisions to be fair, our tests must be accurate in the sense that they must provide information that is both reliable and valid.

In the area of language testing, a common screening instrument is termed an *aptitude test* (Carroll, 1965). It is used to predict the success or failure of students prospective in a language-learning program.

Placement

Closely related to the notions of diagnosis and selection is the concept of placement. In this case tests are used to identify a particular performance level of the student and to place him or her at an appropriate level of instruction. It follows that a given test may serve a variety of purposes; thus the UCLA *Placement Exam* may be used to assign students to levels as well as to screen students with extremely low English proficiency from participation in regular university instruction.

Program Evaluation

Another common use of tests, especially *achievement tests*, is to provide information about the effectiveness of programs of instruction. In this way the focus of evaluation is not the individual student so much as the actual program of instruction. Therefore, group mean or average scores are of greater interest in this case than are isolated scores of individual students. Often one or more *pretests* are administered to assess gross levels of student proficiency or "entry behavior" prior to instruction. Following the sequence of instruction, one or more *posttests* are administered to measure postinstructional levels of proficiency or "exit behavior." The differences between pretest and posttest scores for each student are referred to as *gain scores*.

Frequently in program evaluation tests or quizzes are administered at intervals throughout the course of instruction to measure "en route behavior." If the results of these tests are used to modify the program to better suit the needs of the students, this process is termed *formative evaluation*. The final exam or posttest is administered as part of the process of what is called *summative evaluation* (Scriven, 1967).

Sometimes language programs may be evaluated by comparing mean posttest or gain scores of one program or partial program with those of other programs. Whatever the method of evaluation, the importance of sensitive, reliable, and valid tests is obvious.

Providing Research Criteria

Language test scores often provide a standard of judgment in a variety of other research contexts. Comparisons of methods and techniques of instruction, textbooks, or audiovisual aids usually entail reference to test scores. Even examination of the structure of language itself or the physiological and psychological processes of language use may involve some form of measurement or testing. If we are to learn more about effective methods of teaching, strategies of learning, presentation of material for learning, or description of language and linguistic processes, greater effort will need to be expended in the development of suitable language tests.

Assessment of Attitudes and Sociopsychological Differences

Research indicates that only from one-quarter to one-half of the variability in academic achievement is explainable in terms of cognitive aptitude (Khan, 1969). The importance of noncognitive factors in achievement is seldom more evident that in the field of language learning, where the level of persistence and application needed for significant achievement is enormous. Attitudes toward the target language, its people, and their culture have been identified as important affective correlates of good language learning (Naiman et al., 1978; Saadalla, 1979). It follows that appropriate measures are needed to determine the nature, direction, and intensity of attitudes related to language acquisition.

Apart from attitudes, other variables such as cognitive style of the learner (Witkin et al., 1977), socioeconomic status and locus of control of the learner (Morcos, 1979), linguistic situational context (Henning, 1978), and ego-permeability of the learner (Henning, 1979) have been found to relate to levels of language achievement and/or strategies of language use. Each of these factors in

3

turn must be measured reliably and validly in order to permit rigorous scientific inquiry, description, explanation, and/or manipulation. This is offered as further evidence for the value of a wide variety of tests to serve a variety of important functions.

1.2 Types of Language Tests

Just as there are many purposes for which language tests are developed, so there are many types of language tests. As has been noted, some types of tests serve a variety of purposes while others are more restricted in their applicability. If we were to consider examples of every specific kind of test, or even of language tests alone, the remainder of this text might not suffice. There are, however, many important broad categories of tests that do permit more efficient description and explanation. Many of these categories stand in opposition to one another, but they are at the same time bipolar or multipolar in the sense that they describe two or more extremes located at the ends of the same continuum. Many of the categorizations are merely mental constructs to facilitate understanding. The fact that there are so many categories and that there is so much overlap seems to indicate that few of them are entirely adequate in and of themselves—particularly the broadest categories.

Objective vs. Subjective Tests

Usually these types of tests are distinguished on the basis of the manner in which they are scored. An objective test is said to be one that may be scored by comparing examinee responses with an established set of acceptable responses or *scoring key*. No particular knowledge or training in the examined content area is required on the part of the scorer. A common example would be a multiple-choice recognition test. Conversely a subjective test is said to require scoring by opinionated judgment, hopefully based on insight and expertise, on the part of the scorer. An example might be the scoring of free, written compositions for the presence of creativity in a situation where no operational definitions of creativity are provided and where there is only one rater. Many tests, such as cloze tests permitting all grammatically acceptable responses to systematic deletions from a context, lie somewhere between the extremes of objectivity and subjectivity (Oller, 1979). So-called subjective tests such as *free compositions* are frequently objectified in scoring through the use of precise *rating schedules* clearly specifying the kinds of errors to be quantified, or through the use of *multiple independent* raters.

Objectivity–subjectivity labels, however, are not always confined in their application to the manner in which tests are scored. These descriptions may be applied to the mode of item or *distractor* selection by the test developer, to the nature of the response elicited from the examinee, and to the use that is made of the results for any given individual. Often the term *subjective* is used to denote *unreliable* or *undependable*. The possibility of misunderstanding due to ambiguity suggests that objective–subjective labels for tests are of very limited utility.

Direct vs. Indirect Tests

It has been said that certain tests, such as ratings of language use in real and uncontrived communication situations, are testing language performance directly; whereas other tests, such as multiple-choice recognition tests, are obliquely or indirectly tapping true language performance and therefore are less valid for measuring language *proficiency*. Whether or not this observation is true, many language tests can be viewed as lying somewhere on a continuum from natural-situational to unnatural-contrived. Thus an *interview* may be thought of as more direct than a *cloze* test for measuring overall language proficiency. A contextualized vocabulary test may be thought more natural and direct than a synonym-matching test.

The issue of *test validity* is treated in greater detail in chapter seven. It should be noted here that the usefulness of tests should be decided on the basis of other criteria in addition to whether they are direct or natural. Sometimes *cost-efficiency*, and statistical measures of reliability or predictive validity, are more reflective of test utility than the naturalness or directness of the testing situation. Sometimes tests are explicitly designed to elicit and measure language behaviors that occur only rarely if at all in more direct situations. Sometimes most of the value of direct language data is lost through reductionism in the manner of scoring.

Discrete-Point vs. Integrative Tests

Another way of slicing the testing pie is to view tests as lying along a continuum from *discrete-point* to *integrative*. This distinction was originated by John B. Carroll (1961). Discrete-point tests, as a variety of diagnostic tests, are designed to measure knowledge or performance in very restricted areas of the target language. Thus a test of ability to use correctly the perfect tenses of English verbs or to supply correct prepositions in a cloze passage may be termed a discrete-point test. Integrative tests, on the other hand, are said to tap a greater variety of language abilities concurrently and therefore may have less diagnostic and remedial-guidance value and greater value in measuring overall language proficiency. Examples of integrative tests are random cloze, dictation, oral interviews, and oral imitation tasks.

Frequently an attempt is made to achieve the best of all possible worlds through the construction and use of *test batteries* comprised of discrete-point *subtests* for diagnostic purposes, but which provide a total score that is considered to reflect overall language proficiency. The comparative success or failure of such attempts can be determined empirically by reference to data from test administrations. Farhady (1979) presents evidence that "there are no statistically revealing differences" between discrete-point and integrative tests.

Here again, some tests defy such ready-made labels and may place the label advocates on the defensive. A test of listening comprehension may tap one of the four general language skills (i.e., listening, speaking, reading, and writing) in a discrete manner and thus have limited value as a measure of overall language proficiency. On the other hand, such a test may examine a broad range of lexis and diverse grammatical structures and in this way be said to be integrative.

Aptitude, Achievement, and Proficiency Tests

Aptitude tests are most often used to measure the suitability of a candidate for a specific program of instruction or a particular kind of employment. For this reason these tests are often used synonymously with intelligence tests or screening tests. A language aptitude test may be used to predict the likelihood of success of a candidate for instruction in a foreign language. The Modern Language Aptitude Test is a case in point (Carroll and Sapon, 1958). Frequently vocabulary tests are effective aptitude measures; perhaps because they correlate highly with intelligence and may reflect knowledge and interest in the content domain (Henning, 1978).

Achievement tests are used to measure the extent of learning in a prescribed content domain, often in accordance with explicitly stated objectives of a learning program. These tests may be used for program evaluation as well as for certification of learned competence. It follows that such tests normally come after a program of instruction and that the components or items of the tests are drawn from the content of instruction directly (Mehrens and Lehmann, 1975). If the purpose of achievement testing is to isolate learning deficiencies in the learner with the intention of remediation, such tests may also be termed *diagnostic tests*.

Proficiency tests are most often global measures of ability in a language or other content area. They are not necessarily developed or administered with reference to some previously experienced course of instruction. These measures are often used for placement or selection, and their relative merit lies in their ability to spread students out according to ability on a proficiency range within the desired area of learning.

It is important to note that the primary differences among these three kinds of tests are in the purposes they serve and the manner in which their content is chosen. Otherwise it is not uncommon to find individual items that are identical occurring in aptitude, achievement, and proficiency tests.

Criterion- or Domain-Referenced vs. Norm-Referenced or Standardized Tests

There is no essential difference between *criterion-referenced tests* and *domain-referenced tests*; but a third related category, *objectives-referenced tests*, differs from the other two in that items are selected to match objectives directly without reference to a prespecified domain of target behaviors (Hambleton et al., 1978). There exists such controversy between the advocates of *criterion-referenced tests* and the advocates of *norm-referenced tests* that greater description and explanation is warranted at this point (Ebel, 1978; Popham, 1978).

Characteristically criterion-referenced tests are devised before the instruction itself is designed. The test must match teaching objectives perfectly, so that any tendency of the teacher to "teach to the test" would be permissible in that attaining objectives would thereby be assured. A criterion or *cut-off* score is set in advance (usually 80 to 90 percent of the total possible score), and those who do not meet the criterion are required to repeat the course. Students are not evaluated by comparison with the achievement of other students, but instead their achievement is measured with respect to the degree of their learning or mastery of the prespecified content domain. Consistent with a view of teacher or environmental responsibility for learning, the failure of a large proportion of the learners to pass part or all of the test may result in the revision of the course or a change in method, content, instructor, or even the objectives themselves.

When applied to the field of language measurement, these tests have both strengths and weaknesses. On the positive side, the process of development of criterion-referenced tests is helpful in clarifying objectives. Such tests are useful in ascertaining the degree to which objectives have been met, both in ongoing, formative evaluation and in final, summative evaluation. The tests are useful when objectives are under constant revision. The tests are useful with small and/or unique groups for whom *norms* are not available. Test security is considered less of a problem since students know in advance the precise content domain for which they are held responsible on the test. For the same reason, students' test anxiety is believed to be reduced with this type of test.

On the negative side, the objectives measured are often too limited and restrictive, as is frequently true when objectives must be specified operationally. Another possible weakness is that scores are not referenced to a norm, so students typically are unable to compare their performance with that of other students in the population of interest. Bright students, who easily attain the criterion level of mastery, may not be encouraged to reach higher standards of excellence. The very establishing of the criterion or cut-off score is in practice usually highly arbitrary. Until rate of success is compared with other students in other years and other settings (as in norm-referenced testing), it is difficult to know what is meant by reaching criterion. Techniques of estimating reliability and validity of such tests are only beginning to be developed, so it is not yet clear in most cases whether a given test is reliable or valid in any scientific sense (Popham, 1978).

Norm-referenced or *standardized* tests are quite different from criterion-referenced tests in a number of respects; although, once again, some of the identical items may be used under certain conditions. By definition, a norm-referenced test must have been previously administered to a large sample of people from the target population (e.g., 1,000 or more). Acceptable standards of achievement can only be determined after the test has been developed and administered. Such standards are found by reference to the mean or average score of other students from the same population. Since a broad range or distribution of scores is desired, items at various levels of difficulty are purposely included. Commensurate with a felt need to discriminate between low-achieving and high-achieving students, and consistent with a philosophy of learner responsiblity for achievement, the failure of a large number of students to pass all or a given portion of the test usually results in the revision of the test itself rather than revision of the program or dismissal of the teacher.

For purposes of language testing and testing in general, norm-referenced tests also have specific strengths and weaknesses. Among the strengths is the fact that comparison can easily be made with the performance or achievement of a larger population of students. Also, since estimates of reliability and validity are provided, the degree of confidence one can place in the results is known. To the extent that the test is available, research using the test is readily replicable. Since acceptable standards of achievement are determined empirically with reference to the achievement of other students, it may be argued that such standards are fairer and less arbitrary than in the case of criterion-referenced tests. Since examinees are purposely spread on the widest possible range of performance results, it may be argued that more comparative information is provided about their abilities than in the case where only pass-fail information is available.

Norm-referenced tests are not without their share of weaknesses. Such tests are usually valid only with the population on which they have been normed. Norms change with time as the characteristics of the population change, and therefore such tests must be periodically renormed. Since such tests are usually developed independently of any particular course of instruction, it is difficult to match results perfectly with instructional objectives. Test security must be rigidly maintained. Debilitating test anxiety may actually be fostered by such tests. It has also been objected that, since focus is on the average score of the group, the test may be insensitive to fluctuations in the individual. This objection relates to the concept of reliability discussed in chapter six, and may be applied to criterion-referenced as well as to norm-referenced tests.

Speed Tests vs. Power Tests

A purely *speed test* is one in which the items are so easy that every person taking the test might be expected to get every item correct, given enough time. But sufficient time is not provided, so examinees are compared on their speed of performance rather than on knowledge alone. Conversely, *power tests* by definition are tests that allow sufficient time for every person to finish, but that contain such difficult items that few if any examinees are expected to get every item correct. Most tests fall somewhere between the two extremes since knowledge rather than speed is the primary focus, but time limits are enforced since weaker students may take unreasonable periods of time to finish.

Other Test Categories

The few salient test categories mentioned here are by no means exhaustive. Mention could be made of *examinations* vs. *quizzes, questionnaires*, and *rating schedules* treated more fully in chapter two. A distinction could be made between single-stage and multi-stage tests as is done in chapter nine. Contrast might be made between language skills tests and language feature tests, or between production and recognition tests.

At a still lower level of discrimination, mention will be made of cloze tests, dictation tests, multiple-choice tests, true/false tests, essay/composition/precis tests, memory-span tests, sentence completion tests, word-association tests, and imitation tests, not to mention tests of reading comprehension, listening comprehension,

8

grammar, spelling, auditory discrimination, oral production, listening recall, vocabulary recognition and production, and so on. Figure 1.1 provides a partial visual conceptualization of some types of language tests.

1.3   Evaluation of Tests

A consideration of the purposes and types of tests is only preparatory to the selection or development of tests for any stipulated use. When faced with the responsibility of having to choose or develop an appropriate test, we should take still further matters into consideration, including such information as *the purpose of the test, the characteristics of the examinees, the accuracy of measurement, the suitability of format and features of the test, the developmental sample, the availability of equivalent or equated forms, the nature of the scoring and reporting*

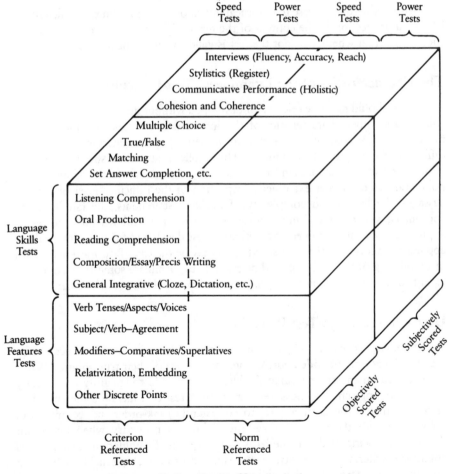

FIGURE 1.1   A partial conceptualization of types of language tests

9

of scores, the cost, the procurement, and *the political acceptability of the test.* These considerations are examined in greater detail in this section of the chapter.

The Purpose of the Test: Test Validity

Perhaps the first and foremost consideration in selecting or developing a test is, "What is the test going to be used for?" Most standardized tests come equipped with a manual reporting validity coefficients for a variety of uses. The overriding concern here is that the test should adequately measure what it is supposed to measure. Nearly all tests are valid for some purposes, but not for others. Validity is discussed in greater detail in chapter seven. At this point it is sufficient to ask ourselves, "Is the content of the test consistent with the stated goal for which the test is being administered?" If, for example, the test is to be an achievement test, accurately reflecting the extent to which students have mastered the content of instruction, the test itself must not contain material which was not encountered by the students in the program of instruction.

So, whether by recourse to empirical indicators such as validity coefficients or by careful inspection of the content of the test in light of its avowed purpose, we should ascertain whether or not the test is valid for its intended use.

The Characteristics of the Examinees: Test Difficulty

A test should never be selected or developed without due consideration of the abilities and other characteristics of the intended examinees. Violation of this principle is most commonly observed in the setting of examinations that are too difficult or too easy for the examinees. This implies that the test should usually be piloted or tried out beforehand on a sample of persons from the same general population as the target examinees. Inspection of the difficulty level of reading passages, the length and complexity of problem statements, the familiarity of vocabulary, and other common indicators can often reveal whether the test is appropriate for the examinees. Sometimes a test developed for use with adults is applied to children, or the reverse situation may be the case. By critical inspection or by piloting of the test, it should be possible to formulate some estimate of the extent to which the test is appropriate to the overall abilities of the examinees.

Decision Accuracy: Test Reliability

All examinations are subject to inaccuracies. The ultimate scores received by the examinees only provide approximate estimations of their true abilities. While some measurement error is unavoidable, it is possible to quantify and greatly minimize the presence of measurement error. A test that has little measurement error and that is found, therefore, to consistently rank-order the examinees in accordance with their comparative true abilities is necessary when important decisions are being made on the basis of test results. Examinations that serve as admissions criteria to university, for example, must be highly reliable; whereas a quiz used to determine which children may be rewarded with a longer recess

10

period between classes would be less critical. Both should be reliable, but the importance of the decision in the former situation requires greater reliability than the decision in the latter situation. When we consider the nature of the decision to be based upon the results of the test, and when we determine in this way the extent of reliability required, related decisions, such as the desired length of the test, can be made. Since test reliability is related to test length, so that longer tests tend to be more reliable than shorter tests, knowledge of the importance of the decision to be based on examination results can lead us to use tests with different numbers of test items. Here again, for standardized tests, accompanying test manuals usually report the reliability levels estimated. In developing our own tests, we should estimate test reliability using procedures described in chapter six.

Suitability of Format and Features: Test Applicability

The actual test format, or the way in which the author has chosen to measure the target ability, may be unfamiliar to the examinees. Consider the example of cloze tests rashly applied to students who have never encountered tests of this type or format before. Certainly their performance will suffer because of lack of familiarity with the test. Their results will not, however, be a reflection of their actual ability or underlying linguistic competence. Consider another example, that of a test that requires the use of tape-recording equipment which may not be available in the actual testing situation. The teacher or test administrator may choose to administer such a test using live voices; but, while such a decision may make the test applicable, it may also seriously alter the nature of what is being measured by the test. The actual choice of a test should be contingent on whether the format and features of the test may fairly be applied in the real testing situation.

The Developmental Sample: Test Relevance

Most widely used tests were originally normed on a sample of persons from a particular population. Often in the case of tests of English as a Foreign Language developed in the United States or in Britain, the developmental sample consisted of entering university students from diverse national backgrounds. One unfortunate artifact of this procedure is that such tests may turn out to be more reliable and valid as indicators of language proficiency for persons from one particular language background than for those from some other background. Or the tests may prove to be less reliable for persons from either of these hypothetical backgrounds than would tests of equivalent length developed exclusively for persons from one or the other of the language backgrounds. All this is by way of pointing out that it is important to consider the characteristics of the sample on which the test was developed before it is blindly applied to some sample from a different underlying population.

Just as we may speak of a sample of persons drawn from a particular population and the relevance of a test developed on that sample when it is applied to a sample from a different population, so we may speak of a sample of test items drawn from a particular domain of items and the relevance of this domain to

11

particular teaching objectives. It follows that certain items drawn from certain domains are irrelevant to certain specified objectives. By considering both the sample of persons on which a test was developed as well as the sample of items drawn from a particular domain, we can judge the relevance of a test for a particular group of people and for a particular stated objective. This notion is closely related to the concept of validity already mentioned. The distinction here is that focus is on the relevance of the examinees and/or the test item domain.

Availability of Equivalent or Equated Forms: Test Replicability

Usually when a testing program is established, there is the intention to test examinees repeatedly over a period of time. Perhaps there is a plan to administer a similar test at the end of every term of instruction or to apply the same test repeatedly as an admissions or a screening instrument. Such procedure is often necessary as an indication of trends over time, reflecting a need to compare examinees from one administration to another. In such circumstances one should choose or develop a test that has equivalent or equated forms, otherwise there will probably be a security breakdown and the test will no longer function as intended. Equivalent or alternative forms are so developed that a raw score on one is nearly equal in meaning to that on another, although the same exact items usually do not appear on the two tests. Equivalent forms are extremely difficult to develop and are therefore highly uncommon. More common are equated forms, which are accompanied by some conversion table whereby the test scores obtained on one form of the test may be converted or transformed to scores on the same scale as the scores of some other test. In this way scores may be compared across forms, even though the test forms may differ in length, difficulty, and so on. Procedures for developing equated or equivalent forms are discussed in chapter six.

Scoring and Reporting: Test Interpretability

Before a test is selected, developed, or applied, it is crucial to understand how the test is to be scored, how the scores are to be reported, and how the scores are to be interpreted. For some tests, such as the Foreign Service Institute Interview (Clark and Swinton, 1980), the scoring procedure requires extensive training and experience. Moreover, once scores have been recorded it is necessary to understand what the scores mean in order to communicate this information most efficiently to the examinees and to those who make decisions on the basis of scores obtained. In most instances a test whose scores can be more efficiently obtained, reported, and interpreted is to be preferred over a test that involves considerable delay, expense, and inconvenience for the same process.

Cost of Test Procurement, Administration, and Scoring: Test Economy

Ultimately one must consider the cost of the test. If the purchase price and the scoring services are too expensive, one may choose to develop one's own test. But if the cost of test development is greater than the cost of purchasing a test already available, then one should usually opt for the latter. Economics of the test should be considered in terms of the cost of purchase or development, the cost of administration including duplicating and proctoring, the cost of scoring, and the cost of reporting, storing, and interpreting scores.

Procurement of the Test: Test Availability

Many tests employed in research literature were developed for one particular research situation and are not available for public use. Even popular standardized tests are not made available to every person for every purpose. Many of these tests will be released only to qualified persons or institutions after special application is made and permission is granted. The point here is that, even after a test is determined to be appropriate in every way including price, there is the possibility that the test is not available. In beginning a testing program one should determine which tests are actually available before final decisions are made.

Political Considerations: Test Acceptability

From the start, any test advocated must satisfy societal and institutional demands. In developing English tests for the ministry of education of one foreign country, the test developers learned that certain constraints existed from the outset (Henning et al., 1981). Any test developed was required to have an equal number of production and recognition items; furthermore, objective tests of reading, writing, and grammar had to be included. In accordance with existing classroom space, no more than 5 percent of the students could be failed at any given level. Some innovation was possible within these existing constraints. It is incumbent on the test developer or test selector to determine what the limits of acceptability are. Many excellent tests have been abandoned simply because they were not found acceptable in the eyes of teachers, parents, or administrators. One does well at this point to involve a wide spectrum of the community in the decision-making process.

These ten considerations in the selecting and developing of appropriate tests are summarized in the checklist of Table 1.1. One may use such a checklist by rating any given test on a scale of one to ten for each of the ten criteria cited. In this way a perfect test would obtain a combined rating of 100. Rough comparisons may be made among tests competing for selection.

1.4 Summary

This chapter has been concerned with testing terminology; introductory notions of *reliability* and *validity* have been presented. Six specific purposes of tests have been described. Categories of tests have been introduced, including *objective/subjective, direct/indirect, discrete-point/integrative, aptitude/achievement/proficiency, criterion-referenced/norm-referenced, speed/power,* and so on.

TABLE 1.1 A checklist for test evaluation

Name of Test _____

Purpose Intended _____

Test Characteristic	Rating (0 = highly inadequate, 10 = highly adequate)
1. Validity	_____
2. Difficulty	_____
3. Reliability	_____
4. Applicability	_____
5. Relevance	_____
6. Replicability	_____
7. Interpretability	_____
8. Economy	_____
9. Availability	_____
10. Acceptability	_____
	_____ Total

Finally, a checklist was presented for the rating of the adequacy of any given test for any given purpose using ten essential criteria.

Exercises

1. Give examples of what is intended by the terms *reliable* and *valid*.
2. List five common purposes for language tests and explain the purpose for which you have used a test most recently—either as examiner or examinee.
3. Considering the test categories presented in this chapter, how would you label a cloze test* employing a passage with every fifth word deleted, beginning from a randomized starting point, which was scored in such a way that only the exact original words of the passage were accepted, and students' scores were compared with those of other students to determine comparative language proficiency?
4. List three kinds of language tests that are not explicitly named in this chapter. Provide a brief description.
5. Distinguish between objective and subjective tests.
6. Distinguish between direct and indirect tests.
7. Distinguish between norm-referenced and criterion-referenced tests.
8. Distinguish between discrete-point and integrative tests.
9. Distinguish between speed tests and power tests.
10. Choose a particular test and rate it for adequacy for a given purpose by reference to the checklist of Table 1.1

---

*For additional information on cloze testing, consult Oller (1979).

Chapter Two

Measurement Scales

2.1 What Is a Measurement Scale?

Scales are most frequently thought of in conjunction with the measurement of weight. But scales are also used in psychological and educational measurement. If tests are the instruments of measurement, scales are the gauges of measurement. The magnitude of any measurement is indicated by some point or position on a scale, expressed as a number or a score. In this chapter we consider a variety of measurement scales, their purposes, and their characteristics.

2.2 What Are the Major Categories of Measurement Scales?

Table 2.1 summarizes the four major types of psychological measurement scales and their purposes with examples of how they are used. Each category appears in the research literature of education, psychology, and linguistics. Indeed, it is only insofar as these metrics have been applied that such behavioral and social fields of study can be termed sciences.

Nominal Scales

Nominal scales are used with *nominal* or *categorical* variables such as sex, native-language background, eye color, preferred teaching method, or phrasal and nonphrasal verbs occurring in speech. Such variables are not normally thought of as existing along a continuum as a matter of degree. They are either present or not

TABLE 2.1   Types, purposes, and examples of measurement scales

Type of Scale	Purpose of Scale	Example of Scale Use
Nominal	Counting frequency	Finding number of native speakers of French in an ESL class
Ordinal	Rank ordering	Ranking students according to frequency of spelling errors
Interval	Measuring intervals	Determining z-scores or standard scores on a grammar test
Ratio	Measuring intervals from a real zero point	Measuring height, weight, speed, or absolute temperature

present in any given situation or observance, and the task of the examiner is to count or tally their frequencies of occurrence. While such frequency counts may be made within a given category, the results are not additive across categories. Combining five native speakers of Tagalog with six brown-eyed persons would give a meaningless result. But the five Tagalog speakers in one class may be combined with the six Tagalog speakers in another class to provide a measure of the total number of Tagalog speakers in both classes; i.e., eleven.

Nominal data are often elicited in demographic questionnaires or socio-linguistic surveys requiring background information about the examinees. Such information can be of vital importance, but care must be taken in the manner in which it is handled. Only a limited range of statistical tests can be applied or inferences drawn from such data. (Cf. Tuckman, 1972, p. 229, for a table of appropriate statistical tests.)

Ordinal Scales

Ordinal scales, as the name implies, are used to rank-order examinees accord-ing to ability on some ability continuum, or according to frequency of a particular kind of error in writing, for example. Reference to an ordinal scale will, for example, provide us with information about which student is first, second, or third in achievement of specified objectives in a program of language instruction. It will not, however, shed light on the distance or interval between examinees. Thus we would not know if student number one is vastly superior to student number two or just slightly more capable. More to the point, we could not be sure whether the amount of achievement superiority exhibited by the first student with regard to the second student was the same as that of the second student with reference to the third student. Nor could we infer that the achievement of the first student was twice as great as that of the second student. Here again, the range of appropriate statistical tests applicable to ordinal data is limited (Tuckman, 1978).

Since tests measure performance from which we infer competence, and since the raw scores of all language tests present us with ordinal data, we here confront a major problem of language measurement and all psychological measurement. When a student gets a score of 68 on a 100-item vocabulary test, chances are this student has greater knowledge of vocabulary than a student who scores 62 on the same test, provided the test is reliable. But since there is not a one-to-one correspondence between number of items passed and degree of underlying competence, still another student scoring 70 may be vastly more knowledgeable of vocabulary than the student scoring 68, while the student scoring 68 may be only slightly more knowledgeable than the student scoring 62 — even if the particular items missed are similar for each student. The problem is usually solved by conversion of our ordinal scale to an interval scale, described on pages 18–21. Several kinds of ordinal scales are illustrated in Table 2.2.

Raw Scores or Obtained Scores

A raw score is merely the total number of correct items, the total score possible minus the cumulative penalties due to errors, or the numerical score of the examinee before any transformations are performed on the test score data.

Ordinal Ratings

An ordinal rating is a rank assigned to the examinee designating his or her status on some ability continuum being measured, with respect to other examinees on the same continuum. An ordinal rating may be inferred from the raw scores in Table 2.2, or it may be determined by direct examiner observation as in an interview.

Percentage Scores

Percentage scores may be easily obtained by dividing the raw score by the total score possible and multiplying the result by 100. In the example of Table 2.2, the percentage score of the examinee with a raw score of 5 was determined as follows:

$$\tfrac{5}{25} \times 100 = 20$$

Since 25 was the maximum possible, that figure was divided into the obtained raw score, and the result was multiplied by 100. While percentage scores have the advantage of adjusting the range of possible scores to extend from zero to 100, they do not add information nor alter the ordinal nature of the score scale.

TABLE 2.2 Ordinal scales for a 25-point dictation subtest for six students

Raw Scores	0	5	12	12	14	19
Ordinal Ratings	5th	4th	3rd	3rd	2nd	1st
Percentage Scores	0	20	48	48	56	76
Cumulative Percentage Scores	16.67	33.33	50.00	66.67	83.33	100.0
Percentile Ranks	8.33	25.00	50.00	50.00	75.00	91.67

Cumulative Percentage Distribution Scores

Since there were only six students in Table 2.2, each student accounts for one-sixth or 16.67 percent of the total number of students. By the same standard, consideration of the lowest-scoring three students accounts for 50 percent of the total number of students, cumulatively. Having arranged the students from lowest to highest according to raw score, we could simply assign a cumulative frequency distribution score to each student in accordance with the percentage of students accounted for at each point on the raw score continuum. Not only does computation of these cumulative percentage distribution scores not improve on the ordinal nature of the raw score scale, it adds arbitrary distortion by assigning different values to examinees who obtained the same raw score and may have equal ability (e.g., the two students in Table 2.2 with a raw score of 12 obtained cumulative percentage distribution scores of 50 and 66.67).

Percentile Scores or Percentile Ranks

Percentile scores or ranks, also termed *centile ranks* (Guilford and Fruchter, 1973), are obtained by adding the number of examinees scoring below a given examinee of interest to one-half the number of examinees obtaining the same score as this examinee, dividing this total by the total number of examinees, and multiplying by 100. In Table 2.2 the percentile score of the examinee with a raw score of 19 was obtained as follows:

$$\frac{5 + 1/2}{6} \times 100 = 91.67$$

Although percentile scores are extremely useful and considerably more meaningful than the other ordinal scales mentioned, they still do not provide us with equal interval measurement of the underlying competence of interest to the examiner.

Interval Scales

Interval scales have the profound advantage of providing all of the information of ordinal scales in terms of rank-ordering students and in addition a meaningful interval for considering comparative distances between scores. Interval scales are usually obtained by the transformation or normalization of ordinal scales. Inferences are drawn about the metric of underlying competencies measured based on the size and shape of the distribution of raw scores obtained.

The most common interval scales include *z-score, T-score, normal distribution area proportion, stanine,* and *I.Q.-equivalent scales*. In Table 2.3 the raw scores from Table 2.2 have been transformed into a variety of interval scale scores.

Table 2.3 illustrates interval scale computations. Such transformations imply the existence of an underlying normal distribution and a much larger sample of examinee scores. More information on normal distributions is provided in chapter three.

TABLE 2.3   Interval scales for a 25-point dictation subtest for six students

Raw Scores	0	5	12	12	14	19
z-Scores	−1.86	−0.96	0.30	0.30	0.66	1.56
T-Scores	31.4	40.4	53.0	53.0	56.6	65.6
Normal Distribution Area Proportions	.03	.17	.62	.62	.74	.94
Stanines	1	3	6	6	6	8
I.Q.-Equivalents (WISC)	72.1	85.6	104.5	104.5	109.9	123.4

z-Scores

For the computation of z-scores from raw scores, the following formula is used:

$$z = \frac{X - M}{S} \qquad (2.1)$$

where,   X refers to the raw score of a given examinee
M indicates the mean or average score
s refers to the *standard deviation* of the raw score distribution

The concept of standard deviation and how it is derived mathematically is further explained in chapter three. For the distribution of raw scores in Table 2.3, the mean is found to be 10.33, and the standard deviation is 5.55. Therefore the z-score of the examinee with raw score zero is determined as follows:

$$z = \frac{0 - 10.33}{5.55} = -1.86$$

Normalized standard scores or *z-scores* equal the number of standard deviations the raw score is found away from the mean score. Thus a raw score equal to the mean of raw scores would have a z-score of zero. z-scores have a number of important functions in addition to that of providing us with this particular interval scale. These functions are discussed below and on pages 20, 21 and 59.

T-Scores

T-Scores are designed to have a mean of 50 and a standard deviation of 10. Thus one can use the following formula for the computation of T-scores from z-scores:

$$T = 10z + 50 \qquad (2.2)$$

In the case of the examinee in Table 2.3 with raw score zero, the T-score is determined as follows:

$$T = 10(-1.86) + 50 = 31.4$$

19

Normal Distribution Area Proportions

Normal distributions have the interesting characteristic that there is a direct correspondence between the magnitude of the z-scores and the area under the curve of the normal distribution. Since, as has been noted, a z-score of zero corresponds to the mean of the raw score distribution, we can readily see that it divides the distribution of scores in half. Therefore a z-score of zero can be said to be at a point above 50 percent of the test scores and below 50 percent of the test scores if the distribution is normal. In the same way, every z-score corresponds to a proportion of the distribution of scores represented. To obtain normal distribution area proportions, we have only to compare the z-scores and consult Table B in Appendix A for the corresponding proportions. Thus, for the student with raw score zero in Table 2.3, an area proportion of .03 was found in Table B to correspond to a z-score of -1.86.

Stanines

Stanine scores, derived from "standard nines," comprise a nine-point interval scale that is often used in test-score profiles, but is generally less sensitive and discriminating than T-scores for the same purpose. Stanine scores have a mean of 5 and a standard distribution of 1.96, except at the ends of the distribution where there is slight distortion due to the desire to maintain just nine points. To determine stanine score from any normal distribution of scores, one may assign a score of 1 to the lowest 4 percent, 2 to the next 7 percent, 3 to the next 12 percent, 4 to the next 17 percent, 5 to the next 20 percent, 6 to the next 17 percent, 7 to the next 12 percent, 8 to the next 7 percent, and 9 to the final 4 percent. Table 2.4 relates stanine scores to cumulative area proportions.

The stanine scores of Table 2.3 were easily obtained from Table 2.4 by taking the normal distribution area proportions of Table 2.3 and consulting Table 2.4 for the corresponding stanine scores.

I.Q.-Equivalent Scores

I.Q. or intelligence quotient scores are traditionally calculated by dividing *mental age* by *chronological age* and multiplying the result by 100. Thus an I.Q. score of 100 would be average in the sense that one's mental age is exactly equivalent to one's chronological age. I.Q. scores have fallen under disrepute for a number of reasons, including the fact that intelligence does not seem to follow a regular continuum throughout the possible range of scores and the fact that the

TABLE 2.4 Stanine scores and their normal distribution area cumulative proportions

Stanine Score	1	2	3	4	5	6	7	8	9
Normal Distribution Area Cumulative Proportion	0.00–.044	.046–.106	.107–.221	.222–.396	.397–.593	.594–.768	.769–.889	.890–.955	.956–1.00

standard deviation for I.Q. varies from test to test (usually from about 10 to 15). The Wechsler Intelligence Scale for Children (WISC) uses a standard deviation of 15 and is among the most widely used I.Q. measures. The same scale was used to compute the I.Q.-equivalent scores in Table 2.3. Such scores may be computed as follows:

$$\text{I.Q.-equivalent} = 15z + 100 \qquad (2.3)$$

In the case of the student with a dictation raw score of zero in Table 2.3, the I.Q.-equivalent was computed in the following way:

$$\text{I.Q.-equivalent} = 15(-1.86) + 100 = 72.1$$

Ratio Scales

Ratio scales provide all of the information of ordinal scales in that they permit a rank-ordering according to magnitude of score. Such scales also provide all the benefits of interval scales in that every point on the scale is equidistant from the adjacent points. But ratio scales have an added feature: they join all measures to a real or absolute zero-point on the scale. Ratio scales are more typical of the physical sciences than of language testing in the behavioral and social sciences. If we find someone is 2 meters tall, we know that that person is 2 meters above a known zero-point. Furthermore, we know that such a person is exactly twice as tall as a one-meter-high table. In the realm of testing language proficiency, even after converting raw scores to an interval scale, we do not know that someone with a T-score of 60 is twice as proficient as someone with a T-score of 30. Nor can we be sure that someone with a raw score or an interval score of zero has no proficiency whatever.

Measures of height, weight, absolute temperature, speed, and time from a known starting point are said to be on a ratio scale. Time and speed or rate are the only ratio scales commonly occurring in the field of language or psychological measurement.

2.3   Questionnaires and Attitude Scales

Frequently in research in the behavioral sciences we have need of questionnaires designed to elicit attitudes and opinions of respondents. Such questionnaires or rating schedules usually employ some sort of artificial scale in order to gather information in the most efficient way. In this section we consider various kinds of these artificial scales of use in the construction of our own questionnaires. Of particular interest will be demographic, Likert, semantic differential, and general rating scales.

Demographic Scales

As the name indicates, with demographic scales we are mostly concerned with the elicitation of vital statistics or other personal information about the respondents. Table 2.5 presents examples of demographic items about language background.

As you can see from Table 2.5, there are many ways to elicit demographic information, even about a topic so limited as language background. Item 1 in the table will be recognized as using a nominal scale, since respondents are required only to list the number of languages known. Item 2 makes use of a four-point scale in the rating of each language skill. Item 3 involves a percentage scale. The selection of the scale depends upon the exact nature of the information sought.

TABLE 2.5   Sample demographic items regarding language background

1. Indicate the number of languages in which you are fluent. _____

2. Rate your mastery in your first foreign language.
   Name of language: _____

Level of mastery:	Poor	Fair	Good	Excellent
Listening	_____	_____	_____	_____
Speaking	_____	_____	_____	_____
Reading	_____	_____	_____	_____
Writing	_____	_____	_____	_____

3. If you are bilingual or multilingual, list the languages you know and indicate the percentage of time you usually use each language in any given day or week.

Name of Language	Percent
_____	_____
_____	_____
_____	_____
_____	_____
	100% total

4. Opposite each language you know indicate (X) the degree of confidence you would feel in a normal speaking situation.

Name of Language	Highly Confident	Somewhat Confident	Not Confident
_____	_____	_____	_____
_____	_____	_____	_____
_____	_____	_____	_____
_____	_____	_____	_____

5. List the languages you know and opposite each indicate the number of years you have studied or used that language.

Name of Language	Number of Years
_____	_____
_____	_____
_____	_____
_____	_____

Demographic items are often used to elicit other information such as age, level of education, father's occupation, income, place of birth, etc.

The Likert Scale

The Likert scale is a popular five-point scale used most commonly to elicit extent of agreement with some statement of opinion or attitude. The respondent is usually requested to circle the number or letters coinciding with his or her reaction to a statement. Table 2.6 provides examples of Likert scale questions designed to elicit attitudes toward the French language and people.

Notice that each of the questionnaire items in Table 2.6 represents an opinion or attitude about the French people, language, or culture. Respondents indicate the extent of their agreement by circling the letters corresponding to their reaction to each statement.

Scoring the Likert Scale

For scoring purposes, the letters SA to SD must be converted to numbers 1 to 5 respectively. It is not particularly important whether the scale runs from 1 to 5 or from 5 to 1; that is, whether SA is coded as 1 or 5, so long as the significance of the direction is borne in mind and the same procedure is consistently applied. The point here is that the item scores are usually intended to be additive so as to form a total attitude score.

Avoiding the "Halo" Effect

Some respondents, particularly those who are favorably disposed toward the subject of a given questionnaire, may tend indiscriminately to supply positive ratings for every item without due consideration of the import of each individual item. To avoid this, it is usually necessary to include negatively stated items or items for which the direction is reversed. Item 3 of Table 2.6 is an illustration of this procedure. This item, unlike the other items, is negatively stated. This is done purposely to avoid a "halo" effect. There is, however, a cautionary reminder necessary here. When scoring Likert scales with mixed positive and negative items, we must remember to invert the negative item scales so that their scores will be additive with those of the other items of the questionnaire.

TABLE 2.6   Likert scale items for the measurement of attitudes toward French

Instructions: Indicate the extent of your agreement or disagreement with the following statements. Do this by circling the letters corresponding to your opinion about each statement. (SA – strongly agree; A – agree; U – undecided; D – disagree; SD – strongly disagree)

1. I like to have French people for friends.	SA	A	U	D	SD
2. The French language is beautiful to hear.	SA	A	U	D	SD
3. Culturally I have little to gain from learning French.	SA	A	U	D	SD

Use of Filler Items

Sometimes it is necessary to disguise the purpose of a questionnaire in order to ensure that item responses will be valid. If respondents realize that we are measuring dogmatism or locus of control, this awareness may color their responses. To avoid this possibility, it is sometimes necessary to include filler items. These are items unrelated to the purpose of the questionnaire which are randomly dispersed among the actual items to prevent respondents from inferring the purpose of the questionnaire. In scoring, these items are disregarded.

Checking Reliability and Validity

When devising questionnaires for use in research, it is always desirable to check on the reliability and validity of such instruments. Reliability and validity are discussed in chapters six and seven, and procedures for their estimation are presented there. Suffice to note at this point that one common method for estimating reliability of a questionnaire is simply to administer it more than one time to the same group of persons over a period of time to determine whether their responses are consistent or not. Validity might be partially established by correlating each item with the total score and discarding items with low or negative correlations. In this way we can be certain that the items are homogeneous, measuring the same underlying trait.

The Semantic Differential

The semantic differential, as devised by Osgood, Suci, and Tannenbaum (1957), is a common scale for eliciting affective responses. Typically this scale consists of seven-point ratings on a series of bipolar continua. A series of antonymous adjectives such as *good/bad*, *hot/cold*, *friendly/hostile* are placed at extreme ends of the seven-point scale. The task of the respondent is, for each item, to mark the point on the scale that most nearly approximates his or her affective response to the subject being rated. An example of a semantic differential questionnaire, which might be employed in the rating of the recorded speech of a person using a nonstandard dialect of English, is provided in Table 2.7.

Notice that, in this instance, the adjectives were carefully selected to be descriptive of people—we did not, for example, include *wet/dry* or *shiny/dull*. It is most irritating for respondents to provide ratings on highly irrelevant characteristics. Osgood and his colleagues determined through factor analytic techniques that the various bipolar dimensions may be reduced to three major categories: *good/bad*, *active/passive*, and *strong/weak*. These categories were restated as *evaluative*, *activity*, and *potency* dimensions. Adjective pairs for inclusion in our questionnaires may now be selected to represent these important dimensions.

Scoring the Semantic Differential

As in the case of the Likert scale, responses to the semantic differential must be translated into numerical form for analysis. The numbers 1 to 7, possibly ranging

TABLE 2.7   A sample semantic differential scale for measuring affective response to nonstandard dialects of English

Directions: Indicate your attitude toward the person whose voice you hear on the tape. Place a mark (X) at the point between each pair of opposing adjectives that best represents your opinion about the person. Please mark each line between pairs only once.

Example: naughty |—+—+—+—+—+—X—+—| nice

friendly		—+—+—+—+—+—+—+—		hostile
passive		—+—+—+—+—+—+—+—		active
intelligent		—+—+—+—+—+—+—+—		dull
weak		—+—+—+—+—+—+—+—		strong
educated		—+—+—+—+—+—+—+—		uneducated
small		—+—+—+—+—+—+—+—		large
quiet		—+—+—+—+—+—+—+—		loud
cowardly		—+—+—+—+—+—+—+—		brave
rich		—+—+—+—+—+—+—+—		poor
lazy		—+—+—+—+—+—+—+—		industrious

from the negative to the positive characteristic, are assigned to each rating in accordance with the position of the mark on the scale. Here again it may be observed that the positions of positive and negative characteristics have been randomly reversed in Table 2.7 to avoid any "halo" effect. Notice that, unlike the items of the Likert scale, the items of the semantic differential are not additive. Each bipolar dimension must be evaluated separately, unless the dimensions are aggregated statistically as with factor analytic techniques.

Research Applications of the Semantic Differential

Aside from ascertaining attitudes toward speakers of nonstandard dialects in sociolinguistic research, the semantic differential has been used to identify and measure cultural stereotypes, cultural empathy, and proximity to native-speaker attitudes on the part of nonnative speakers of second or foreign languages.

In any of the various applications of this scale, care must be exercised not to alienate the respondents by employing irrelevant adjectives or insisting on *forced-choice* alternatives. With forced-choice alternatives the researcher compels the respondents to express a preference, when no preference may exist. An example of this would occur if we devised a semantic differential with only six points on the scale. Respondents would be forced to show preference toward one end of the scale or the other since no middle ground is available. Sometimes such procedure is warranted, but often it is found to alienate respondents and lose their cooperation. Bear in mind that we are usually already requiring judgments based on very limited information. To add further unreasonable constraints may antagonize the respondents, who may in turn respond in some haphazard or antagonistic manner that will contaminate the data.

Other Common Rating Scales

A wide variety of other rating scales or schedules have been devised for a multitude of purposes. A few brief examples of such scales are presented in Table 2.8. Consider the various examples of rating schedules or scales presented in this table. Example A illustrates how we might elicit information about the frequency with which certain activities are performed.

Example B is a typical anxiety scale for use in gathering respondents' self-reports regarding level of test anxiety.

Example C presents a simple fluency rating scale. In this example a rating is supplied for the fluency of every person on the list. Of course, such a scale could be employed for rating a great number of other traits or characteristics.

Example D presents a typical classroom observation schedule. Each observed teacher activity is tallied in this way and an activity rate is calculated. The Flanders Interaction Process Analysis (1965) system works according to a similar principle. Only that method, called time-coding, seeks to ascertain what percentage of the time is devoted to each behavior. Also, student behaviors are coded in addition to teacher behaviors. Other coding systems, such as that of Bales (1950), seek to tabulate the frequency of occurrence of each behavior of each person in the classroom. This latter method is called sign-coding as opposed to the time-coding of the former method.

Example E illustrates another common five-point rating scale. In this instance it is being used to elicit ratings of teacher ability and performance.

Another use of an evaluative scale is illustrated in example F. Here we are shown a typical Need-Press Interaction questionnaire. This kind of questionnaire is used to determine whether the instructional press of an academic program is commensurate with the felt needs of the participants in the program. Areas of vast discrepancy between felt importance and perceived emphasis become the focus of curricular reform (cf. chapter ten).

2.4   Scale Transformations

Frequently it becomes desirable to transform one type of scale into another. Such transformations may be necessary in order to make test data more easily interpreted, such as when raw scores are transformed into percentage scores. Or the purpose of the transformation may be to make the test scores more amenable to computation and statistical manipulation, as when raw scores are transformed into normal distribution area proportions. Some statistical analyses assume a normal distribution of the data, and when the actual distribution fails to meet assumptions of normality, certain logarithmic, trigonometric, or other normalization transformations are applied. The two major categories of transformations are *linear* and *normalization*.

TABLE 2.8   Sample rating schedule items for various research purposes

A. Directions: Circle the number corresponding to the frequency with which you perform each activity on any average day.

	Never	Seldom	Occasionally	Often	Usually
1. Listen to English radio broadcasts	1	2	3	4	5
2. Read English books and newspapers	1	2	3	4	5

B. Directions: Indicate with a mark (X) approximately what percentage of the time you experience unpleasant anxiety when sitting for examinations.

5% _____   25% _____   50% _____   75% _____   100% _____

C. Directions: Rate each speaker for fluency on a scale of zero to 5. (0 = unable to speak; 1 = unable to complete utterances; 2 = halting, simple speech; 3 = frequent pauses to find words; 4 = fluent in most topics, hesitant in a few; 5 = as fluent as a native speaker)

Name	Fluency Rating
1. _____	0 1 2 3 4 5
2. _____	0 1 2 3 4 5
3. _____	0 1 2 3 4 5

D. Directions: Indicate the duration of the observation period in minutes. Then record each occurrence of the activities listed. Finally calculate the rate per hour of the occurrences by multiplying the total occurrences for each activity by 60 and dividing by the number of observation minutes, as in the formula:

$$\text{rate} = \text{occurrence} \times 60/\text{observation minutes}$$

Teacher's Name: _____   Class: _____   Date: _____
Observation Period: From: _____   To: _____   Minutes: _____

Teacher Activity	Frequency	Rate
Asks question _____		
States information _____		
Uses blackboard or other AV _____		
Praises student(s) _____		
Criticizes student(s) _____		
Corrects mistakes _____		
Presents assignment(s) _____		
Responds to question _____		
Personal interaction _____		
Listening and observing _____		

E. Directions: Underline your rating of your teacher on each of the following qualities:

1. Knowledge of the subject:

Below Average   Average   Good   Very Good   Outstanding

2. Clarity of explanation:

Below Average   Average   Good   Very Good   Outstanding

F. Directions: Rate each of the following components of the program in regard to importance and emphasis. First, indicate its importance to your future success. Next, indicate how much emphasis was given to it in the program. (1 = none at all; 2 = a little; 3 = moderate; 4 = above average; 5 = very great)

Component	Importance	Emphasis
Pronunciation skills	1 2 3 4 5	1 2 3 4 5
Reading skills	1 2 3 4 5	1 2 3 4 5
Spelling skills	1 2 3 4 5	1 2 3 4 5

Linear Transformations

The simplest transformations are termed linear transformations, since they entail altering each score in the distribution by a constant. One example of a linear transformation is the conversion of raw scores to percentage scores. This procedure involves the formula,

$$Y = X \, \frac{100}{C} \qquad (2.4)$$

where, Y = the percentage score
X = the raw score (i.e., number of correct items)
C = the total number of items (i.e., highest possible score)

Here C and 100 are constants applied to X in order to determine Y. A straight line could be drawn on a graph showing every possible Y score corresponding to every given X score.

Another common linear transformation formula, this one used in regression and prediction in chapter five, is,

$$Y = a + bX \qquad (5.4)$$

Here a and b are constants used to determine a predicted value of Y for any value of X.

Normalization Transformations

Normalization transformations are used to standardize or normalize a distribution of scores. The most common of these is the z-score transformation discussed earlier in the chapter. By means of this transformation, ordinal data is changed to interval data, and scores are anchored to a norm or a group performance mean as a point of reference. Other interval scales discussed in the chapter also accomplish this end. Size and representativeness of the reference group must always be considered when one is making decisions based on normalized scores.

Fisher Z Transformation

One important transformation is named the Fisher Z transformation after its originator. This is quite distinct from z-score transformations discussed earlier. Fisher Z is used to transform correlation coefficients from a distorted ordinal to a normal interval scale so that arithmetic computations may be done using the coefficients. For example, if one wished to compare the ratio of two coefficients to that of two other coefficients as in the formula below, it would be appropriate to transform the coefficients first, then perform the arithmetic, and finally convert back to correlation coefficients.

$$X = \frac{r_1}{r_2} - \frac{r_3}{r_4}$$

The distortion that results from arithmetic operations involving nontransformed correlation coefficients is negligible when the coefficients are of mid-range magnitude, but becomes great as the coefficients approach unity.

28

The formula for the Fisher Z transformation is given below.

$$Z = \tfrac{1}{2} \ln (1+r) - \tfrac{1}{2} \ln (1-r) \tag{2.5}$$

where, Z = the value of Fisher Z
   r = the value of the correlation coefficient
   ln = the natural or Napierian logarithm

One may transform the coefficient using this formula and making use of a table of natural logarithms, or one may consult Table C in Appendix A where the transformation has been calculated for every value of the correlation coefficient.

2.5 Summary

This chapter has presented important information about scaling in measurement. The four major scales (i.e., *nominal, ordinal, interval,* and *ratio*) were presented along with numerous examples of each and indications of purpose and methods of computation. Artificial scales used in the construction of questionnaires were presented with examples, including the Likert scale, the semantic differential, and other common rating schedules and scales. Finally, examples were given of scale transformations, including linear, normalization, and Fisher Z transformations.

Exercises

1. Name the four major measurement scales and their purposes, giving an example of each.
2. What is the main advantage of interval scales over ordinal scales in measurement?
3. Identify the scales represented by the following kinds of data:
   Raw scores from a listening comprehension test
   Adjectives on a word-association test
   Percentile scores from a spelling test
   Speed of note-taking in words per minute
   I.Q.-equivalent scores on a vocabulary test
   z-scores on the TOEFL
   The number of instrumentally motivated students in class
4. Compare and contrast the Likert scale and the semantic differential.
5. Name and give an example of two major scale transformations.
6. Given the following raw score distribution on a spelling test of 25 items, calculate (a) ordinal ratings, (b) percentage scores, (c) percentile ranks: 6, 9, 11, 12, 12, 13, 15, 17, 17, 21.
7. If you administered a multiple-choice test of phrasal verb usage to a class of ten students and got the following distribution of scores: 11, 13, 16, 16, 18, 20, 20, 25, 27, 29, what would be the corresponding z-scores, T-scores, and normal distribution area proportions if the standard deviation is 5.95?

8. If you administered a test of idioms to a class of 15 students and got the following raw score distribution: 10, 12, 15, 20, 21, 21, 21, 23, 26, 29, 32, 37, 38, 41, 42, what would be the corresponding stanines, and I.Q.(WISC)-equivalents, if the standard deviation is 10.29?

9. What score would a questionnaire respondent receive if she or he obtained a raw score of 36 on a ten-item Likert scale questionnaire assessing degree of motivation, and you performed a linear transformation to a percentage score?

10. If you performed a Need-Press Interaction analysis of an academic program, and students and faculty reported *mean importance* and *mean emphasis* of vocabulary expansion as 4.5 and 2.3 respectively, what would you probably conclude about the program curriculum?

Chapter Three

Data Management in Measurement

In measuring achievement or proficiency in the use of language, we usually administer one or more tests to one or more students. What we can infer about student competence or ability depends on (1) what we can discover about the characteristics of the testing instrument(s) and (2) what we can interpret as the significance of performance scores on the instrument(s). These two important steps in measurement require facility in the management of scores of the test and its component items. Accordingly, this chapter is devoted to the management of test data.

3.1 Scoring

Tests with Items

Most language tests are composites of individual items, and scores on these tests are obtained by summing the correct answers. Each item response is scored as either correct or incorrect. Typical varieties of these tests include *multiple-choice, true/false, cloze completion,* or *question-answer* types of items. Because it is possible to guess the correct answers with multiple-choice or true/false type items, correction-for-guessing procedure is often used. The net result is that measurement error due to guessing is reduced, and test scores become slightly more reliable. One common formula applied in correction-for-guessing procedure is the following:

$$S_{cg} = N_r - \frac{N_{wa}}{N_o - 1} \qquad (3.1)$$

where, S_{cg} = the score corrected for guessing
 N_r = the number of right item responses

N_{wa} = the number of wrong items attempted (Note that this does not count omitted items.)

N_o = the number of options available per item

As is obvious from the formula, this procedure introduces a weighted penalty for responding without comparative certainty. Typically the amount of reliability gained by this procedure is only substantial when items use few (i.e., two or three) options. With increase in response options, the advantages of correction for guessing diminish rapidly. Part of the reliability, or person-separability, of some tests is a function of speededness. In a test of reading comprehension, less capable students are partially distinguished from more capable students in that the less capable students are unable to finish the test. When correction for guessing is used for these tests, the contribution to reliability from speededness is partially removed. Slower, but more accurate, students are not penalized as much for not finishing the test when correction for guessing is used.

Latent trait approaches to scoring, as employed on the Test of English as a Foreign Language (TOEFL), and an increasing number of modern examinations have the potential of identifying and controlling for guessing. Scoring according to latent trait methodology does not require the sum of a person's correct responses but can be determined with reference to performance on a very small subset of items, the difficulties of which closely match the person's ability. Latent trait methodology is introduced in chapter eight.

Tests with Prose Passages

The scoring of prose passages produced by the students may introduce measurement error due to rater subjectivity unless appropriate precautions are taken. *Precis, composition,* and *dictation* tasks are common examples of this category of tests.

Dictation passages may be scored by treating each word as a separate item, counting it correct if present and incorrect if absent. However, research on this technique found improved reliability of scoring to be at the expense of validity (Shereaf, 1981). The more common procedure is to allot a maximum score possible, often corresponding to the number of words in the passage, and then systematically to subtract points for errors of grammar, spelling, or punctuation, depending on the purpose of the test.

Oller (1979) suggests two basic scoring techniques: *correct words-in-sequence* and *error counting.* By the latter technique, a student may receive a negative score if error penalties exceed the total mark possible. Shereaf (1981) provides a thorough discussion of statistical advantages and disadvantages of a variety of techniques of scoring dictation.

Similarly, free-writing tasks may be scored by deduction for errors from a maximum permissible score. However, the problems in scoring free-writing tests are manifold. Some examinees write longer passages than others and so produce more errors as a function of their greater effort. This suggests that rate of errors per specified passage length is more useful than an actual frequency tally of errors. Some examinees avoid all complex structures and sophisticated vocabulary for fear of mistakes, while others attempt more creative use of language and thus generate comparatively more errors. Such problems suggest that an element of subjective judgment on the part of the person scoring the test may be necessary. Subjectivity of this judgment may be minimized in at least four ways. *First*, a rating schedule may be used which operationally distinguishes between superior and inferior performance. One example is provided in Table 3.1.

Notice that this particular rating schedule permits a maximum of ten points for any given composition or essay. The schedule calls for equal weighting of mechanics and content, with one point awarded for satisfactory performance in each component area. Depending on the level of the particular student sample, the operational definition of acceptable or satisfactory performance will vary. One might say for a given sample length that more than two errors of spelling on the part of the examinee would result in forfeiting the possible one point awarded for spelling, etc. Using such a rating schedule tends to "objectify" the rater's task in the sense that ratings by various persons at various times will tend to reflect the same underlying criteria and thus become more consistent.

There is still a problem with such a scale; that is, that the selection of component areas and weights is somewhat arbitrary. Thus, one teacher may prefer to allow comparatively more weight for grammar usage, or for organization, and so on. A more scientific procedure for assigning appropriate weights to component parts of an examination or rating schedule is discussed under the multiple regression section of chapter ten. Another variety of rating schedule might specify in advance the kind of writing behavior that warrants specific marks. An example of such a schedule is provided in Table 3.2.

Here it may be desirable to allow partial scores, as 3.5, 2.5, etc., for persons whose performance is located between points on the scale.

A *second* way to reduce the subjectivity of scoring beyond the use of rating schedules is to insist on rater competence or expertise. This is to say that selection criteria be imposed in the choice of raters. Obviously no one should undertake the task of rating who does not know the language well or who has not had sufficient prior training and/or experience in rating.

A *third* possible procedure for reducing the subjectivity in the scoring of compositions or other written passages is to employ multiple independent raters. In this way every composition is read and marked independently by more than one

TABLE 3.1   Sample rating schedule* for use with precis, essay, and composition

MECHANICS		CONTENT	
Area	Weight	Area	Weight
Spelling	1	Organization	1
Grammar usage	1	Relevance to topic	1
Punctuation	1	Creativity/interest	1
Orthography	1	Range and sophistication of syntax	1
Paragraphing	1	Richness of vocabulary/expression	1
	5		5

*Other more sophisticated schedules are available (Cf. Jacobs et al.).

33

TABLE 3.2   A sample behavior-specific rating schedule for use in foreign language writing evaluation

BEHAVIOR	RATING
1. Writing is indistinguishable from that of a competent native speaker.	5
2. Writing is grammatically correct but employs nonnative usages.	4
3. Writing contains infrequent errors of grammar, lexis, spelling, or punctuation.	3
4. Writing contains numerous errors of grammar, lexis, spelling, and punctuation.	2
5. Writing is incomprehensible. Orthography is illegible.	1

rater. Such ratings must be independent in the sense that raters do not confer nor see the mark assigned by the other rater(s) before they have made their own judgment. The ratings of each rater for each examinee are then totaled or averaged to give a composite score for each examinee that reflects the combined judgments of all raters.

It is often desirable to employ all three of these "objectifying" procedures simultaneously. Thus, an ideal procedure is to use a rating schedule with multiple independent raters who are experts. Mansour (1978) found that the use of multiple independent raters who did not employ rating schedules necessitated the use of as many as seven raters rating each composition in order to attain acceptable reliability of scoring.

A *fourth* "objectifying" procedure is to elicit multiple writing samples from the examinee, preferably at various times on various topics. This would control for the fact that writing ability may vary with topic and time of day, etc.

Tests of Oral Communication

Many comments already made on scoring written passages apply equally well to scoring oral communication or production performance. It is equally desirable to have rating schedules and multiple independent raters who are experts. It is equally preferable for raters to judge performance in more than one topic or situational context. In addition to these scoring procedures, it may be desirable to record examinee performance on cassette or video-cassette in order to permit repeated or more thorough judgment by the rater(s) involved. Use of recording equipment must be considered thoroughly beforehand, not only to ensure quality of recording but also to determine whether or not subjects find such equipment threatening or intimidating and whether resultant speech samples become unnatural or otherwise invalid.

A sample rating schedule for use in judging speaking ability in a foreign language is reported in Table 3.3. In it the interviewer or rater records the name of the examinee and then proceeds to rate examinee performance on a scale of 1 to 5, depending on how nearly it approximates native-speaker performance. Further information on techniques of scoring samples of oral production, such as interviews, is available from Foreign Service Institute and Educational Testing

TABLE 3.3 A sample rating schedule for rating oral communication performance

Name of Examinee	Fluency (1–5)	Pronunciation Accuracy (1–5)	Grammar Accuracy (1–5)	Expressive Content (1–5)	Total (4–20)

Service (1962). The present grouping of tests with prose passages and tests of oral communication is not intended to imply that writing and speaking may not be tested well using tests with items rather than tests with extended free samples of language. The classifications mentioned have been introduced because of their usefulness in promoting understanding of scoring procedure. Additional rating schedules have been presented by Harris (1969) and others.

3.2   Coding

Once a set of dependable scores is in hand, reflecting the performance on a test or a battery of tests for a sample of examinees, the task becomes one of organizing and recording this raw test data. For tests with items, it is helpful to record data on a *scoring matrix*, normally on computer coding sheets or ordinary graph paper. An example is provided in Table 3.4.

Notice that the numbers on the left correspond to the identification numbers assigned to the papers of the students (p). The numbers across the top correspond to the 15 individual items (i) on the vocabulary subtest of the Ain Shams University Proficiency Examination (ASUPE) (Henning, 1978). Actual item performance data is recorded in the matrix with ones and zeroes. A *one* signifies that the examinee got that particular item correct, while a *zero* means that the examinee response was incorrect.

The next step in working with such a scoring matrix is to obtain the marginal totals. The totals at the right represent the total subtest scores for each student. The totals at the bottom of the matrix signify the number of persons getting correct scores on each item. As such they provide one measure of the comparative difficulty of the items.

Use of such a matrix is essential in the analysis of test data, particularly when there are large numbers of items and examinees and reliance must be placed upon a computer. Even when item data is not being considered, it is useful to resort to scoring matrices for recording subtest total scores for each examinee.

35

		ITEMS (i)															
		1	2	3	4	5	6	7	8	9	10	11	12	13	14	15	TOTAL
THIRD YEAR STUDENTS (p)	1	1	1	0	1	0	0	1	0	1	1	1	1	0	1	0	9
	2	1	1	1	1	0	0	0	0	1	1	0	1	0	0	0	7
	3	1	1	1	0	1	1	1	1	1	0	1	0	0	0	0	9
	4	1	0	1	1	1	1	1	1	1	1	1	1	0	0	0	11
	5	1	1	0	1	1	1	1	1	1	1	1	1	1	1	1	14
	6	0	0	1	0	1	0	0	0	0	1	1	1	0	0	0	5
	7	1	1	1	1	1	0	0	1	1	1	1	1	1	1	0	12
	8	0	1	1	1	1	1	1	1	1	1	1	1	1	1	0	13
	9	1	1	1	1	1	1	0	1	0	1	1	1	0	1	1	12
	10	0	0	0	0	1	0	1	1	0	1	1	0	0	0	0	5
	11	1	0	0	0	1	0	0	0	1	1	1	1	0	1	0	7
	12	1	1	0	1	0	0	0	0	1	1	1	1	1	0	0	8
	13	1	0	0	0	1	1	1	1	0	1	1	1	0	0	1	9
	14	1	1	1	0	1	0	0	1	0	0	0	1	0	1	0	7
	15	0	1	0	0	0	1	0	0	1	0	1	1	0	1	0	6
	16	1	1	1	1	1	1	1	0	1	1	0	0	0	0	0	9
	17	0	0	0	1	0	1	0	1	0	0	0	0	0	0	0	3
	18	0	1	1	1	1	1	0	0	0	0	1	0	0	0	0	6
	19	1	1	1	1	0	0	1	1	1	1	1	1	1	1	0	12
	20	1	1	0	1	1	1	0	0	0	0	0	1	0	0	0	6
	21	1	1	0	0	1	0	0	1	1	0	0	0	0	0	0	5
	22	0	1	1	1	1	0	1	1	1	0	0	0	0	0	0	7
	23	1	0	0	0	0	0	0	0	0	0	1	1	1	1	1	6
	24	0	1	1	0	1	0	1	0	1	0	1	1	0	1	0	8
	25	1	1	1	1	1	1	1	1	1	1	1	1	1	1	0	14
	26	1	1	1	1	1	1	1	1	1	1	1	1	1	1	0	14
	27	0	1	1	0	1	0	0	0	0	0	0	0	0	0	0	3
	28	0	1	1	0	1	1	1	1	1	1	0	0	0	0	0	8
	29	1	1	0	1	1	0	0	0	0	0	0	0	0	0	0	4
	30	1	1	1	1	1	1	0	1	1	1	0	0	0	0	0	9
TOTAL		20	23	18	18	23	15	14	17	19	18	19	19	8	13	4	

3.3   Arranging and Grouping of Test Data

Range and Distribution

In order to better understand the nature of the test and the comparative abilities of the examinees, it is desirable to arrange the scores in such a way that we can readily visualize the overall results. If we arrange the total test scores from Table 3.4 in this way, the result would appear as in Table 3.5.

TABLE 3.5   A frequency distribution of scores from the ASUPE Form A Vocabulary Subtest

Score	0	1	2	3	4	5	6	7	8	9	10	11	12	13	14	15
Frequency	0	0	0	2	1	3	4	4	3	5	0	1	3	1	3	0

Notice from Table 3.5 that no students obtained a score of less than 3 or more than 14. We could say therefore that the *actual range* of scores was 3–14, or 11. The *possible range* was 0–15, or 15. Since this was a multiple-choice type test with four options, one would expect the examinees to get a score of at least 25 percent by mere guessing. Thus, a score of 3.75 or below would actually be meaningless for discriminating among students in the ability being tested. Therefore we conclude that the *effective range* of this test was 4–14, or 10. Generally tests with the broadest possible effective range are most useful in discriminating among examinees on the ability under consideration.

The information presented in Table 3.5 is called a *frequency distribution* because it reports the frequency with which examinees obtained particular scores. This same information might have been presented graphically as in Figure 3.1.

Several kinds of frequency distribution are of interest in the field of test development or measurement theory. One kind of scoring distribution is called *skewed* distribution. Examples of this type of distribution are provided in Figure 3.2.

Notice from the example of *positive skew* at the top of Figure 3.2 that, in this case, the examinees found the examination too difficult. Most of the student scores are clustered near the zero point of the scoring range. In the case of the distribution with *negative skew*, just the opposite is true. Here the examinees found the test too easy, and a high percentage of them obtained a perfect score. Negative skew is not always considered a problem. In the case of criterion-referenced tests, this type of distribution is desirable as an indication that a majority of the students attained the objective of the program of instruction.

Another useful concept in the consideration of the shape of a scoring distribution is the notion of *kurtosis*, or peakedness. Figure 3.3 illustrates two extremes of kurtosis called a *leptokurtic* or peaked distribution and a *platykurtic* or flat distribution.

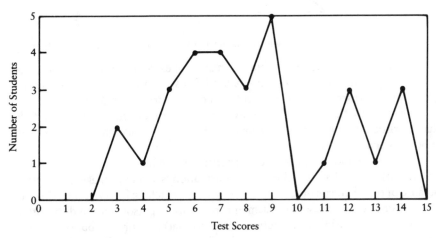

FIGURE 3.1 A frequency distribution of ASUPE scores

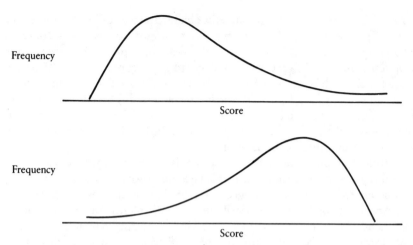

FIGURE 3.2   Typical shapes of skewed distributions. Positive skew is illustrated above, and negative skew is shown below.

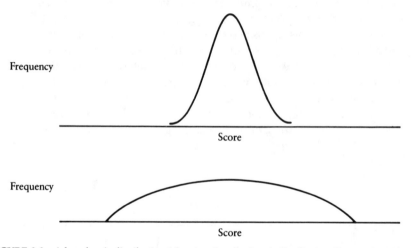

FIGURE 3.3   A leptokurtic distribution (above) and a platykurtic distribution illustrated (below).

Notice that all of these distribution shapes are extreme deviations from some standard or *normal distribution*. In practice both skew and kurtosis exist as some degree of departure from the expected shape of a normal distribution.

For reasons that now become evident, it is important to understand the characteristics of the normal distribution. Figure 3.4 illustrates some of these important characteristics for us.

Perhaps the most important characteristic of the normal distribution is *symmetry*. This means that each side of the distribution is a mirror image of the other. Because of this characteristic, it can be shown that matching intervals on either side of the distribution represent the same proportions of persons in the distribution.

A second important characteristic of the normal curve or distribution is closely related to the first: that, for the normal distribution, the *mean*, the *median*, and the

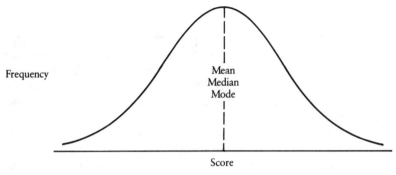

Frequency

Mean
Median
Mode

Score

FIGURE 3.4   The normal distribution

mode fall at the same point on the scoring axis. These three measures of central tendency or numerical average are discussed in greater detail in the following section.

The third property of the normal distribution is that the curve is *asymptotic*; that is, it never intersects the horizontal axis. This means that in a theoretical sense there is always the possibility that some one person's score may extend infinitely far to the right or to the left on the horizontal axis. In practice, however, because we cannot test an infinitely large sample and because tests have a finite number of items, this characteristic is not so important to us as the other two properties of the normal distribution.

Measures of Central Tendency or Statistical Average

There are at least three ways to locate a mid-point of the distribution. The most common method is by using the arithmetic *mean*. To obtain the mean we sum the individual scores of the distribution and divide by the total number of scores in the distribution.

This relationship is shown in the following formula:

$$\bar{X} = \frac{X}{N} \tag{3.2}$$

where, $\bar{X}$ = the arithmetic mean
X = the sum of all scores
N = the number of persons in the sample

Applying this formula to the data of Table 3.5, we obtain the following:

$$\bar{X} = \frac{248}{30} = 8.27$$

A second measure of central tendency is termed the *median*. This is the numerical point in the distribution at which half of the obtained scores lie above and half below. With an odd number of scores in the distribution, this is simply the centermost score. When there is an even-numbered distribution, as in Table 3.5, the median is the midpoint of the interval between the two centermost scores. This can be determined by summing the two centermost scores and dividing the result by two, as in the following example: from the data of Table 3.5

39

$$\text{Median} = \frac{8 + 8}{2} = 8$$

The third measure of central tendency is termed the *mode*. This is simply the most frequently occurring score which is easily located as the peak of the curve. For the data of Table 3.5, since the score of 9 occurs five times, it is the most frequent score and therefore the mode of the distribution. Sometimes distributions have more than one mode. A distribution with two distinct peaks or modes is called a *bimodal* distribution.

We observe from our example of Table 3.5 that there is a slight difference between these three kinds of average. There the mean was 8.23, the median was 8, and the mode was 9. We will rely almost entirely on the mean as a measure of central tendency in this text.

Measures of Dispersion or Variability

Another concern in describing the shape of a distribution is to quantify the density or *dispersion* of the scores around the mean. Consider the leptokurtic distribution at the top of Figure 3.3. Most of the scores are closely gathered around the mean. Such a distribution is said to have low *variability*. By contrast, the platykurtic distribution at the bottom of the same figure is said to have high variability because the scores are spread widely.

Two measures of variability are commonly used in test development. The first is called the *variance*. It is determined for a sample of scores by the following formula:

$$s^2 = \frac{\Sigma(X - \bar{X})^2}{N-1} \tag{3.3}$$

where, s^2 = the variance
X = any observed score in the sample
$\bar{X}$ = the mean of all scores
N = the number of scores in the sample
Σ = the symbol for summation

The second measure of variability is called the *standard deviation*. It is obtained by taking the square root of the variance, as shown by the following formula:

$$s = \sqrt{s^2} = \sqrt{\frac{\Sigma(X - \bar{X})^2}{N-1}} \tag{3.4}$$

It is important to note that these formulas are designed to provide an unbiased estimate of the variability in an underlying *population* of scores based on a *sample* of scores drawn from that population. If it were possible for us to obtain or conceptualize all of the scores in the population, we would rely on slightly different formulas: i.e.,

$$\sigma^2 = \frac{\Sigma(X - \bar{X})^2}{N} \tag{3.5}$$

$$\text{and } \sigma = \sqrt{\frac{\Sigma(X - \bar{X})^2}{N}} \tag{3.6}$$

Notice that for *population parameters*, as opposed to *sample statistics*, reliance is placed upon Greek rather than Latin symbols and N replaces $N-1$ in the denominator.

3.4 Summary

In this chapter we considered management of test data, including a review of scoring procedures for a variety of language tests. Coding test data through the use of scoring matrices has been discussed. And the grouping of test data according to the range and shape of the distribution of scores was the final general topic. Skew and kurtosis have been considered along with the properties of the normal distribution. Three measures of central tendency and two measures of variability or dispersion were introduced. A final comment was offered on the difference between population parameters and sample statistics.

Exercises

1. What would the score be after correction for guessing for a student who got 72 out of a possible 90 correct on a three-option multiple-choice test? Assume the student attempted all but five of the 90 items.
2. What are three techniques which may be used to reduce subjectivity of scoring for compositions or oral interviews?
3. What are some advantages of a scoring matrix?
4. How does the *effective range* differ from the *possible range* or the *actual range*?
5. What does the presence of positive and negative skew in the distribution of scores tell us about the nature of the test?
6. Given the following set of scores from a 25-item reading comprehension test: 11, 7, 13, 9, 14, 6, 17, 12, 14, 14, 10, 13, 12, 10, 19, compute the mean, the median, and the mode.
7. Name three properties of a normal distribution.
8. Using the data from problem 6, compute the standard deviation and the variance.
9. What is the difference between a population parameter and a sample statistic?
10. In a normal distribution, what proportion of the scores lie between plus and minus one standard deviation? Between plus and minus two standard deviations?

Chapter Four

Item Analysis: Item Uniqueness

In most language testing situations we are concerned with the writing, administration, and analysis of appropriate items. The test is considered to be no better than the items that go into its composition. Weak items should be identified and removed from the test. Very often, however, weak items cannot be identified and modified or removed without a "pilot" administration of the test. Thus, we must "test the test" before we use it to measure person abilities. There are, nevertheless, certain principles we can follow in writing items that may ensure greater success when the items undergo formal analysis.

4.1 Avoiding Problems at the Item-Writing Stage

Mixed Response

Items are sometimes prepared to test a specific skill or competence, but close examination of the response options reveals that the options actually measure ability in skill areas other than those intended. Consider the following example:

John _____ flowers to the party last night.
    a) carries   c) lifts
    b) carried   d) lifted

If an item such as this were used to measure knowledge of grammar with particular focus on simple past tense, the obvious flaw would be that the response options require choice of lexical items as a task. This item is as much a vocabulary item as it is a grammar item. A more consistent set of response options would be the following:

a) carries	c) is carrying
b) carried	d) has carried

A still more common example of a problem of this type is provided when tense is said to be tested but the options confound the notion of tense with that of agreement, as in the following example:

The woman _____ to the same shop every week.

a) go	c) have gone
b) goes	d) am going

Clearly distractors (a), (c), and (d) of this item can be eliminated, not on the basis of inappropriateness of tense, but due to lack of subject-verb agreement.

The basic problem with such items is not that they may be unreliable indicators of general proficiency, but that they lack validity as measures of what they are purported to measure.

Response Cues

Perhaps the most difficult task in preparing multiple-choice distractors is to avoid giving response cues. Students who have had much prior exposure to these kinds of examinations may be said to have developed "test wiseness"; that is, such students may be capable of selecting the correct option independently of any knowledge of the content field being tested. Such students usually succeed in making correct selections merely by attending to response cues in the options themselves. Following are some examples of response cues:

Length Cues

Frequently the longest and most explicit option available is the obvious answer. Consider the following example:

In the story, the merchant was unhappy because it

a) rained.	c) was windy.
b) was dark.	d) was windy and rainy and he had forgotten his raincoat.

If we had neither read nor understood the story in question, still we might choose option (d) and stand a reasonable chance of getting the item correct.

Convergence Cues

Consider the following set of options:

a) tea	c) party
b) tee	d) dinner

Even though we do not have the item stem, we can venture an intelligent guess about the correct option because of convergence. Notice that options (a), (c), and (d) pertain to a gathering at which food or refreshment is served. Option (b) is merely a homonym for option (a), providing additional distraction of a phono-logical nature. The option at which the two kinds of distraction (i.e., semantic and phonological) converge is (a) *tea,* which is the correct option in this case.

Inconsistent Distractor Cues

Examine the following set of distractors:

a) ran   c) is running
b) runs   d) fast

Obviously option (d) differs from the other options both in lexical root and in part of speech. We would probably be right in eliminating that option at the start. In effect, the item has only three viable options, making it a simpler item than originally intended.

There are many other kinds of cues that should be avoided, but these examples constitute some of the more common ones. The presence of such cues may not always be detected in formal item analysis, so the item writer must be sensitive to such matters if student scores are to reflect knowledge of the desired content area.

Number of Options

Care should be taken to ensure the proper number of options for any given set of items. Problems may arise when the number of response options are *too few.* True/false type items allow only two options. This implies that an unusually large set of items will be needed to increase the effective range of the test and ensure overall test reliability. It is not wrong to have few options unless there are also few items on the same test.

Options may also be *too many.* Consider for example a test of listening comprehension for which five options are employed. Very often on such a test the examinee forgets the aural stimulus before he or she has had time to review all of the options. In this way the test becomes a test of memory recall beyond the constraints of natural speech communication, and thus it may become invalid as a test of listening comprehension.

Options may be *irregular in number,* as in the case where the same test or subtest employs some items with three distractors, some with four, etc. Tests with such items may satisfy requirements of reliability and validity but they pose certain problems in analysis. For example, such items do not permit application of the correction-for-guessing formula introduced in chapter three. When such items are indicated by analysis to be weak or faulty, it is not immediately apparent whether the problem is inherent in the content of the item or its options or whether the problem is an artifact of the variant number of options.

Nonsense Distractors

For most purposes, nonsense distractors are to be avoided. Nonsense options have two basic problems. First, they tend to be weak distractors. Second, they frequently have negative "wash-back" on instruction; i.e., the students may learn errors from the examination itself. Consider the following example:

They said they
a) had gone.   c) have went.
b) had go.   d) had went.

Obviously distractors (b), (c), and (d) contain structures that do not occur in grammatically acceptable English for classroom use. On the one hand, the selection of the correct options can be made without consideration of use in context, merely because three of the options may be disallowed on separate criteria. On the other hand, if this item happened to comprise one of the early exposures of an examinee to perfect tenses, it is conceivable that the examinee might begin to entertain such nonsense structures as within the range of allowable alternatives of the language.

Review Options

Care must be taken in the use of review options, as shown in the following example:

The stranger had left his native land because he
a) wished to seek his fortune.
b) wanted to avoid his creditors.
c) preferred the new land.
d) none of the above
e) *a* and *b* but not *c* above
f) *b* and *c* but not *a* above

Options such as (d), (e), and (f) in the example require the examinee to review the previous options and form conclusions about their interrelatedness or cooccurrence. As such, these latter options are qualitatively different from the former options. Not only this, such options require considerable concentration and focus on the comparatively small information presented in the three former options. Such items may be more useful as measures of concentration and reasoning power than of reading comprehension or other purely linguistic skills.

Trick Questions

For some teachers it is always a temptation to include trick quesions on an examination. It is difficult to say whether the teacher's motive is to display cleverness, to embarrass the students for revenge, or merely to ensure test difficulty. The point is that such questions make for both inaccurate measurement and poor pedagogy. Consider the following example:

When is it not appropriate not to be absent from class?
a) When you are sick.
b) When you are young.
c) While class is in session.
d) Whenever the teacher is angry.

Notice that the example item stem employs a double negative structure in a way that seriously violates the range of structures employed in ordinary speech communication. A more suitable question for the item stem would be, "When should you be absent from class?" Trick questions promote guessing, poor motivation, unfavorable attitudes toward the teacher and the target language, and bad measurement.

Common Knowledge Responses

Particularly when testing the skill of reading comprehension, it may happen that an item may test common knowledge. In this way the correct response may be chosen without comprehension of the reading passage. An example would be the following:

> We learn from this passage that Napoleon was
> a) British   c) Polish
> b) French   d) German

The answer is common knowledge for most persons regardless of the content of the reading passage.

Matching Material

In testing reading comprehension, another common mistake is to allow the task to degenerate into a simple matching of words or phrases in the options with words or phrases in the passage. Unfortunately, in this case, the person providing the correct answer may not have comprehended the passage but is simply adept at matching words. For this reason response options should require some transformation of the material on the part of the examinee. This can be accomplished by requiring recognition of synonyms in the questions rather than actual vocabulary from the passage.

Redundancy

Another common mistake to be avoided is the repetition of redundant material in the response options. Consider the following example:

> The boy took the newspaper
> a) because he wanted to read it.
> b) because he wanted to wrap a gift in it.
> c) because he wanted to dispose of it.
> d) because he wanted to remove an article.

In this example the examinee is called upon to read an excess of redundant material. This makes the exam inefficient in the sense that too much time is required to elicit the information gained. A better format for the same item would be:

The boy took the newspaper because he wanted to
   a) read it.   c) dispose of it.
   b) wrap a gift in it. d) remove an article.

Medium of Response

Sometimes in testing a given language skill the person preparing the test resorts to an inappropriate medium of response. The author found that, to measure reading comprehension, requesting students to write short-sentence answers to written questions was less valid a procedure than multiple-choice sentence selection, synonym-antonym selection, or cloze recognition (Henning, 1975). It follows that the way in which the response is elicited becomes a part of the measured task itself. Care should be taken to ensure that the response medium be consistent with the objective of the test. For a more complete list of 20 common test development mistakes to avoid, see Henning (1982).

4.2   Appropriate Distractor Selection

We may well ask what techniques of distractor selection would provide suitable distractors that actually appeal to the examinees. To do this we must attend to the language production of the examinees. One technique that has been used to good advantage is the use of cloze passages for distractor selection. The test developer administers a cloze test and records the erroneous responses for any given item of interest. It is assumed that the most frequent errors elicited would become the most attractive or appealing distractors for use with a multiple-choice type test.

It is also very useful to attend to the free composition or free speech samples of the students. Frequent composition errors form ideal items for use with error identification format. Consider the following example used to measure the usage of third person singular s:

   A   B   C   D
The man frequently / go walking alone / when he is / tired or sad.

The task here is to identify B as the segment of the sentence containing the error. But the choice of the sentence itself may have been based on the occurrence of the error in a student composition. In this way the error will likely go undetected by some students. In addition, such items, with appropriate feedback, may result in improved composition writing on the part of the students.

4.3   Item Difficulty

As we move from considerations of item writing and distractor selection, we encounter empirical considerations of item analysis. Although the foregoing principles of this chapter may serve as guidelines in the writing of good items, ultimately it is not until the test has been tried out or "piloted" on an appropriate sample of examinees, and until performance data has been collected and analyzed, that we can be certain of the worth of any given item.

Perhaps the single most important characteristic of an item to be accurately determined is its difficulty. Often, when tests are rejected as unreliable measures for a given sample of examinees, it is due not so much to the carelessness of the item writers as to the misfit of item difficulty to person ability. Tests that are too difficult or too easy for a given group of examinees often show low reliability. But the same tests used with examinees of appropriate ability often prove highly reliable. Item difficulty is determined as the proportion of correct responses, signified by the letter "p". The formula for item difficulty then is

$$p = \frac{\Sigma C_r}{N} \qquad (4.1)$$

where, p = difficulty, proportion correct
ΣC_r = the sum of correct responses
N = the number of examinees

By the same token, the proportion incorrect is equal to 1 minus the proportion correct and is represented by the symbol "q". This may be stated in algebraic form as follows:

$$q = 1 - p \qquad (4.2)$$

where, q = the proportion incorrect
p = the proportion correct

The scoring matrix of Table 3.4 provides an example of scores for 30 students on 15 vocabulary items of the Ain Shams University Proficiency Exam (ASUPE). We can now make use of the data of that table to compute item difficulty for each of the 15 items. Observe Table 4.1 to see how the computation of item difficulty and proportion incorrect was done.

Notice that the higher the difficulty, the lower the proportion correct and the higher the proportion incorrect. Thus, the difficulty index, "p", is inversely related to the actual difficulty of any given item.

At this point we are ready to ask the question, "What constitutes appropriate item difficulty for any given set of examinees?" In general it can be shown that item difficulty is most appropriate when it approaches the mid-point of the difficulty range. Thus item 6 of Table 4.1 can be said to have the most appropriate difficulty for this particular sample of students (.50). A more difficult question to answer is,

TABLE 4.1   Item difficulty as proportion correct and proportion incorrect for 15 ASUPE A items (N = 30 examinees)

Item No.	1	2	3	4	5	6	7	8	9	10	11	12	13	14	15
Correct	20	23	18	18	23	15	14	17	19	18	19	19	8	13	4
p	.67	.77	.60	.60	.77	.50	.47	.57	.63	.60	.63	.63	.27	.43	.13
q	.33	.23	.40	.40	.23	.50	.53	.43	.37	.40	.37	.37	.73	.57	.87

When should we reject items as too difficult or too easy? Some authors advocate rejection of items with a proportion of correct answers that is less than .33 or that exceeds .67 (e.g., Tuckman, 1978). This is not a bad general rule of thumb, but there are several additional constraints that may need to be imposed on the decision to reject items as too difficult or too easy. Consider the following:

The Need to Include Specific Content

Popham (1978) has correctly pointed out that the systematic rejection of all items that are at the extremes of the difficulty continuum may result in a test that is insensitive to the objectives of instruction. When measuring achievement, we may need to include some very easy or very difficult items to ensure that the test itself has face or content validity. The fact that students find a particular item easy may be a useful piece of information — an indication of how well the instructional objectives were realized. Insensitivity to instructional objectives is one of the arguments advanced against norm-referenced examinations by advocates of criterion-referenced testing. Careful selection of item content and a degree of flexibility in the setting of item difficulty may obviate this objection.

The Need to Provide an Easy Introduction

Many test developers prefer to begin each section of their tests with a few very easy items. This is done to overcome psychological inertia on the part of the examinee. It is thought that persons experiencing test anxiety in particular might benefit from an initial positive experience with the test. In some cases these initial "warm-up" items are not included in the actual scoring of the test. Similarly, for some purposes it is desirable to arrange items in order of difficulty, presenting the easy items first. This is especially useful when testing small children. After having experienced three or four successive item failures they are exempted from the remaining items. In this way they are relieved of needless frustration.

The Need to Shape the Test Information Curve

By systematically sampling items at a specific difficulty level for inclusion in the test, it is possible to create a test that is more sensitive or discriminating at a given cut-off score or scores. This procedure is called "shaping the information curve" and is discussed more thoroughly in chapters eight and nine. Here again we may choose to violate a general rule of thumb in item difficulty limits if our purpose is to make the test function in a certain way for certain examinees.

The Availability of Items

One obvious constraint is that we cannot reject all of the items of inappropriate difficulty when the total number of items is insufficient. This consideration should encourage us to prepare an abundance of items at the pilot stage so that, if we must reject some items, there is still a sufficient pool of good items left.

Otherwise we are forced to relax our standards of item difficulty and include items we would otherwise reject.

4.4   Item Discriminability

Another important characteristic of a test item is how well it discriminates between weak and strong examinees in the ability being tested. Difficulty alone is not sufficient information upon which to base the decision ultimately to accept or reject a given item. Consider, for example, a situation in which half of the examinees pass a given item and half fail it. Using difficulty as the sole criterion, we would adopt this item as an ideal item. But what if we discovered that the persons who passed the item were the weaker half of the examinees, and the persons who failed the item were the stronger examinees in the ability being measured. This would certainly cause us to have different thoughts about the suitability of such an item. If our test were comprised entirely of such items, a high score would be an indication of inability and a low score would be an indication of comparative ability.

What we need at this point is a method of computing item discriminability. There are, in fact, several. Some involve the correlation of item responses with other variables, and some entail the comparison of response patterns of examinees who are strong in the ability being measured with those who are weak in this ability. Logic rules in favor of the latter methods because they entail direct comparison of the performances of strong and weak examinees. However, other considerations—such as the need for additional computer programming to separate the strong and weak students—sometimes cause us to adopt other, more traditional, approaches.

Item Discriminability with Sample Separation

Table 4.2 shows the procedure in computing item discriminability by sample separation for item six of Table 3.4. Notice that the first step is to separate the highest scoring group and the lowest scoring group from the entire sample on the basis of total score on the test. In Table 4.2 the ten students with highest total scores are compared in their performance on item six with the ten students with lowest total scores, using the formula,

$$D = \frac{H_c}{H_c + L_c} = \frac{7}{7+4} = 0.64 \qquad (4.3)$$

where, D = discriminability
   H_c = the number of correct responses in the high group
   L_c = the number of correct responses in the low group

The decision to employ ten students in each of the two groups was somewhat arbitrary. Research indicates that the optimal size of each group is 28 percent of the total sample. Often, with very large samples of examinees, the numbers of examinees in the high and low groups are reduced to 25, or even 20, percent, for computational convenience.

TABLE 4.2   Computation of item discriminability for item 6 of Table 3.4 by sample separation

	Examinee No.	Item 6	Total Score
	5	1	14
	25	1	14
	26	1	14
High	8	1	13
Scoring	7	0	12
Group	9	1	12
(N = 10)	19	0	12
	4	1	11
	1	0	9
	3	1	9
		7	
	17	1	3
	27	0	3
	29	0	4
Low	6	0	5
Scoring	10	0	5
Group	21	0	5
(N = 10)	15	1	6
	18	1	6
	20	1	6
	23	0	6
		4	

Notice that the discriminability found for item six was .64. This is considered poor discriminability according to this particular method. By this method, discriminability may range from zero to one. The higher it is, the better. Acceptable discriminability usually begins about two-thirds of the way along the discriminability continuum. Thus a discriminability index of .67 is considered the lowest acceptable discriminability by this method.

Point Biserial Methods

A more common technique for the computation of item discriminability is to compute the correlation between item responses and total scores for any given test. Since item scores in this instance are binary, i.e., zero or one, and total scores are continuous, the resultant correlation coefficient is called a *point biserial correlation coefficient*. The formula for point biserial correlation is given as follows:

$$r_{pbi} = \frac{\bar{X}_p - \bar{X}_q}{s_x} \sqrt{pq} \qquad (4.4)$$

where, r_{pbi} = the point biserial correlation

$\bar{X}_p$ = the mean total score for examinees who pass the item

$\bar{X}_q$ = the mean total score for examinees who fail the item

s_x = the standard deviation of test scores

p = the proportion of examinees who pass the item
q = the proportion of examinees who fail the item

Using item six of Table 3.4 again as an example, we can compute the point biserial correlation with total score as follows;

X_p	X_q
9	9
11	7
14	5
13	12
12	5
9	7
6	8
9	7
3	12
6	5
6	7
14	6
14	8
8	3
9	4

$$s_x = \sqrt{\frac{\Sigma(X-\bar{X})^2}{N-1}} = 3.25$$

$$p = \frac{15}{30} = .50$$

$$q = 1 - .50 = .50$$

$\Sigma = 143 \quad 105$

$\bar{X} = 9.53 \quad\quad 7.00$

$$r_{pbi} = \frac{\bar{X}_p - \bar{X}_q}{s_x} \sqrt{pq} = \frac{9.53-7.00}{3.25} \sqrt{.50 \times .50} = .39$$

The point biserial correlation in this case was .39. In general, point biserial correlations of .25 and above are acceptable, but here again flexibility is required. Correlation magnitude is partly a function of sample size and ability range, so that the point biserial correlation may change for the same item when different samples of examinees are used. For this reason it is best to treat the coefficient as an inter-item comparative measure rather than as an absolute. It is usually identical to the Pearson product-moment correlation introduced in chapter five; however, it permits simplified computation because of binary item responses.

In measuring discriminability, a point biserial correlation may also be computed with level or years of training as an indirect continuous measure. Here it is assumed that a high correlation of the items with level indicates which items effectively discriminate among students with the most training. Of course this procedure cannot be used with poor instructional programs where no learning is taking place.

Biserial Methods

The same correlations between binary item responses and total score or level can be computed using biserial instead of point biserial correlation. The advantage of biserial correlation is that it assumes that the pass and fail on a test item represent the dichotomy of an underlying normally distributed ability variable. Thus the maximum and minimum values of r_{bi} are independent of the point of dichotomy and are $+1$ and -1. With the r_{pbi}, slight distortion causes the maximum and minimum values never to reach $+1$ or -1. The formula for biserial correlation is as follows:

$$r_{bi} = \frac{\bar{X}_p - \bar{X}_q}{s_x} \frac{pq}{y}$$ (4.5)

where, r_{bi} = the biserial correlation coefficient
         $\bar{X}_p$ = the mean test score of those who pass the item
         $\bar{X}_q$ = the mean test score of those who fail the item
         s_x = the standard deviation of test scores
         p = the proportion of correct scores on the item
         q = the proportion of incorrect scores on the item
         y = the height of the ordinate of the unit normal curve at the point of division between the p and q proportions of cases

In practice y can be determined by consulting Table D in Appendix A. The relationship between point biserial and biserial correlation is given by the following formula:

$$r_{bi} = r_{pbi} \frac{\sqrt{pq}}{y}$$ (4.6)

4.5   Item Variability

The variability of individual items is the final item characteristic we shall consider in this chapter. For calculation of variance we have already confronted the general formula,

$$s^2 = \frac{\Sigma(X - \bar{X})^2}{N-1}$$ (3.3)

In the case of binary item response data, the variance computation reduces to the expression,

$$s^2 = pq$$ (4.7)

where, s^2 = the variance
         p = the proportion correct
         q = the proportion incorrect

The maximum item variance obtainable then is .25, when 50 percent of the examinees pass and 50 percent fail an item. This variance characteristic is sometimes referred to as the information function of the item. The higher the item variance, the more information it is providing us about the abilities of the particular sample of examinees measured. In general, test developers seek to maximize the information value of the test by including items with high variance.

4.6   Distractor Tallies

Ultimately with multiple-choice type items, we do not know whether distractors are functioning adequately until we try them out. We can easily tally the number of responses given for each option of an item. The frequency with which the correct option is chosen is a measure of item difficulty already discussed. We are also interested in determining the frequency of selection of the incorrect, distractor options. If a distractor elicits very few or no responses, then it may not be functioning as a distractor and should be replaced with a more attractive option. Also some distractors may be too appealing, causing the item to be too difficult. Very often items which have been rejected as having inappropriate difficulty, discriminability, or variability can be redeemed by the revision of one or two of the response options. In this way a distractor tally can serve to pinpoint item weaknesses.

4.7   Summary

In this chapter we have considered elements of item writing and analysis that distinguish unique properties of items. Suggestions were provided for eliminating item deficiencies at the writing stage. Various techniques of computation of item difficulty, item discriminability, and item variance were introduced. And a brief discussion of distractor analysis was presented.

Exercises

1. List five common problems at the item writing stage. Provide one example of each problem type and correct the item in each case.
2. What are some advantages of "piloting" a test before using it to measure examinee ability?
3. What general relationship exists between test reliability and the number of items on the test?
4. Describe a method for finding effective distractors on a multiple-choice test. How may we be certain whether distractors are functioning as desired?
5. What are a few considerations that may cause us to relax standards when faced with the decision of whether or not to reject items?
6. Compute item difficulty and the proportion incorrect for each of the items in the following scoring matrix. Identify items for rejection.

		Items				
		1	2	3	4	5
	1	1	0	1	1	1
	2	1	1	0	0	0
	3	1	1	0	0	1
Examinees	4	1	0	1	0	1
	5	0	1	0	0	0
	6	1	1	1	1	0
	7	1	1	0	0	1

7. Using the matrix of problem six, compute the discriminability for each item by sample separation. Indicate which items may be rejected as having weak discriminability.

8. Using the matrix of problem six, compute discriminability for each item using point biserial correlation. Compare the results with those of the technique used in problem seven.

9. Using the matrix of problem six, compute item variability for each item. Tell which items provide the most information about the examinees.

10. Using the scoring matrix of Table 3.4, tell which items you would reject on the basis of a) difficulty, b) discriminability, c) information value.

Chapter Five

Item and Test Relatedness

In the previous chapter we considered some of the unique properties of items and how they may be evaluated on those properties or characteristics. It is also useful to consider the extent to which items and tests in general relate to other criteria. The present chapter is concerned with methods of determining relatedness rather than uniqueness.

One of the most useful and pervasive concepts in testing theory is the concept of correlation. It would be impossible to conceive of language test development without a thorough appreciation of the correlation coefficient, what it means, and how it is derived. We have already encountered the correlation coefficient in the discussion of point biserial and biserial measures of discriminability in chapter four. It is now time to explore correlation at a deeper conceptual and computational level.

5.1 Pearson Product-Moment Correlation

Perhaps the most common method for quantifying the strength of a relationship is known as product-moment correlation. Karl Pearson (1901) is credited with the development of this method. Before examining the actual computational formulas, we need to conceptualize what is meant by the magnitude and direction of a relationship.

Magnitude and Direction of Correlation

If we wanted to know the strength and direction of the relationship between scores in vocabulary recognition and scores in reading comprehension for the same sample of persons, we might choose to plot these scores on a scatterplot or scattergram, as in Figure 5.1(a).

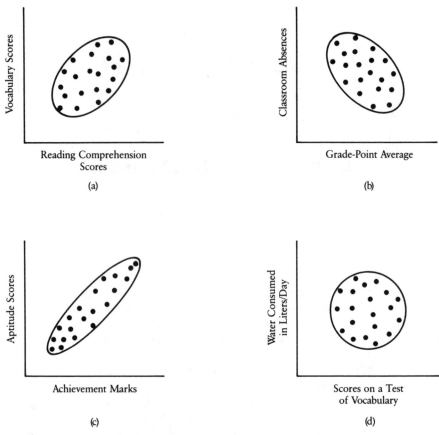

FIGURE 5.1 Various relationships contrasted in magnitude and direction

In Figure 5.1(a) a dot has been inserted for each person in the sample at the point where his or her vocabulary score and reading comprehension score coincide. Since the scores on the horizontal axis increase from left to right, and the scores on the vertical ordinate increase from bottom to top, considering the sample as a whole, we can see a relationship: as vocabulary score increases, reading comprehension score also increases. This relationship is termed *positive correlation*.

Figure 5.1(b) depicts a relationship of similar strength but different direction. According to this illustration, the more a person is absent from class, the lower that person's grade-point average or achievement becomes. This kind of relationship — where one variable increases as the other decreases — is called *negative correlation* and is indicated by the presence of a minus sign before the correlation coefficient.

The relationship portrayed between aptitude and achievement in Figure 5.1(c) is in the same direction as that shown in Figure 5.1(a), but the dots fall very close together in a comparatively narrower or more elongated ellipse. This shows us that the relationship between our measures of aptitude and achievement is comparatively stronger than the relationship between our measures of vocabulary and reading comprehension. When all of the dots fall exactly on one straight line, we have the strongest possible relationship, known as *perfect correlation*. The correlation coefficient ranges in value from minus 1.00 to plus 1.00. Perfect correlations are depicted at the extremes as a negative or positive value of one. Such a relationship is so strong that all that may be known about a person with regard to the one variable is perfectly revealed by the other variable. If, for example, aptitude and achievement were perfectly related, which they are not, then it would not be necessary to test achievement. Some measure of aptitude would be sufficient.

Figure 5.1(d) takes the form of an amorphous blob. Here we see that our vocabulary test score bears no relationship to how much water a person drinks. In this case the correlation coefficient would be approaching zero magnitude, and knowledge of water consumption would provide no information about whether or not an individual is likely to pass the vocabulary test.

Mean Cross-Product of z-Scores

Part of the difficulty in quantifying the strength of a relationship is that the tests or measures used are usually on a different scale, as explained in chapter two. Relating a score on a test with five items to a score on a test with fifty items becomes a problem. At this point we can apply the concept of z-score transformation introduced on pages 18 and 19. By converting raw scores to z-scores, summing the cross products for every person, and averaging the total, we derive the correlation coefficient. This relationship is given in the following formula:

$$r_{xy} = \frac{\Sigma z_x z_y}{N-1} \tag{5.1}$$

Table 5.1 provides an example of the computation of the correlation coefficient by means of this formula. Notice that the correlation coefficient expressed here by the symbol r_{xy} is a sample statistic, and therefore $N - 1$ appears in the denominator. The correlation coefficient as a population parameter is expressed by the symbol ρ_{xy} and employs N in the denominator.

TABLE 5.1 Computation of the correlation coefficient as the mean cross-product of standard scores

Case	X	$\bar{X}$	$(X-\bar{X})$	$(X-\bar{X})^2$	z_x	Y	$\bar{Y}$	$(Y-\bar{Y})$	$(Y-\bar{Y})^2$	z_y	$z_x z_y$
1	2	2.5	−.5	.25	−.39	3	3	0	0	0	0
2	3	2.5	.5	.25	.39	3	3	0	0	0	0
3	4	2.5	1.5	2.25	1.16	4	3	1	1	1.22	1.42
4	1	2.5	−1.5	2.25	−1.16	2	3	−1	1	−1.22	1.42
	10			5.00		12			2		2.84

$s_x = \sqrt{\frac{\Sigma(X-\bar{X})^2}{N-1}} = \sqrt{\frac{5}{3}} = 1.29$ $s_y = \sqrt{\frac{\Sigma(Y-\bar{Y})^2}{N-1}} = \sqrt{\frac{2}{3}} = .82$

$z_x = \frac{X-\bar{X}}{s_x}$ $z_y = \frac{Y-\bar{Y}}{s_y}$

$r_{xy} = \frac{\Sigma z_x z_y}{N-1} = \frac{2.84}{3} = .95$

In the example of Table 5.1 we are shown how the correlation coefficient was computed for two sets of measures, X and Y, taken on four persons. In this example the X and Y values stand for ratings of composition quality by two independent judges, on a scale of one to five. The high positive correlation of 0.95 indicates that there was a high degree of agreement between the two raters, and thus their ratings, especially when combined, may be considered highly reliable.

Computational Formulas

While the formula presented in the previous section helps us understand the concept of correlation, it is not at all the most convenient formula for computational purposes. For most practical purposes it is not necessary to compute each z-score transformation individually. The following two formulas are easier and more efficient to apply:

$$r_{xy} = \frac{\Sigma(X - \bar{X})(Y - \bar{Y})}{\sqrt{\Sigma(X - \bar{X})^2 \Sigma(Y - \bar{Y})^2}} \qquad (5.2)$$

$$r_{xy} = \frac{N\Sigma XY - \Sigma X \Sigma Y}{\sqrt{[N\Sigma X^2 - (\Sigma X)^2][N\Sigma Y^2 - (\Sigma Y)^2]}} \qquad (5.3)$$

Of these two formulas, formula 5.3 is usually preferable in situations where a calculator is available and where large sample sizes are involved. The solutions of both formulas applied to the data of Table 5.1 are as follows:

$$r_{xy} = \frac{3}{\sqrt{5 \times 2}} = .95$$

$$r_{xy} = \frac{4 \times 23 - 10 \times 12}{\sqrt{(4 \times 30 - 100)(4 \times 38 - 144)}} = \frac{12}{\sqrt{20 \times 8}} = .95$$

Meaningfulness and Statistical Significance of Correlation

Very often in language test development we want to know not only the exact value of the correlation coefficient, but also whether or not that value is important or significant. This is especially true since the value of the correlation coefficient, like that of the variance, is somewhat affected by the size of the sample in our computations. Moreover, it may be that our sample of persons is biased in the relationship we are measuring, even though we may have drawn them randomly from the population of interest. We would like to know how accurate we would be in generalizing our finding of a correlation in the sample to the population at large. We can estimate the probability of error in such a generalization. Such a probability estimate depends on the strength of the correlation we observed, and on the number of persons or cases in our sample.

In our example of ratings of composition writing quality shown in Table 5.1, we found a high correlation of 0.95 between the ratings by two different judges. This adds to our confidence in the reliability of the ratings. Unfortunately, however, there were only four persons in our sample, and it may have been just a matter of chance that four persons were chosen for whom the judges happened to express agreement. How can we test to find out whether the probability of accuracy is strong enough so that we can generalize to the population from which our sample was drawn? The easiest way is simply to consult Table E in Appendix A. Table E lists those values of the correlation coefficient that must be exceeded in order for the probability of *error of generalization* to the population to be smaller than the amount listed at the top of the table. Usually we want the error of generalization to be as small as possible if we want to affirm that the relationship we noted in the sample also exists in the entire population.

The proportion of probable error of generalization is also known as the *level of significance*, or the *p-value* of the statistic. As a convention, educators and other behavioral scientists have come to accept $p < 0.05$ as the maximum level of error permissible in order for generalization to take place. This means that, with a correlation coefficient having a level of significance of $p < 0.05$, we are confident that more than 95 times out of 100 a similar sample drawn at random from the population will exhibit the same relationship.

As we shall see in the next section, correlation usually is used to describe a linear relationship, one that can be illustrated by a straight line. In drawing a straight line, we often connect the two dots at the extreme ends of the line. These two points are given, and it is the points in between that must be determined by the drawing of the line. We say that the two points are not free to vary, while the other points are said to have freedom to vary, and must be specified along the line for us to know where they are. Therefore the correlation coefficient loses two *degrees of freedom*, corresponding to the two points, when we seek to test its level of significance. The degrees of freedom associated with the correlation coefficient then become the number of persons in the sample minus two. In Table E, the left-hand column labeled "df $= N - 2$" lists the degrees of freedom associated with any correlation coefficient being tested. In our example of composition ratings in Table 5.1, the sample consisted of four persons, therefore the degrees of freedom associated with the correlation coefficient calculated would be $N - 2$, which equals $4 - 2$, or two degrees of freedom. We must look at the row corresponding to two degrees of freedom in order to find the value which the correlation coefficient must exceed if the probability of error is to be no more than the acceptable level of $p < 0.05$.

Notice that the level of significance varies according to whether we are making a *one-tailed* or *two-tailed* test of significance. This refers to the hypothesized direction of correlation. If we say, as in our example again, that the correlation between our two judges' ratings in the entire population should be positive, then we will make a one-tailed test of significance. On the other hand, if it is not important to us whether the relationship is positive or negative, then we would accept correlations on both the negative and the positive sides of the continuum, and this would be said to be a two-tailed test of significance. Of course, in our example we assume that the relationship between judges' ratings should be positive, and we are making a one-tailed test of significance. According to Table E, the value of the correlation coefficient found with our sample must exceed 0.900 if we are to be able to generalize to the population at a level of significance of $p < 0.05$. Since our observed correlation was 0.95, we say that this correlation is significant and we can generalize to the population from which the sample was randomly chosen. We are 95 percent confident that there is a positive relationship in the

61

population of students rated that exceeds zero magnitude. If we wanted to be 99 percent confident of the relationship, we would look in the table under the p-value of 0.01. For this level of confidence, our correlation coefficient would have had to have exceeded the value of 0.980. Since it did not exceed this value, we cannot have this level of confidence in our generalization to the population.

We have seen how a correlation coefficient can be termed *significant*. With very large sample sizes it is possible for comparatively small correlation values to be found significant. For this reason, it is good to consider the absolute size of the coefficient in addition to its significance as a determinant of the importance of the correlation. Usually coefficients above 0.50 are said to be *meaningful* for research purposes. Thus we should consider both the significance and the meaningfulness of the correlation coefficient.

Regression and Prediction

One of the many nice things about correlation is that, once the magnitude and direction of the correlation coefficient have been established, it is possible to predict scores on the one variable by knowledge of scores on the other variable of the correlation. Suppose, for example, we want to estimate or predict what persons' scores would be on the *Test of English as a Foreign Language* (TOEFL) on the basis of their scores on a 50-item proficiency test of our own making. If we were to find a sufficiently large sample of students who had actually taken both tests under similar conditions, without allowing too much time to elapse between the two test administrations (say, no more than two weeks), then we could use the correlation between the two sets of scores to estimate TOEFL scores for any additional students from the same population who had only been administered our proficiency exam. We would be able to do this by referring to the line of best fit.

The Line of Best Fit

Figure 5.2 provides a scatterplot of paired scores on the TOEFL and on a locally constructed proficiency exam for 15 persons who were administered both examinations. In the center of the scatterplot a straight line has been drawn known as the *regression line* or the *line of best fit*. As the latter name implies, the line has been drawn in such a way that the sum of the distances of all the dots in the figure from the line itself is at a minimum. If we were to draw perpendicular lines from the dots to the regression line and measure their lengths, we would find that the regression line has been so positioned that the sum of all their lengths is at a minimum.

This line becomes the basis of our estimating scores on one variable from scores on the other variable. As this line serves such an important function, it is useful for us to be able to position the line mathematically without having to plot

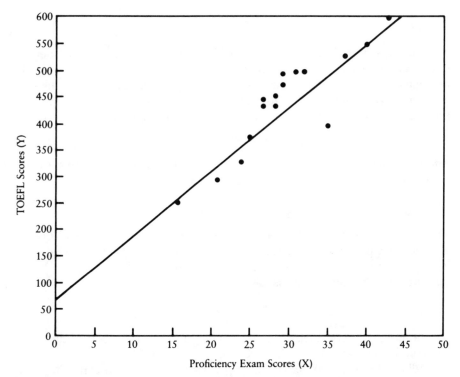

FIGURE 5.2   A scattergram of the relationship between TOEFL and proficiency exam scores, showing the line of best fit (N = 15)

all of the data each time we wish to estimate scores. We do this by means of the following algebraic formula for a straight line:

$$Y = a + bX \qquad (5.4)$$

where,   Y = a given score to be predicted on the *dependent variable*
         a = the *Y-intercept*, the point where the line crosses the vertical ordinate
         b = the *slope* of the line
         X = a given score being the basis of prediction from the *independent variable*

A simple variation of this formula, which we can apply in making predictions from raw score information, is the following:

$$\hat{Y} = r_{xy} \frac{s_y}{s_x} (X - \bar{X}) + \bar{Y} \qquad (5.5)$$

Before we apply this formula in the prediction of TOEFL scores as indicated in our example, it is worthwhile to understand what is meant by the various parts of Formula 5.4 and how the parts are derived.

The Slope

The *slope* of the line refers to the rate of ascent or descent of the line from the horizontal plane, and is indicated by the letter "b" in Formula 5.4. The slope is determined by dividing the number of vertical units of ascent, known as the *rise*, by the associated number of horizontal units, known as the *run*. If, for example, the line rises four vertical units for every ten horizontal units, we say

$$\text{the slope} = \tfrac{\text{rise}}{\text{run}} = \tfrac{4}{10} = 0.4$$

Another more common method for determining slope is by referring to the correlation coefficient in the following relationship:

$$b_{yx} = r_{xy} \frac{s_y}{s_x} \qquad (5.6)$$

This is akin to stating that the slope or *regression coefficient* for the prediction of Y from X is equal to the correlation of X with Y, times the standard deviation of Y, divided by the standard deviation of X. If we were predicting X from Y, the formula would change slightly as follows:

$$b_{xy} = r_{xy} \frac{s_x}{s_y} \qquad (5.7)$$

In terms of trigonometry, the slope is the same as the *tangent* of the angle between the regression line and the X-axis.

When the X and Y variables are transformed to z-scores, the slope or regression coefficient in the regression equation has other interesting properties. Under the specific condition that the raw scores have been converted to z-scores, and the correlation coefficient has been computed from the z-score data, it can be shown that the correlation coefficient will equal the regression coefficient. And since the Y-intercept will assume the value of zero under this condition, the formula for z-score prediction may be written as follows:

$$\hat{z}_y = bz_x = r_{xy}z_x \qquad (5.8)$$

In this case the regression coefficient will also be exactly the same for the prediction of the z-score of Y and the z-score of X.

The Y-Intercept

Another component term of the formula for the regression line, 5.4, is the Y-intercept, a. As the name implies, the Y-intercept identifies the point where the regression line crosses the Y-ordinate, and its value is given in the number of units it lies above or below the zero point. The Y-intercept, a_{yx}, for the prediction of Y from X may be computed using the following formula:

$$a_{yx} = \bar{Y} - b_{yx}\bar{X} \qquad (5.9)$$

The Y-intercept, a_{xy}, for9 the prediction of X from Y may be computed by means of the following formula:

$$a_{xy} = \bar{X} - b_{xy}\bar{Y} \qquad (5.10)$$

In general, if only one prediction is being made, it may be simplest to employ Formula 5.5. But in the situation where many predictions are being made from the independent to the dependent variable, it is best to compute the Y-intercept and derive the slope for using regression Formula 5.4.

Figure 5.2 reported a scatterplot of local proficiency exam scores and TOEFL scores obtained by 15 imaginary students. Table 5.2 reports the raw scores and the steps of computation of the formula for the prediction of TOEFL scores from this local proficiency exam data. A much larger sample of scores would ordinarily be used for regression than the 15 in this example.

Now that we have the regression equation for the prediction of TOEFL scores from local proficiency exam scores, given any new local proficiency exam scores

TABLE 5.2   Raw scores and computational steps for the prediction of TOEFL scores from a locally constructed exam

Person No.	TOEFL Score (Y)	Local Exam (X)
1	395	35
2	444	27
3	253	16
4	597	42
5	482	29
6	328	24
7	488	31
8	432	28
9	294	21
10	525	37
11	372	25
12	476	29
13	435	27
14	496	32
15	451	28
	6468	431

Step No.	Task	Formula	Result
1.	Compute Means of X and Y	$\bar{X} = \frac{\Sigma X}{N}$ $\bar{X} = 28.73,$	$\bar{Y} = 431.20$
2.	Compute s_x and s_y	$s_x = \sqrt{\frac{\Sigma(X-\bar{X})^2}{N-1}}$ $s_x = 6.35,$	$s_y = 90.60$
3.	Compute r_{xy}	$r_{xy} = \frac{\Sigma(X-\bar{X})(Y-\bar{Y})}{\sqrt{\Sigma(X-\bar{X})^2\Sigma(Y-\bar{Y})^2}}$	$r_{xy} = 0.88$
4.	Compute b_{yx}	$b_{yx} = r_{xy}\frac{s_y}{s_x}$	$b_{yx} = 12.59$
5.	Compute a_{yx}	$a_{yx} = \bar{Y} - b_{yx}\bar{X}$	$a_{yx} = 69.49$
6.	Construct formula	$Y = a + b_{yx}X$	$Y = 69.49 + 12.59X$

using our same test with persons from the same population, we can estimate the TOEFL scores of the persons taking the proficiency exam even though they have not taken the TOEFL exam. Suppose, for example, a student from the same population takes our local proficiency exam and gets a score of 33. By referring to the formula derived in step 6 of Table 5.2, we would estimate that person's TOEFL score as

$$69.49 + 12.59 (33) = 485$$

When to Use Regression and Prediction

Our data should meet certain assumptions in order for regression procedure to be warranted:

1. There should be a simple linear relationship between the variables.
2. A sample should be of sufficient size to define a probable, stable regression line. Some authorities suggest that a minimum of 30 paired observations be required.
3. Caution must be used when dealing with *truncated samples*. If a sample of students is used to promulgate the regression formula, and the students were initially selected by performance on a test the scores of which define one of the correlated variables, then this sample is said to be truncated on the variable. Correlation and prediction will be biased against the selection variable in many applications.
4. There should be *homoscedasticity*; that is, the variance of the Y-score distribution should be constant at all points along the regression line where predictions are being made. This assumption applies to the underlying population and may not necessarily be satisfied in the sample data.
5. A true line must be defined. If the breadth of the *confidence* interval of interest is equal to or greater than the length of the regression line in the range of interest, then no true line has been defined.
6. Estimates of Y should only be made from X values of persons from the same population as those on whom the calculation of the regression equation was based.
7. Confidence in estimates diminishes in proportion to the distance on the regression line away from the point where the means for X and Y coincide. Therefore, caution is needed regarding estimates at the extreme ends of the regression line, especially when they are beyond the range of existing data used in the computation of the regression equation.

The Confidence Interval

When we estimate scores on a test by means of regression procedure, there is always an element of error of estimation unless there is a perfect correlation between the two variables in the regression equation. The amount of error in the estimate depends on the strength of the correlation and the magnitude of the variability of the distribution of the dependent or predicted variable. This relationship is summarized as follows:

$$s_{y \cdot x} = s_y \sqrt{1 - r_{xy}^2} \qquad (5.11)$$

where, $s_{y \cdot x}$ = the *standard error of estimate*
s_y = the standard deviation of the dependent variable
r_{xy} = the correlation coefficient

The term *standard error of estimate* implies that if we computed a set of predicted Y-scores and subtracted from these the values of the actual Y-scores, we could form a distribution of errors of estimation using the absolute deviations of estimated scores from observed scores. This distribution of errors of estimate has a standard deviation known as the standard error of estimate.

We know from the properties of z-scores, and their relationship to the area under the normal curve described in Table B of Appendix A, that approximately 68 percent of a normal distribution is contained in the interval between one standard deviation below and one standard deviation above the mean. Similarly, 95 percent of the distribution is bounded by the interval ±1.96s. We can now apply this concept to determine the confidence we can place in our estimates of Y. We say we are 95 percent confident that the actual value of Y lies somewhere between the interval plus or minus 1.96 times the standard error of estimate. Similarly, to find the 99 percent confidence interval, we start with the predicted Y value and add and subtract 2.58 times the standard error of estimate to bracket the interval of confidence around the estimated Y value.

Returning to our sample data of Table 5.2, we can now compute the standard error of estimate and the confidence interval for any level of confidence desired. Since the correlation was 0.88 and the standard deviation of Y was 90.60, we determine the standard error of estimate by referring to Formula 5.11 as follows:

$$s_{y \cdot x} = 90.60 \sqrt{1 - (.88)^2} = 43.03$$

The 95 percent confidence interval would then be

$$\pm 1.96(43.03) = \pm 84.34$$

If a student scored 33 on our locally developed proficiency exam, we would estimate his or her TOEFL score at 485, and we would be 95 percent confident that his or her actual TOEFL score lies somewhere in the interval, 485 ± 84.34, or 400.66 to 569.34.

5.2 The Phi Coefficient

In many instances we may wish to correlate scores for two items the scores of which are binary, i.e., either correct or incorrect. We do this to determine how highly interrelated the items of a test may be, whether we wish to ensure homogeneity or eliminate redundancy. To do this we may resort to the following

TABLE 5.3   Phi coefficient pass-fail contingency table based on items 10 and 11 of Table 3.4

		Item 11 Fail	Item 11 Pass
Item 10	Pass	A 4	B 14
	Fail	C 7	D 5

formula, which produces the same product-moment correlation coefficient, but computation has been simplified because of the binary nature of the item scores:

$$r_{phi} = \frac{p_{ik} - p_i p_k}{\sqrt{p_i q_i p_k q_k}} \qquad (5.12)$$

where, r_{phi} = the phi coefficient
p_{ik} = the proportion of persons getting both items correct
p_i = the proportion of persons getting item i correct
p_k = the proportion of persons getting item k correct
q_i = the proportion of persons getting item i incorrect
q_k = the proportion of persons getting item k incorrect

Another formula for the computation of r_{phi} is based on a pass-fail contingency table, as indicated in Table 5.3.

$$r_{phi} = \frac{BC - AD}{\sqrt{(A+B)(C+C)(A+C)(B+D)}} = \frac{(14)(7) - (4)(5)}{\sqrt{(4+14)(7+5)(4+7)(14+5)}} = 0.37 \quad (5.13)$$

In testing the significance of the phi coefficient as a departure from zero correlation, we can use a chi square formula with one degree of freedom as follows:

$$\chi^2 = N r_{phi}^2 \qquad (5.14)$$

To test significance we have only to consult table of significance for chi square in Appendix A (Table F).

5.3   Point Biserial and Biserial Correlation

Point biserial and biserial correlation were introduced on pages 52 and 53. Methods of computation and comparative advantages and disadvantages are discussed there. Suffice to add here that these methods may be applied to situations where any binary variable, such as scores on a test item, is to be correlated with a continuous variable, such as total score on a test. The point biserial correlation would give the same result as the product-moment correlation; however, some computational ease is introduced by Equation 4.4, as an artifact of the presence of a binary variable.

5.4 Correction for Part-Whole Overlap

It frequently happens that an inflated correlation is computed between an item and a total score or between a subtest and a total score. In these cases it must be remembered that part of the magnitude of the coefficient is due to the presence of the item or subtest in the total score itself. Of course, a relationship will exist when one of the variables is a component of the other variable. It is usually desirable to remove the contribution of the component variable to the total variable before reporting the correlation coefficient. This can be done in two ways.

The item or subtest can be removed from the total score. Thus correlation would be between the item or subtest and the combination of all other items or subtests. This procedure becomes extremely tedious when one is dealing with a large test or test battery and comparisons are being made among all component score correlations with total score. This is because a new total score variable must be computed for every correlation computation.

A more common procedure is to compute correlations between component variables and total score and then to correct these correlations for part-whole overlap. In this way the contribution of item or subtest score to total score may be removed in a post hoc manner by means of the following formula:

$$r_{(t-i)} = \frac{r_{it}s_t - s_i}{\sqrt{s_i^2 + s_t^2 - 2r_{it}s_is_t}} \qquad (5.15)$$

where, $r_{(t-i)}$ = the correlation corrected for part-whole overlap
r_{it} = the item or subtest total score correlation
s_t = total score standard deviation
s_i = item or subtest standard deviation
s_t^2 = the total score variance
s_i^2 = the item or subtest variance

This procedure becomes particularly useful in the computation of internal item validity discussed in chapter seven.

5.5 Correlation and Explanation

The correlation coefficient has another interesting property of use to us in language test development. Since correlation is a measure of the relatedness of two variables, the square of the correlation coefficient tells us the proportion of variance in one variable accounted for by the other variable. Consider Figure 5.3.

If, according to Figure 5.3, we found that reading comprehension correlated 0.70 with general EFL proficiency then by taking r^2, 0.49, we can say that reading comprehension accounts for 49 percent of the variability in EFL proficiency. In this case, r^2 is termed the *coefficient of determination*.

It is useful to point out here that correlation does not necessarily imply causation. If, for example, we found a high correlation between annual rainfall in a region and sales of umbrellas, we could not infer that our purchase of an umbrella would cause it to rain. Similarly, high correlation does not tell us which of the two

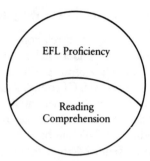

FIGURE 5.3   Illustration of the explanatory relationship between reading comprehension and EFL proficiency

variables causes the other, or indeed whether both are brought about by a third variable or a combination of other variables.

5.6   Summary

This chapter has been concerned with item and test relatedness. The use and methods of computation of the product-moment correlation coefficient, the phi coefficient, biserial and point biserial correlation, and the coefficient of determination have been presented. The computation and application of regression and prediction have been discussed. Computation of the confidence interval and correction for part-whole overlap have been introduced.

Exercises

1. If one variable increases as the other decreases, what is the direction of correlation?
2. What is the essential difference between scatterplots of low-correlated variables and those of high-correlated variables?
3. What can we infer from a perfect correlation?
4. What does it mean if we say a correlation coefficient is significant at the $p < .05$ level?
5. When do we use a one-tailed versus a two-tailed test of the significance of a correlation coefficient?

6. Look at the following paired scores on listening comprehension (X) and general proficiency (Y) for ten students:

X	Y
25	28
13	21
15	22
19	27
17	31
16	22
21	29
24	33
22	26
21	29

Compute the correlation coefficient for these scores. What is the coefficient of determination?

7. Compute the regression equation for the prediction of general proficiency and estimate that proficiency for a listening comprehension score of 23.

8. Find the 95 percent confidence interval around the estimate in exercise 7.

9. Consider the following scoring matrix:

		Items				
		1	2	3	4	5
	1	1	1	1	0	0
	2	0	1	0	1	0
Persons	3	1	0	0	0	0
	4	0	1	1	1	1
	5	1	1	1	1	1

Compute the phi coefficient between items 3 and 4.

10. Using the matrix in exercise 9, compute the point-biserial correlation between item 3 and total score. Correct for part-whole overlap.

Chapter Six

Language Test Reliability

6.1 What Is Reliability?

In chapter one we were introduced to the notion that reliability has to do with accuracy of measurement. This kind of accuracy is reflected in the obtaining of similar results when measurement is repeated on different occasions or with different instruments or by different persons. This characteristic of reliability is sometimes termed *consistency*. We can readily see how measurement with a steel tape measure would give more reliable or consistent results than measurement with an elastic tape measure. Thus, we infer that the steel tape measure is a more reliable instrument.

In thinking of psychological tests in general, and language tests in particular, we say reliability is present when an examinee's results are consistent on repeated measurement. With a group of examinees, reliable measurement is indicated by a tendency to rank order the entire group in the same way on repeated administrations of the test. Even if a slight practice effect is present, such that students do somewhat better on a second administration than they did on the first, if all scores improve equally, students will be rank-ordered in the same way on the two administrations, the intercorrelation of these repeated measures will be high, and the test will be called reliable.

It follows logically that test scoring distributions that have high variance or great distance between scores will be less likely to have persons exchange positions on an ability continuum or change their rank order with repeated administrations of the test. Thus, test reliability is also related to high variance of the *true score* distribution. For this reason, coupled with the fact that *reliability* has many definitions, some authors prefer to use the term *person separability* (Wright and

Stone, 1979). For the individual, however, reliability is said to be associated with the tendency of his or her score not to vary with repeated measurement.

Reliability is thus a measure of accuracy, consistency, dependability, or fairness of scores resulting from administration of a particular examination. It should not, however, be confused with the notion of validity, which is discussed more thoroughly in the next chapter. If reliability is associated with accuracy of measurement, it follows that reliability will increase as error of measurement is made to diminish. We actually quantify reliability so that we can be aware of the amount of error present in our measurement and the degree of confidence possible in scores obtained from the test.

6.2 True Score and the Standard Error of Measurement

Usually when we administer and score a test, some error of measurement is present. Consider by way of example a listening comprehension test of 100 items administered to a class of 25 students. We might imagine two students of exactly equal listening comprehension ability who got different scores on the test. Let us say, one student managed to guess several items successfully and obtained a score of 84. The other student sat at the back of the room, failed to hear the tape recorder clearly, and got a score of 78. Let us say that the score showing the true ability or the true score of both students was 81. As a result of an error due to guessing, the one student obtained a score that was three points above his true score. Due to an error of administration, the other student got a score that was three points below his true score. If we could record the amount of error of measurement for each student as a deviation from his or her true score, we would find the distribution of all errors around their true scores to resemble closely in principle the distribution of errors of estimate around observed Y-scores discussed on page 67. In fact, a close cousin of the standard error of estimate introduced in that section is the *standard error of measurement*, which we are about to consider. The formula for the standard error of measurement is almost identical to Formula 5.11.

$$s_e = s_t \ \sqrt{1 - r_{tt}} \qquad (6.1)$$

where, s_e = the standard error of measurement
s_t = the standard deviation of test scores
r_{tt} = the reliability coefficient

Notice that, as reliability, r_{tt}, increases, error of measurement, s_e, decreases. Notice that as the standard deviation of the observed scores increases, the standard error of measurement also increases. This is because the observed score variance contains error variance, and as you increase the one, the other increases as well, provided the reliability is constant. The relation between the variances of true score, observed score, and error then may be expressed as follows:

$$s_t^2 = s_T^2 + s_e^2 \qquad (6.2)$$

where, s_t^2 = observed score variance

s_T^2 = true score variance

s_e^2 = error variance

Here we are saying in effect that observed scores are composed of true scores and errors of measurement.

Reliability, if we were to express it as a coefficient similar in range to a correlation coefficient (0.0 to 1.00), could be expressed as the ratio of true score variance to observed score variance as follows:

$$r_{tt} = \frac{s_T^2}{s_t^2} = \frac{s_T^2}{s_T^2 + s_e^2} \qquad (6.3)$$

It is obvious from Formula 6.3 that the higher the true score variance in relation to the error variance, the greater will be the reliability of the test. Our task in improving test reliability then is essentially that of reducing measurement error.

It is interesting to note that, if we take Formula 6.1 and solve for reliability using information provided in Formula 6.2, we will derive Formula 6.3.

6.3   Threats to Test Reliability

Reliability has been shown to be another word for consistency of measurement. A variety of kinds of measurement error can introduce fluctuations in observed scores and thus reduce reliability. Here it is important for us to consider these sources of measurement error as threats to reliability and to seek ways of eliminating or minimizing their influence.

Fluctuations in the Learner

A variety of changes may take place within the learner that either will introduce error on repeated administrations or will change the learner's true score from time one to time two. If true scores change, correlations between repeated sets of observed scores will go down, causing us to underestimate the reliability of the test.

Changes in True Score

Changes in the examinee such as maturation, further learning, or forgetting may bring about fluctuations in true score. When this occurs, correlations between the scores obtained from two separate administrations of the same test on the same persons will be reduced in magnitude. As a result, reliability calculated by test-retest procedures will be underestimated. To minimize this problem in language testing the following procedures should be followed: (a) the time interval between administrations should be no greater than two weeks, (b) no feedback should be provided to students regarding correct and incorrect answers on the first administration of the test, (c) examinees should not be forewarned that the test will be administered

75

a second time, and (d) the test itself should contain sufficient items so that it will not be possible for examinees to remember a significant portion of the items of the test.

Temporary Psychological or Physiological Changes

Temporary changes in the examinee may introduce measurement error. Influences such as fatigue, sickness, emotional disturbance, and practice effect may cause the examinee's observed score to temporarily deviate from his or her true score, or that score which reflects his or her actual ability. For this reason, care should be taken to ensure the examinee's physical and emotional comfort during the administration of the test. On repeated administrations of a test to the same persons, sufficient time should elapse between administrations (say, two or three days), and a sufficient number of items should be included to minimize practice effect. Exact decisions of the time of the interval between administrations of the test will depend on such factors as length of the test, maturation, subsequent learning exposure, examinee fatigue, and possible practice effect.

Fluctuations in Scoring

Subjectivity in scoring or mechanical errors in the scoring process may introduce inconsistencies in scores and produce unreliable measurement. These kinds of inconsistencies usually occur within or between the raters themselves.

Intra-Rater Error Variance

Any rater called upon to make subjective estimates of composition quality or speaking ability in a language is liable to be inconsistent in judgment. This is particularly true in situations where the raters are not provided with detailed rating schedules, as discussed in chapter three. The rater himself or herself is liable to become less accurate with fatigue. Experience gained in the course of marking or rating may result in greater accuracy of estimates for later examinees. Changing attitudes or other idiosyncracies on the part of the rater can affect the scoring estimates. It has been observed that many raters are highly influenced by superficial factors, such as handwriting beauty, when marking compositions. If the rater knows the examinee and the examinee's name appears on the paper, personality factors may influence the scoring process. To minimize these kinds of measurement error, raters may be encouraged (a) to use rating schedules, (b) insofar as possible to employ anonymous or "blind" marking procedures, and (c) to mark the writing or speaking sample a second time to ensure consistency of estimate.

Inter-Rater Error Variance

Raters may differ widely among themselves in estimates of appropriate marks for the same sample of language performance. Such differences may arise from various levels of experience in rating or familiarity with the language under consideration. Differences may spring from deep philosophical or personality origins, or they may be mere subjective whims, such that ratings would be found to coincide more closely if the raters were allowed to discuss the reasons for their estimates. In these instances measurement error may be reduced (a) by employing detailed rating schedules for the independent use of all judges, (b) by requesting judges to repeat their estimates in cases where estimates were widely divergent, and (c) by insisting on rater experience and competence.

Fluctuations in Test Administration

Inconsistencies in the administrative process may introduce measurement error and thus reduce test reliability. This is most observable in situations where the test is administered to different groups in different locations or on different days, but may also appear within one administration in one location.

Regulatory Fluctuations

Differences in the clarity of instructions, the time of test administration, the extent of test administrator interaction with examinees, the prevention of cheating behavior, and the reporting of time remaining are all potential sources of measurement error. Prior decisions must be made regarding the administrative procedures that should produce the most reliable test scores, and then these procedures should be followed consistently for all examinees in every administrative instance. To ensure this standardization of procedures, it is often necessary to provide training sessions for the test administrators. At least written guidelines for test administration should be supplied to all administrators. Details should be explicit down to the identification of pauses in dictation passages.

Fluctuations in the Administrative Environment

Environmental inconsistencies may also introduce measurement error. Typical inconsistencies occur when there are interruptions and distractions for one group of examinees and not for another. Also situations arise where the reading light may be better in one situation than in another. Even more typical is a situation where listening comprehension passages may be presented at different rates or volumes for different groups of examinees. Within the same examination room there may be disparities when the people at the back of the room are not able to hear the aural stimuli or instructions clearly. These and many other environmental factors should be made optimally conducive to good results and experienced equally by all examinees. Standardizing such influences in this way will help to minimize measurement error resulting from administrative inequities.

Test Characteristics Affecting Reliability

Often measurement error is an artifact of the nature of the test itself. By becoming aware of test characteristics that may affect reliability, we can avoid measurement error that may be "built into" the test itself.

Length, Difficulty, and Boundary Effects

Reliability is affected by the number of items in the test. We can readily understand how it happens that with more items in the test a greater range of scores is possible, and thus examinees are more widely dispersed along the scoring continuum. In this way it can be said that we have greater *person separability* and less likelihood that examinees would change rank order on repeated administrations of the test. The nature of the relationship between reliability and test length is explored in greater detail later in this chapter, but for now we can see that adding more items of similar kind should improve test reliability up to a point of *asymptote* where little further contribution is made to reliability regardless of how many further items are added. Figure 6.1 illustrates this point more clearly. In this example we can readily see that, for these particular items with this particular sample of persons, little reliability is gained by adding more than 75 items. 75 items and 0.78 reliability may be thought of as the point of asymptote.

Test difficulty as well may be shown to have an influence on reliability of the test. When tests are overly easy or difficult for a given group of examinees, skewed scoring distributions will result, as noted in Figure 3.2. With skewed distributions, scores are unnaturally compacted at one end of the scoring continuum or the other. These phenomena of compacting of scores at either end of the scoring continuum are also referred to as *boundary effects*. As a result of such effects it becomes more difficult to distinguish among persons in their ability at the compacted ends of the scoring distribution. There is a loss of person separability or reliability. As is self-evident, such unreliable tests should not be used for purposes of program evaluation, for little discriminatory power is available at the compacted ends of the continuum. It is also evident that such tests may be perfectly suitable when applied to examinees of appropriate, median ability. So then it can be shown that the same test may be reliable for one set of examinees and unreliable for another set with a different ability level.

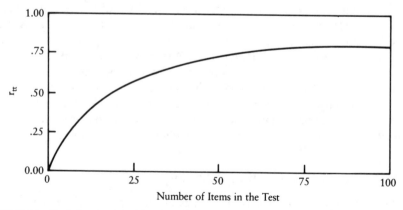

FIGURE 6.1 Depicting the probable relationship between reliability and test length for a test with 0.70 reliability with 50 items.

78

Discriminability, Speededness, and Homogeneity

Other features of tests and items that will influence reliability include *discriminability*, *speededness*, and *homogeneity*. We have already considered item discriminability in chapter four. It follows logically on that discussion that if we include items in the test with high discriminability, the test as a whole will have greater power to discriminate among people who are low and high in the ability of interest. In other words, the test will have greater person separability or reliability.

In chapter one we reflected briefly on the difference between speed tests and power tests. It was pointed out that most tests fall somewhere on a continuum between the two extremes. Here we should consider the fact that any element of speededness in a test should increase the person separability beyond that which accrues from mere differences in examinee knowledge about the test content. By introducing an element of speededness, we are discriminating among persons not only in their knowledge of the facts, but in the speed with which they are able to report that knowledge. Of course, if all of the facts are known to all of the examinees, then the test becomes a pure speed test, and examinees are discriminated only in the speed with which they respond to the items of the test. This influence of speededness upon reliability should be carefully considered during the administration of the test. For most power tests for which *internal consistency* measures of reliability are calculated, failure to allow examinees a reasonable amount of time to complete the test will result in overestimates of test reliability. On the other hand, if the test becomes too difficult as a result of the element of speededness, reliability will diminish, as indicated in the previous section. Special procedures must be followed in the calculation of reliability of speed tests, (e.g., test-retest and parallel forms methods), and these procedures are introduced later in this chapter.

Another test characteristic which will influence estimates of reliability is the homogeneity of item type. When reliability is determined by internal consistency methods such as the *split half method*, where performance on half of the test is correlated with performance on the other half in order to determine how internally consistent the test may be, it follows that the greater similarity of item type there is, the higher the correlation of the parts of the test will be. We can increase reliability and reduce measurement error by including items of similar format and content, assuming that the overall pattern of performance will be similar for all items. At this point we can see that reliability and content validity are not always compatible. Often, to ensure content validity, we must include items with wide diversity of content. This procedure will tend to reduce reliability estimated as internal consistency. The relation between reliability and validity is discussed in greater detail in the next chapter.

Error Associated with Response Characteristics

Certain characteristics of the manner in which examinees respond to the examination may also introduce measurement error. Some of these response characteristics relate to the degree of arbitrariness or chance associated with the response itself. Other response characteristics relate to examinee traits.

Response Arbitrariness

An important source of measurement error, particularly with objective type tests, is *guessing*. Understandably, guessing takes place more frequently when these objective-type tests are too difficult for any given group of examinees. Some persons, especially young boys, are impulsive rather than reflective in test-taking behavior. In extreme cases impulsive persons may need help in giving more careful consideration to the quality of their responses. To ensure greater reliability of measurement, correction-for-guessing procedures are often employed, as described in chapter three. *Latent trait* testing procedures have been used effectively to identify guessers and isolate them from the sample. Such techniques are introduced in chapter eight.

Response arbitrariness may stem from insincerity or lack of cooperation on the part of the examinee. It may be important to the accuracy of the results of a test to convince the examinees that the test-taking experience is for their personal benefit or for the good of mankind. To promote such cooperation it may help to provide confidential results to the examinees. If the examinees are students in an academic program, it will help to confine the examination content to matters relating to their course of instruction. Incentives may need to be offered in some instances.

Wiseness and Familiarity Responses

Tests will tend to be less reliable for persons who have had no prior exposure to the test format, and for persons who have developed a high degree of "test-wiseness." For the former category of persons, time will be lost in interpreting the nature of the task. For the latter category, because of the developed ability to respond correctly to objective items without anticipated content mastery, success on the examination may not reflect actual ability in the content field. In other words, observed scores may overestimate true scores because of measurement error due to test-wiseness. In general, this source of measurement error may be minimized by providing familiarization tasks and strategy guidelines for all examinees prior to the examination, and by eliminating convergence and divergence cues from the item response options.

6.4 Methods of Reliability Computation

While reliability normally exists in the zero to one range, and while it always represents the ratio of true score to observed score variances, a variety of methods exists for the computation of reliability in any given instance. The choice of the method of computation will depend on such factors as the nature of the threats to reliability present, ease of computation, and the nature of the test and the testing situation.

Test-Retest Method

The simplest computational method, *test-retest*, is calculated by means of product-moment correlation of two sets of scores for the same persons. The same test is readministered to the same people following an interval of no more than two weeks. The purpose of the interval limitation is to prevent changes in the examinee's true score, which would cause underestimation of reliability by this method. A formula might be expressed for this method as follows:

$$r_{tt} = r_{1,2} \tag{6.4}$$

where, r_{tt} = the reliability coefficient using this method

$r_{1,2}$ = the correlation of the scores at time one with those at time two for the same test used with the same persons

Parallel Forms Method

By this method of computation of reliability, two tests are administered to the same sample of persons and the results are correlated using product-moment correlation. However, the tests employed in this method must satisfy rigid requirements of equivalence. Thus, these tests are termed *parallel forms, equivalent forms,* or *alternate forms*. To demonstrate equivalence of tests, these tests must (1) show equivalent difficulty as indicated by no significant difference in mean scores when the tests are administered to the same persons and their means are compared using the t-test, (2) show equivalent variance when the variances of the scoring distributions of the two tests are compared for the same sample of persons by means of an F-Max test, and (3) show equivalent covariance as indicated by no significant differences in correlation coefficients among equivalent forms or among correlation coefficients of equivalent forms with a concurrent criterion, all administered to the same persons and compared by means of the t-test.

According to classical reliability theory, the correlation between the scores of two parallel forms administered to the same persons at the same time should be the same as the correlation between the scores of either of the two forms readministered to the same persons by the test-retest method, assuming there is no practice effect. One of the benefits of this method is that practice effect is controlled, since the examinees do not encounter the same items twice. In practice, however, it is almost impossible to satisfy conditions of *equality* of means, variances, and correlations. And even the requirements for establishing less restrictive *equivalence* explained above are difficult to meet. For these reasons, test developers usually attempt to *equate* tests rather than establish *equivalence*. Equated tests are tests that yield different scores for the same persons, but the scores of these tests have been equated in the sense that we are informed that a score of X on one test is equivalent to a score of Y on the other. Usually equated tests are accompanied by tables of score equivalencies, so that one may readily equate scores on one form with those on another form.

The term *random parallel tests* has been used to describe tests that have been composed of items drawn randomly from the same population of items. By this less restrictive definition, tests are said to be randomly parallel when the same numbers of items with equivalent content are randomly drawn from a pool of such items. Consider, for example, a pool of items for measuring perfect tense. Imagine that each of these items has a stem with the same number of words and the same multiple-choice distractors appearing beneath the stem. If we had a collection of such items built around the same "shell," we could argue that a random selection of these items assigned to the various tests would produce random parallel tests if the same number of such items were used in each form.

In general, the procedure for calculating reliability using parallel forms is to administer the tests to the same persons at the same time and correlate the results as indicated in the following formula:

$$r_{tt} = r_{A,B} \qquad\qquad (6.5)$$

where, r_{tt} = the reliability coefficient

$r_{A,B}$ = the correlation of form A with form B of the test when administered to the same people at the same time

If the tests used by this method satisfy the most rigid requirements of parallel tests, which almost never happens in fact, the coefficient derived is called the *coefficient of precision*, and is usually high in magnitude, approaching 1.00. If the tests satisfy the requirements of equivalence described above, but the true score on one differs slightly from the true score on the other for the same person, the coefficient derived is only an estimate of the coefficient of precision, and is termed the *coefficient of equivalence*. If we have the least-restrictive situation described above, random parallel tests, then the coefficient derived is called an *internal consistency coefficient* and merely serves to indicate the extent to which the items are homogeneous, measuring the same content.

Inter-Rater Reliability

Another procedure for estimating reliability is used when scores on the test are independent estimates by two or more judges or raters. This is usually the situation when the test is measuring composition writing ability or speaking ability, for example. In these instances reliability is estimated as the correlation of the ratings of one judge with those of another. But because the final mark given to the examinee is a combination of the ratings of all judges, whether an average or a simple sum of ratings, the actual level of reliability will depend on the number of raters or judges. In general, the more raters present in the determination of the mark, the more reliable will be the mark derived from all ratings. So there are two steps in the estimation of inter-rater reliability. *First*, the ratings of all judges must be intercorrelated. If more than two raters are involved in the rating of all examinees, an average of all correlation coefficients is derived. For this average, use is made of a Fisher Z transformation, especially when a correlation coefficient is far above or below 0.50. This is because the correlation coefficient itself is on a non-interval scale. *Second*, the correlation coefficient or average coefficient is adjusted by means of the Spearman-Brown Prophecy Formula to make the final reliability estimate reflect the number of raters or judges who participated in the rating of the examinees. These steps are summarized in the following formula:

$$r_{tt} = \frac{nr_{A,B}}{1 + (n-1)r_{A,B}} \qquad (6.6)$$

where, r_{tt} = inter-rater reliability

n = the number of raters whose combined estimates form the final mark for the examinees

$r_{A,B}$ = the correlation between the raters, or the average correlation among all raters if there are more than two

This formula is known as the *Spearman-Brown Prophecy Formula*, and it is also used to describe the relationship between reliability and test length as we shall see in the next section.

Split Half Reliability

Often situations arise where reliability must be estimated and it is not possible to administer the test twice according to the test-retest method. Also there may be no parallel forms of the test, and only one rater is involved in the scoring. In these instances reliability may be determined with reference to the structure of the test itself. Because the focus of these next methods for estimating reliability is internal, within one administration of the exam itself, these methods are collectively referred to as internal consistency methods, and the reliability estimates derived are termed *internal consistency reliability estimates*. Split half reliability is one variety of internal consistency reliability. According to the split half method, a test is administered once to a group of examinees, it is divided into halves, the scores of each half are correlated with the other half, and the coefficient derived is adjusted by means of the Spearman-Brown Prophecy Formula to allow for the fact that the total score on the test is based on an instrument that is twice as long as each of its halves. The test may be split in a variety of ways. If the test is comprised of items, a common technique is to place all of the odd-numbered items in one half and all of the even-numbered items in the other half. These two halves then are scored separately and are correlated with each other. For tests without items, some other method of dividing the test may be used. If, for example, the test consisted of a series of compositions, each group of compositions may be scored separately and correlated with the other. A formula for the split half method may be expressed as follows:

$$r_{tt} = \frac{2r_{A,B}}{1 + r_{A,B}} \qquad (6.7)$$

where, r_{tt} = reliability estimated by the split half method

$r_{A,B}$ = the correlation of the scores from one half of the test with those from the other half

Unfortunately, as one can readily imagine, the reliability estimated provided by this method will change according to the manner in which the test is divided. For tests with binary item scores, this deficiency may be corrected by means of one of the following methods.

Kuder-Richardson Formula 20

If we were to use the split half method described above, and we were able to divide the test into a series of halves according to every possible combination of items, and for each division we correlated scores from the two halves, we would obtain a series of correlation coefficients. If we adjusted these coefficients by means of the prophecy formula and then averaged them by use of Fisher Z transformations, we would obtain an estimate of reliability that would control for the arbitrariness of the way in which the test was divided. Kuder-Richardson Formula 20 permits us to arrive at the same final estimate of reliability without having to compute reliability estimates for every possible split half combination. The KR method employs the following formula:

$$r_{tt} = \frac{n}{(n-1)} \left(\frac{s_t^2 - \Sigma s_i^2}{s_t^2} \right)$$
(6.8)

where, r_{tt} = the KR 20 reliability estimate

n = the number of items in the test

s_t^2 = the variance of the test scores

Σs_i^2 = the sum of the variances of all items, which may also be expressed as Σpq

The KR 20 formula yields the same results as Cronbach's alpha approach to estimation of internal consistency (Cronbach et al.; 1963).

Kuder-Richardson Formula 21

A variation of the previous method may be used when it is not possible or not desirable to calculate the variances of each of the items. It should be remembered, however, that this KR 21 shortcut method is less accurate than KR 20, as it slightly underestimates the actual reliability. Both KR 20 and KR 21 tend to provide distorted estimates when only a few items occur in the test. KR formula 21 is expressed as follows:

$$r_{tt} = \frac{n}{(n-1)} \left\{ 1 - \frac{\bar{X} - \bar{X}^2/n}{s_t^2} \right\}$$
(6.9)

where, r_{tt} = the KR 21 reliability estimate

n = the number of items in the test

$\bar{X}$ = the mean of scores on the test

s_t^2 = the variance of test scores

It should be noted briefly here that internal consistency methods of estimating test reliability have not been found acceptable in recent U.S. court decisions, where test-retest reliability was deemed more appropriate (Fisher, 1980). This may be less of a commentary on the inadequacy of internal consistency measures than on their difficulty of interpretation by the non-specialist.

6.5   Reliability and Test Length

We have already observed, in Figure 6.1, how reliability increases as items are added to the test. We have also encountered the Spearman-Brown Prophecy Formula, which summarizes the exact relationship between reliability and test length. This formula may be used not only to estimate what the reliability of the test would become if we increased the test to a specified length, but also to determine how much longer a given test would need to be in order to achieve a specified level of reliability. Bear in mind that use of the Spearman-Brown Prophecy Formula to estimate reliability with changes in test length assumes that any items added to a test are of the same kind as those already in the test. If the test is lengthened by addition of heterogeneous items, the formula will overestimate adjusted reliability. To relate test length to reliability we may use the formula as follows:

$$r_{ttn} = \frac{nr_{tt}}{1 + (n-1)r_{tt}} \qquad (6.10)$$

where, r_{ttn} = the reliability of the test when adjusted to n times its original length
r_{tt} = the observed reliability of the test at its present length
n = the number of times the length of the test is to be augmented (e.g., for a test of 20 items, if 5 items are added, n would equal 1.25)

To determine the test length, or the number of raters needed to achieve a desired level of reliability, we may employ the following formula:

$$n = \frac{r_{ttd}(1 - r_{tt})}{r_{tt}(1 - r_{ttd})} \qquad (6.11)$$

where, n = the number of times the test length must be increased with similar items, or the number of raters needed
r_{ttd} = the level of reliability desired
r_{tt} = the present observed level of reliability, or the correlation between two raters

Notice that n in these formulas is not the same as the n employed in the Kuder-Richardson formulas.

6.6   Correction for Attenuation

Now that we can estimate the reliability of any given test, it is possible to hold reliability constant when comparing the correlation between tests. When we compute a correlation matrix from a battery of subtests, for example, we should bear in mind that the magnitudes of these correlation coefficients is affected by the reliabilities of the subtests. Consider the example in Table 6.1. Notice that the highest correlation with speaking is exhibited by the reading subtest. So we might be tempted to conclude that reading is more highly related to speaking than is grammar. However, since the magnitude of the observed correlations is partially a function of reliabilities of subtests, this conclusion may be unwarranted. A correc-

TABLE 6.1 A hypothetical correlation matrix showing the intercorrelations of three subtests of a language test battery

	Grammar	Reading	Speaking
Grammar	1.00		
Reading	0.75	1.00	
Speaking	0.55	0.60	1.00

tion must be made in the correlation coefficients to hold reliability constant. This procedure is called *correction for attenuation* and employs the following formula:

$$r_{CA} = \frac{r_{xy}}{\sqrt{r_{ttx}r_{tty}}} \qquad (6.12)$$

where, r_{CA} = the correlation coefficient corrected for attenuation
r_{xy} = the correlation between any two variables X and Y
r_{ttx} = the reliability coefficient for the measure of the X variable
r_{tty} = the reliability coefficient for the measure of the Y variable

Let us suppose, for the correlation matrix of Table 6.1, that the reliability coefficients for the three subtests of language proficiency are as follows: Grammar, 0.70; Reading, 0.90; and Speaking, 0.80. Although the initial correlations with Speaking were 0.60 for Reading and 0.55 for Grammar, the varying levels of reliability for these subtests suggest that we should disattenuate, i.e., correct these correlation coefficients for attenuation. Using the formula given above, we find that the disattenuated correlation of Reading with Speaking becomes

$$\frac{.60}{\sqrt{.90 \times .80}} = .71$$

On the other hand, the disattenuated correlation of Grammar with Speaking becomes

$$\frac{.55}{\sqrt{.70 \times .80}} = .73$$

This tells us that, when we control for the differences in reliability among the subtests in this hypothetical example, we find that Grammar is actually more highly related to Speaking than is Reading.

6.7 Summary

In the present chapter we have considered the nature of reliability. We have seen its relationship to *true score* and *standard error of measurement*. We have considered threats to reliability in testing, including fluctuations in the learner, fluctuations in scoring, fluctuations in test administration, test characteristics affecting reliability, and threats to reliability arising from the characteristics of the responses of the examinees. We have noted common methods for the computation of reliability, including *test-retest, parallel forms, inter-rater, split half, Kuder-Richardson 20*, and *Kuder-Richardson 21* methods. A discussion was provided about the relationship between reliability and test length, and the purposes and methods of *correction* for *attenuation* were presented.

Exercises

1. What happens to reliability as the variance of observed scores increases, providing the error of measurement remains constant?
2. If all error of measurement could be removed from a person's observed score, what would we call the remaining quantity?
3. Imagine a situation where an interview was conducted to ascertain speaking ability in English as a Foreign Language. Assuming that only one rater was available and each interviewee was interviewed twice to provide an estimate of test-retest reliability, list as many threats to this reliability estimate as you can.
4. What are the advantages of KR 20 reliability over split half and KR 21 reliability estimation methods?
5. What are two primary uses of the Spearman-Brown Prophecy Formula in its various expressions?
6. If the reliability of a certain listening comprehension test was estimated as 0.80 and the variance of the observed scores was 25, what would the standard error of measurement be?
7. Consider the following scoring matrix for a multiple-choice vocabulary test:

		Items					
		1	2	3	4	5	6
	1	1	0	0	1	1	0
	2	1	1	0	1	0	1
Persons	3	1	1	1	1	1	0
	4	1	0	0	0	1	0
	5	1	1	1	1	0	0
	6	0	0	0	0	1	0

Compute split half reliability using the odd-even method.
8. If inter-rater reliability was found to be 0.60 for two raters using a rating schedule for EFL compositions, how many independent raters would be needed to attain a reliability of 0.85?
9. If a test of composition writing correlated 0.65 with a test of grammar usage, disattenuate this correlation, assuming that KR 20 reliabilities of the tests were 0.75 for composition writing and 0.85 for grammar usage.
10. Compute KR 20 and KR 21 reliability using the matrix of exercise 7.

Chapter Seven

Test Validity

7.1 What Is Validity of Measurement?

We encountered the idea of validity in chapter one. There it was asserted that invalid tests were those that had undesirable content mixed in with the desirable content. We shall see now that this is only a small part of what is intended by the term *validity*. Validity in general refers to the appropriateness of a given test or any of its component parts as a measure of what it is purported to measure. A test is said to be valid to the extent that it measures what it is supposed to measure. It follows that the term *valid*, when used to describe a test, should usually be accompanied by the preposition *for*. Any given test then may be valid for some purposes, but not for others. The matter of concern in testing is to ensure that any test employed is valid for the purpose for which it is administered.

Validity, like reliability discussed in the previous chapter, may be determined in a variety of ways. Some of these methods are empirical, involving the collection of data and the use of formulae. Other methods are nonempirical, involving inspection, intuition, and common sense. A primary purpose of the present chapter will be to examine these methods for estimating validity of measurement instruments.

7.2 Validity in Relation to Reliability

For most empirical kinds of validity, reliability is a necessary but not sufficient condition for validity to be present. Stated in another way, it is possible for a test to be reliable without being valid for a specified purpose, but it is not possible for a test to be valid without first being reliable. Since empirical validity is usually expressed as a correlation coefficient, called a *validity coefficient*, it is possible to describe the relationship between reliability and validity, where the criterion measure is perfectly reliable, as follows:

$$r_{xy(max)} = \frac{r_{xy}}{\sqrt{r_{tt(x)}}} \tag{7.1}$$

where, $r_{xy(max)}$ = the maximum validity possible for a given reliability

         r_{xy} = the estimated validity coefficient for test X

         $r_{tt(x)}$ = the estimated reliability coefficient for test X

The theoretical upper limit of the validity coefficient then is 1.0. But in practice this is virtually never achieved because it assumes perfect reliability of the test X, and perfect correlation between test X and criterion Y, implying that criterion Y would also need to be perfectly reliable. Since validity criterion measurements are usually not perfectly reliable, it is desirable when estimating validity to correct for the unreliability of the criterion measure. The following formula indicates how this is done:

$$r_{xy(CV)} = \frac{r_{xy}}{\sqrt{r_{tt(y)}}} \tag{7.2}$$

where, $r_{xy(CV)}$ = the corrected validity coefficient

         r_{xy} = the observed validity coefficient

         $r_{tt(y)}$ = the reliability of the criterion measurement

Knowing that validity cannot exceed unity (1.0), we can substitute 1.0 for $r_{xy(max)}$ in Formula 7.1. It then becomes apparent that the maximum observed validity possible occurs when the observed validity, r_{xy}, equals the square root of the reliability, $r_{tt(x)}$. This means that the maximum validity possible in the most ideal situation is equal to the square root of the reliability of the test, or, $\sqrt{r_{tt(x)}}$.

The reader will note that these formulas are all derived from the formula for correction for attenuation (6.12).

Since validity is so closely related to reliability, it follows that increases in reliability, as by increasing test length, will result in increases in validity. The effect on validity obtained by an increase in test length can be expressed by a derivation of the Spearman-Brown Prophecy Formula (6.10):

$$r_{x(n)y} = r_{xy} \sqrt{n/[1 + (n - 1) r_{tt(x)}]} \tag{7.3}$$

where, $r_{x(n)y}$ = the validity coefficient predicted for an increase of the length of test X by *n* times

         r_{xy} = the observed validity coefficient

         n   = the number of times the length of test X is increased

         $r_{tt(x)}$ = the reliability of test X

It must be remembered that these formulae permit the computation of maximum validity coefficients under certain conditions of test length and test reliability. As has been stressed, however, validity ultimately depends upon the use to which the test is put. Even an ideal test which is perfectly reliable and possessing perfect criterion-related validity will be invalid for some purposes. Also, since validity assumes and entails reliability, but reliability does not necessarily imply validity, it is probably more important that a test be valid than that it be found to be reliable.

These relationships between reliability and validity hold true for empirical measures of validity. In the case of nonempirical content validity, a unique relationship often appears. Since content validity depends in part on the diversity and comprehensive nature of the items of the test, it often conflicts with internal consistency reliability which depends on the homogeneity of the items. In this circumstance it may be found that increasing content validity will reduce internal consistency reliability and, conversely, increasing internal consistency reliability will result in a reduction of content validity. An awareness of this potential conflict may permit the reaching of an appropriate balance or compromise in any given test development situation.

7.3   Threats to Test Validity

Since validity has been defined as the capacity of a test to measure what it is purported to measure, a variety of considerations may bring about a reduction of this validity.

Invalid Application of Tests

The most obvious threat to validity arises from the misapplication of tests. A test that is highly valid for measuring general language proficiency in a foreign language may not be valid as a measure of a specific classroom achievement objective. Even though the scores resulting from the administration of such a test may prove to be highly reliable, still the test is invalid if it fails to measure what it is intended to measure. A test of reading comprehension designed to measure achievement in reading comprehension in accordance with the syllabus of first-year university students will probably be invalid if applied to measure achievement of third-year secondary school students. This is not a criticism of the test itself, which may be highly valid for specified purposes, but it is a criticism of the manner in which the test is used. Careful consideration must be given to the designated purpose of a test, including the exact content or objectives said to be measured and the type of examinee for whom the measurement is to occur.

Inappropriate Selection of Content

Frequently tests are constructed with a kind of built-in invalidity. This commonly occurs when items do not match the objectives or the content of instruction. Also, this may happen when the test items are not comprehensive in the sense of reflecting all of the major points of the instructional program. With language achievement tests in particular, it may happen that the test may wrongly require knowledge of vocabulary and structures to which the students were never exposed. It may also happen that the content of the test is biased in favor of some particular

91

grammatical structure to the neglect or exclusion of others. When this happens, it is said that the test lacks *content* or *face validity*.

Often elaborate specifications and expert opinion must be used to ensure that a test exhibit content validity. Specifications may determine the frequency of each item type to be included on the test. A primitive specification scheme would be to draw one item from each page of the textbook.

Imperfect Cooperation of the Examinee

If the examinees do not approach the testing situation in the expected manner, the results may prove to be invalid. This might occur if the examinees are insincere, misinformed, or hostile with regard to the test or the testing situation. In this case we say that the test lacks *response validity*. Consider an example of students responding to a semantic differential questionnaire. Suppose the respondents feel that the questionnaire is a ridiculous waste of time. They may respond by quickly marking a series of answers which do not at all reflect their true opinions. Or consider a situation where the instructions of the test are not clear. Examinees may respond in an inappropriate manner, and their responses be counted incorrect, when they did in fact know the correct answers to the questions but were misinformed regarding how to respond.

Inappropriate Referent or Norming Population

It often happens that standardized proficiency tests are developed on subjects drawn from a distinct population, and the same tests are subsequently administered to subjects or samples drawn from a qualitatively different population. We have seen how items are analyzed based on the patterns of responses observed among the examinees. The point is that items that are found to be suitable, with high discriminability, etc., for one group of examinees may function quite differently with examinees from a qualitatively different underlying population. Consider the Test of English as a Foreign Language (TOEFL) as a case in point. This is a standardized English Language proficiency examination of high measured reliability and validity for the purpose of screening foreign students for entry to American universities. The sample on whom this test was normed or standardized was drawn primarily from among applicants to American universities from diverse national and linguistic backgrounds. If a university entrance examination of English language proficiency is sought for use with student applicants within a foreign country, all having the same native language background, it follows that an exam of equal length developed and normed on the native population will probably be more valid than tests like the TOEFL or the Michigan ELP for screening purposes. Or even the TOEFL itself, if renormed on the students from the single foreign language background, will be found to have many items rejected as lacking discriminability for the monolanguage population.

It follows that careful consideration must always be made of the referent or norming population when selecting standardized tests for any given purpose.

Poor Criterion Selection

In criterion-related validity, a validity coefficient is derived by correlation with scores obtained using some criterion measure. If the criterion measure itself has low reliability and validity as a measure of the target competence, then validity coefficients obtained by this procedure will tend to underestimate true validity. If the problem exists only with the reliability of the criterion, then correction may be made using Formula 7.2 to estimate the true validity. But in cases where the criterion measure lacks content validity, there is no empirical method for estimating true validity from obtained validity. It follows that the selection of a criterion measure must be done with great care to ensure that obtained validity does not grossly underestimate true validity.

Sample Truncation

Any irregularity in the testing situation that reduces test reliability will be found to produce a corresponding reduction in test validity. It will not be profitable for us to review all of the causes of reduced reliability presented in chapter six. But it is worthy of note that sample truncation, or artificial restriction of the range of ability represented in the examinees, will result in underestimation of both reliability and validity. The effect of truncation may not be important in a study comparing validities of different instruments on the same sample when no tests of significance are being made. But when tests of significance are being made, or comparison is being made with coefficients obtained from nontruncated samples, it may prove necessary to correct for attenuation due to sample truncation using an appropriate derivation of Formula 6.12.

Use of Invalid Constructs

Tests are said to be valid insofar as they measure the particular abilities or constructs they are purported to measure. However, in the situation where the constructs or hypothesized abilities are not valid to begin with, it is not possible that the tests will be valid. Suppose, for example, we devised a test to measure how successful a person is. If our test were heavily weighted with items measuring financial success, a wealthy person might pass the test while a poorer person would fail. The poor person might rightfully object that he has been more successful in relationships, in citizenship, in athletics, or in community service than the wealthy person. The test might be found invalid because our concept of success lacked validity.

If the construct of *success* proves to be controversial and value-laden, the construct of *intelligence* has fallen under similar criticism. Before we can determine whether an intelligence test is valid or not, we must know what kind of intelligence is being measured, whether or not the items accurately reflect that kind of intelligence, and whether or not it is important for a given decision-making process to gather information about the specific kind of intelligence in question.

7.4   Major Kinds of Validity

Several kinds of validity have already been mentioned in this chapter. It is appropriate now to examine these and other types in much greater detail.

A distinction has been made between empirical and nonempirical kinds of validity. Nonempirical validity does not require the collection of data or the use of formulae. There are no coefficients or mathematical computations involved. Examples of this kind of validity include *face* or *content validity* and *response validity*.

Empirical kinds of validity usually involve recourse to mathematical formulae for the computation of validity coefficients. Common kinds of empirical validity include *concurrent* and *predictive validity*, which are also termed *criterion-related validities* because they require reference to external criteria. *Construct validity* is another type of validity we shall examine. When construct validity is determined through a process known as *multitrait-multimethod validation*, certain other kinds of validities are computed known as *convergent* and *discriminant validities*. In latent trait analyses described in the next chapter, validity is assessed in terms of measuring of *fit to a specified model*.

Content or Face Validity

Many testing specialists make no distinction between *content* and *face validity*, but consider them to be synonyms (Magnusson, 1967). Others differentiate between them by noting that face validity, unlike content validity, is often determined impressionistically; for example, by asking students whether the exam was appropriate to their expectations. Content or face validity is intuitive and logical, but usually lacks an empirical basis. There is no such thing as a content validity coefficient. As the name implies, content validity is concerned with whether or not the content of the test is sufficiently *representative* and *comprehensive* for the test to be a valid measure of what it is supposed to measure.

Usually a test cannot be exhaustive but must be selective in content. Important decisions must be made about the method of content selection. For achievement tests, this process is usually easier than for proficiency tests, since in the case of the former the content of the test must be bound to the content of instruction, which in turn is constrained by the instructional objectives; whereas in the case of the latter the only guiding constraint may be the length of testing time allotted.

It is precisely in the area of content validity of achievement measures that criterion- or domain-referenced tests have certain profound advantages over more traditional norm-referenced tests, as contrasted in chapter one. To appreciate these advantages it is necessary for us to carefully consider the illustration of item domains within a general subject area domain provided in Figure 7.1.

Let us assume for the sake of illustration that the largest rectangle of Figure 7.1 represents complete mastery of a foreign language as a general subject domain. The tiny circles distributed throughout the figure represent items selected more or less at random to be representative of language mastery. Notice that, if the pattern of item distribution had continued without interruption by the smaller rectangles, our test of language mastery would have consisted of 50 items spread purposely

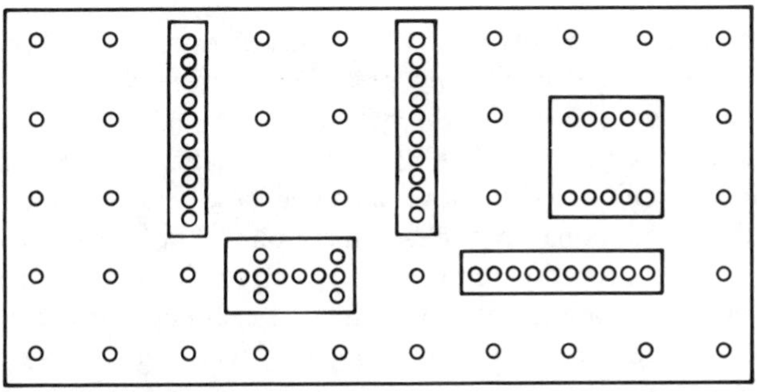

FIGURE 7.1 A conceptual view of items within item domains and their subject domain

over the widest possible representative area. The five smaller rectangles represent five item domains corresponding to five instructional objectives, each containing ten representative items. The 50 items of the large rectangle may be said to comprise a content-valid proficiency exam, in the sense that they are representative and comprehensive. However, 35 of these items are found to lie outside of the areas of a given course content and instructional objectives; therefore, such a test would certainly not have content validity as a measure of the content and objectives of our imaginary language course.

The smaller rectangles contain ten items each, comprising a criterion-referenced exam of 50 items total, measuring achievement corresponding to five specific instructional objectives. This achievement test may be found to be a valid test of the stipulated objectives, but it would not be a valid measure of general language mastery, since so much of the content representative of overall mastery has been neglected in this test.

Some persons will rightfully criticize the criterion-referenced exam in that it is not a comprehensive measure of language mastery. But it is important to remember that no student is likely to attain language mastery as the result of a single course of instruction anyway; and, as Bruner (1966) pointed out, the most pervasive problem of pedagogy is how to design and sequence instruction in the most efficient manner for the most successful learning by the students. The criterion-referenced exam offers the advantage that it is linked to the design and sequencing of instruction. That it is highly selective and limited in the objectives it measures, no one can deny. But so is instruction highly selective and limited in the content it can present.

In order to ensure content validity of both achievement and proficiency exams, it is usually necessary to seek the advice of content experts. It may be desirable to have a panel of experts examine each part of the test and to provide a rating of its local representativeness and global comprehensiveness. Weaker parts of the test would be revised until the experts were in near perfect agreement that the test exhibited content validity. In this way the test developer would have evidence to support the contention that the test was valid.

Another approach would be to develop elaborate specifications for items in a variety of domains representative of the objectives of instruction. A large number of items would then be written in each domain. Random subsets of items could be drawn from each domain at the time of test construction. Less elaborate schemes might involve regular development of a prescribed representative number of items from within each lesson or unit of the syllabus.

Some experts—e.g., Oller (1979); Hinofotis (1981)—have emphasized a distinction between face and content validity. For these persons, content validity is described in the conventional way already mentioned, but face validity becomes a kind of impressionistic reaction to the examination on the part of examinees. This would be ascertained, for example, by asking the examinees afterward how they felt about the examination. If a sizable segment of these examinees expressed the feeling that the exam was not sufficiently representative or comprehensive in terms of their expectations, the exam would be said to lack face validity. Other researchers (Thorndike and Hagen, 1969; Magnusson, 1967), however, do not distinguish between face and content validity.

Response Validity

Another type of nonempirical validity is termed *response validity*. This is intended to describe the extent to which examinees responded in the manner expected by the test developers. If examinees respond in a haphazard or nonreflective manner, their obtained scores may not represent their actual ability. Also, if instructions are unclear and the test format is unfamiliar to the students, their responses may not reflect their true ability, and in this way the test may be said to lack response validity.

It is of utmost importance that the examinees cooperate and participate to the best of their ability during the testing situation. This is particularly true in research contexts where the results of the examination or questionnaire may be of no direct value to the examinee or respondent. Often in such circumstances incentives must be provided to ensure complete cooperation by participants. Violations of response validity can sometimes be detected by asking examinees afterward about the quality of their participation, or by interviewing examinees with unusual or irregular response patterns.

Concurrent Validity

Concurrent validity is a kind of *empirical, criterion-related* validity. It is empirical in the sense that data are collected and formulas are applied to generate an actual numerical validity coefficient. It is criterion-related in the sense that the validity coefficient derived represents the strength of relationship with some external criterion measure.

Typically when one is validating a test of some particular ability in this way, one administers a recognized, reputable test of the same ability to the same persons concurrently or within a few days of the administration of the test to be validated. Scores of the two different tests are then correlated using some formula for the correlation coefficient (e.g., formulas 5.1, 5.2, or 5.3), and the resultant correlation coefficient is reported as a concurrent validity coefficient.

In the situation where the reliability of the criterion measure is known to be less than perfect, it is possible to correct the coefficient obtained above by substituting the known reliability and obtained validity in Formula 7.2. This will produce a more accurate, disattenuated validity coefficient.

In general, care must be taken in the selection of a criterion or concurrent measure. Validities may be grossly underestimated if the criterion measure itself lacks validity.

Predictive Validity

Closely related to concurrent validity is the concept of *predictive validity*. Predictive validity is usually reported in the form of a correlation coefficient with some measure of success in the field or subject of interest. For example, one might administer a university entrance or admissions exam to a group of students at the time of their entry into university. One might then proceed to collect grade-point averages (GPAs) for each of these students after each successive year of university study. Finally, one would correlate admissions exam scores with successive annual GPAs to obtain predictive validity of the admissions exam.

By the procedure described above, entrance exams typically show highest validity after only one year of study. There is a tendency for predictive validity to decrease with each successive year in the program, reflecting maturational changes in the students. Therefore, a further consideration regarding predictive validity is to design and select tests so that they will show the greatest possible stability of validity over time.

Criteria other than GPAs may be selected as success measures. For law students, scores on a bar exam might suffice. For clerical or industrial workers, employer ratings of job performance subsequent to training might serve this purpose.

It should be remembered that, in the computation of validity coefficients where the exam to be validated formed the basis of selection of students or trainees, GPA-type predictive validity will tend to be artificially low because the sample has been truncated on the exam under consideration. For this reason, it is better if the exam being validated not become the basis of selection until after the validation process has been completed. Similarly, if two tests are being compared for predictive validity, and one of the tests formed the basis of selection into the instructional program while the other did not, correlation coefficients will be biased in favor of the test that was not used for selection purposes. The critical matter for decision in the application of selection tests, beyond the issue of their validity as predictors of achievement, is the choice of a cut-off score, below which less desirable applicants are rejected. The determination of cut-off scores is discussed at greater length in chapter eight.

Construct Validity

The notion of *construct validity* was formally originated in 1954 with the publication of technical recommendations of a committee of the American

Psychological Association. While construct validity is empirical in nature because it involves the gathering of data and the testing of hypotheses, unlike concurrent and predictive validity, it does not have any one particular validity coefficient associated with it.

The purpose of construct validation is to provide evidence that underlying theoretical constructs being measured are themselves valid. Typically, construct validation begins with a psychological construct that is part of a formal theory. The theory enables certain predictions about how the construct variable will behave or be influenced under specified conditions. The construct is then tested under the conditions specified. If the hypothesized results occur, the hypotheses are supported and the construct is said to be valid. Often this will involve a series of tests under a variety of conditions.

Group Differences Approach

Let us suppose, for purposes of illustration, that we wish to establish the validity of a construct known as *communicative competence* that we are defining operationally in terms of scores on a test of communicative competence. Let us suppose further that we have a well-articulated, formal, comprehensive theory of communicative competence (Would that we had such a theory!). Moreover, suppose our theory led us to hypothesize the following:

1. Those who possess communicative competence will have a higher rate of successful oral information exchange than those who do not possess it.
2. Those who possess communicative competence will make fewer errors of grammar and pronunciation in speaking, and fewer errors of recognition and comprehension in listening, than those who do not possess it.
3. Those who possess communicative competence will show greater sensitivity and awareness to social and cultural nuances related to the selection and use of appropriate language register than those who do not possess it.

Given these three theory-generated hypotheses, we can construct reliable measures of information exchange, error frequency, and register manipulation to test the hypotheses.

In our testing of these hypotheses we might identify persons who qualify as competent and persons who do not qualify as competent under these three distinct criteria. If our original test used to operationally define communicative competence appears to identify the same persons as competent and incompetent as those so identified under the separate criteria, we might conclude that the construct of communicative competence, as specified by our theory and operationally defined by our test of communicative competence, exhibits construct validity. On the other hand, if our hypothesis testing does not corroborate the person selection and competence identification brought about by our test of communicative competence, we are not certain whether the construct generated by our theory, and thus the theory itself, is invalid, or whether only the operational definition of the construct provided by our test is invalid.

It follows from this discussion that statistical evidence of construct validity might take the form of a table or matrix of correlation coefficients, a vector of discriminant function coefficients, or even t-values or F-values, depending on the hypothesis-testing procedures employed. As can be inferred from the preceding examples, a basic difficulty in establishing construct validity consists in the fact that the construct itself cannot be measured directly.

Further explications of construct validity by a number of experts (Cronbach and Meehl, 1955; Magnusson, 1967; Lord and Novick, 1968) present a variety of approaches including study of the following:

1. Group differences predicted by theory
2. Influence of environmental changes on test results, predicted by theory
3. Correlations among tests measuring the same variable
4. Correlations among items or subscales of a test

The example above of validating the construct of communicative competence would fall under the first category of approaches, the group differences approach.

Internal Construct Validation

The fourth approach to construct validation listed in the preceding section involves correlations among items or subscales of a test. One advantage of this approach is that it usually does not require administration of concurrent tests to serve as validation criteria. Instead, the validation criteria are derived from within the test battery itself.

The validation procedure is demonstrated more clearly by reference to Table 7.1. Notice that this table represents the scoring matrix of a language test battery consisting of a three-item subtest of vocabulary and a three-item subtest of grammar. This simple, hypothetical test battery has been administered to a sample of five persons.

This procedure assumes that, if the vocabulary items have construct validity, the point-biserial correlation between each vocabulary item and the total scores for vocabulary should be higher than the point-biserial correlations of the same items with the total scores for grammar. Mathematically this might be expressed as follows:

TABLE 7.1   A scoring matrix for internal construct validation of a language test battery consisting of vocabulary and grammar subtests of three items each, administered to five persons

S	V_1	V_2	V_3	VT	G_1	G_2	G_3	GT
1	1	1	1	3	1	0	1	2
2	0	1	0	1	1	1	0	2
3	0	1	1	2	0	1	0	1
4	0	0	0	0	1	0	0	1
5	0	1	1	2	1	1	1	3

$$r_{V_1VT} > r_{V_1GT} \tag{7.4}$$

$$r_{V_2VT} > r_{V_2GT} \tag{7.5}$$

$$r_{V_3VT} > r_{V_3GT} \tag{7.6}$$

where the symbols indicate that the correlations of individual items with their own subtest totals should be greater than the correlations of the same items with other subtest totals. By actually computing the correlations from Table 7.1, we obtain the following results:

$$r_{V_1VT} = .69 \ (.42) > r_{V_1GT} = .13$$
$$r_{V_2VT} = .78 \ (.57) > r_{V_2GT} = .53$$
$$r_{V_3VT} = .88 \ (.69) > r_{V_3GT} = .33$$

Notice that each of the vocabulary items showed construct validity in that it correlated more highly with the vocabulary total than with the grammar total. The coefficients in parentheses represent the value of the correlation after correction for part-whole overlap. This latter correction is necessary, as discussed on pages 68 and 69, because the vocabulary items before correction show artificially high correlation with their own subscale since they comprise a portion of that subscale total.

If we choose to reflect the construct validity of the vocabulary subtest as a single coefficient, we might select the proportion of valid items within that subtest, as done by Henning (1979) and Qomos (1981). In this case, since all items are valid, the proportion is 1.00, indicating perfect validity. If we followed the same procedure for the items of the grammar subtest of Table 7.1, we would find it necessary, after correction for part-whole overlap, to reject items G_2 and G_3 as correlating more highly with the vocabulary section than with the grammar section of the test battery. The *Internal Construct Validity Proportion* for the grammar subtest would then be only .33, since only one item in three was found valid by this procedure.

In practice this procedure is followed when there is a larger sample than that of the example—say, a minimum of 25 additional persons; when there are more items per subtest than those of the examples—say, a minimum of ten items; and when there are several other kinds of subtests included in the battery—say, a minimum of two additional subtests. Also, in practice, it is sometimes found that items correlating more highly with unintended than with intended subscales can, after careful inspection, be repositioned into the subtest showing the highest correlation. By this procedure items are not needlessly rejected, provided they are found to be valid in some other part of the test battery.

Another approach to internal construct validity is through the use of confirmatory factor analysis discussed in detail elsewhere (Nie et al., 1979). Such multivariate approaches tend to be sufficiently complex and sophisticated that a separate discussion is warranted to provide explanation.

Multitrait-Multimethod Validation

A final procedure for determining construct validity is termed *multitrait-multimethod validation*. This somewhat elaborate procedure corresponds to approach 3 on page 99; i.e., the study of correlations among tests measuring the same variable.

As the name of this procedure implies, it involves simultaneous comparison of correlations among two or more traits or constructs under two or more methodological conditions. A simple example of the application of this procedure occurred in the analysis of the response data from the children's aphasic language test development project, Measures of Children's Language Performance (Laine et al., 1976). In that test battery it was determined that the four language constructs—phonology, syntax, morphology, and semantics—would be tested under the two methodological conditions of recognition and production. Following analysis involving the computation of a correlation matrix for tests of all constructs under both methods, it was found that all constructs were valid as distinct components of the test battery with the exception of morphology. Morphology was found to merge with syntax under the same linguistic construct. Thus, evidence was provided about the comparative integrity and validity of each of the component subtests of the battery.

The actual computational procedures for multitrait-multimethod validation have been discussed extensively by Campbell and Fiske (1959), Magnussen (1966), and Lord and Novick (1968). What follows here is an expanded interpretation with examples and some practical extensions of the procedure. To understand the procedure we shall need to consider the multitrait-multimethod matrix of Table 7.2, reprinted from Henning (1982). Notice that this matrix reports correlations among five different scoring techniques (Raw Score, Fluency, Pronunciation, Grammar, and Fluency-Pronunciation-Grammar combined) under three general methods of testing oral language proficiency, Imitation, Completion, and Interview.

Variables termed *traits* as opposed to those termed *methods* are frequently so designated somewhat arbitrarily in the sense that the same principles of interpretation apply regardless of which assumes which designation, as in bivariate correlations, $r_{xy} = r_{yx}$. Although in the present example we are dealing with specific techniques and general methods of testing, for the sake of application to different situations, we shall refer to the techniques (fluency, etc.) as *traits* and to the methods (imitation, etc.) as *methods*. The procedural steps in multitrait-multimethod validation then may be detailed as follows:

A. Generate a correlation matrix reporting correlations among all traits and all methods. For ease of interpretation, the matrix should then be partitioned into triangles with solid and broken lines, as in Table 7.2. The solid lines enclose correlations among different traits within the same methods and thus are termed *heterotrait-monomethod* correlations. The broken lines enclose correlations among different traits and different methods and thus are termed *heterotrait-heteromethod* correlations. The diagonals outside the broken triangles report the

101

TABLE 7.2 Multitrait-multimethod matrix for imitation, completion, and interview methods employing conventional, fluency, pronunciation, grammar, and FPG scoring techniques (N = 50)

		I					II					III			
	1	2	3	4	5	6	7	8	9	10	11	12	13	14	15
I. Imitation															
1 Raw Score						.613	.535	.605	.335	.530	.716	.678	.699	.562	.700
2 Fluency	.940					.690	.623	.712	.416	.630	.782	.762	.721	.614	.761
3 Pronunciation	.941	.957				.678	.611	.691	.376	.602	.746	.720	.749	.587	.742
4 Grammar	.955	.968	.971			.699	.603	.682	.405	.608	.763	.710	.741	.595	.738
5 FPG total*	.956	.969	.986	.992		.698	.615	.702	.407	.620	.770	.735	.743	.603	.752
II. Completion															
6 Raw Score											.675	.590	.589	.557	.627
7 Fluency						.567					.589	.542	.457	.356	.496
8 Pronunciation						.646	.873				.577	.514	.540	.409	.528
9 Grammar						.551	.671	.710			.369	.185	.287	.100	.202
10 FPG total						.641	.923	.934	.882		.554	.442	.460	.305	.437
III. Interview															
11 FSI**															
12 Fluency											.892				
13 Pronunciation											.808	.760			
14 Grammar											.813	.844	.716		
15 FPG total											.912	.954	.881	.927	

*FPG refers to an unweighted combination of fluency, pronunciation and grammar
**FSI refers to an adaptation of the foreign service institute

102

correlations among the same traits employing different methods and are therefore termed *monotrait-heteromethod* correlations.

B. Inspect the monotrait-heteromethod correlation coefficients in the diagonals. These coefficients are termed the *convergent validity coefficients* and should be significantly higher than zero if the trait may be claimed to manifest convergent validity. Only Completion Grammar (9) in its correlation with Interview Grammar (14) failed to demonstrate convergent validity by this liberal criterion. This validation procedure is not unlike other criterion-related measures of validity which we have already encountered. Notice, however, that in the present matrix each trait has two such coefficients. If for any reason it became necessary to compare the overall convergent validities for the different traits, it might be desirable to compute a mean of coefficients for the two or more coefficients available for each trait. Averaging correlation coefficients necessitates recourse to Fisher Z transformations, as explained on page 20. Means for the present monotrait-heteromethod convergent validity coefficients are reported in column one of Table 7.3.

C. The next step entails the comparison of the convergent validity coefficients with the corresponding heterotrait-monomethod coefficients within the solid triangles. The $r_{1,6}$ convergent validity (.613) in Table 7.2 would be compared with the variable one heterotrait-monomethod coefficients (.940, .941, .955, .956) and with the variable six heterotrait-monomethod coefficients (.567, .646, .551, .641). If the convergent validity coefficient is found to exceed all of these corresponding heterotrait-monomethod coefficients, which in the present example it does not,

TABLE 7.3   Mean convergent and discriminant validity coefficients for three methods and fifteen techniques of oral language testing

	Monotrait-Heteromethod Mean Convergent Validity	Heterotrait-Monomethod Mean Discriminant Validity Ratio	Heterotrait-Heteromethod Mean Discriminant Validity Ratio
I. IMITATION	.663	.455	.805
1. Raw Score	.668	.517	.802
2. Fluency	.699	.495	.828
3. Pronunciation	.722	.515	.846
4. Grammar	.506	.328	.692
5. FPG total	.692	.422	.821
II. COMPLETION	.541	.413	.718
6. Raw Score	.645	.591	.770
7. Fluency	.584	.449	.756
8. Pronunciation	.621	.484	.769
9. Grammar	.259	.198	.468
10. FPG total	.535	.345	.708
III. INTERVIEW	.613	.458	.773
11. FSI	.696	.586	.812
12. Fluency	.666	.503	.818
13. Pronunciation	.657	.523	.799
14. Grammar	.374	.275	.591
15. FPG total	.619	.398	.768

then the trait is said to manifest *heterotrait-monomethod discriminant validity*. Notice again in the present example that each trait has two convergent validity coefficients; therefore, the above procedure must be repeated twice for each trait. Again, one might wish to make comparisons among the traits in mean heterotrait-monomethod discriminant validity. By averaging all of the corresponding hetero-trait-monomethod coefficients for each trait, and dividing this mean into the mean of the two convergent validity coefficients for that trait, it is possible to compute a kind of mean ratio which would reflect the comparative overall heterotrait-monomethod discriminant validity of each trait. This has been done by use of Fisher Z transformations in column two of Table 7.3. In order for the respective traits to exhibit discriminant validity, the corresponding mean ratio would have to exceed 1.00. Since none of the mean ratios in the present example exceeded 1.00, we can conclude that heterotrait-monomethod discriminant validity was not present overall. Yet we can by comparison conclude that Completion Raw Score (.591) was the most nearly valid of the traits while Completion Grammar (.198) was the least valid, by this criterion.

D. The next procedural step is to compare the convergent validity coefficients of the diagonals with the corresponding heterotrait-heteromethod coefficients enclosed within the broken triangles. In the present example the correlation between variables one and six (.613) would be compared with the corresponding heterotrait-heteromethod coefficients for variable one (.535, .605, .335, .530, .678, .699, .562, .700) and for variable six (.690, .678, .699, .698, .590, .589, .557, .627). If the convergent validity, .613, were found to exceed all of these coefficients, which it does not, the trait would be said to exhibit *heterotrait-heteromethod discriminant validity*. Once again we can average all of the heterotrait-hetero-method coefficients for a given trait by using Fisher Z transformations, and then we can divide this mean into the mean convergent validity for that trait in order to obtain an overall heterotrait-heteromethod discriminant validity ratio. A trait which is said to exhibit overall validity of this type will show a ratio in excess of 1.00. For the present example these mean ratios are reported in column three of Table 7.3. Although none of the traits showed overall heterotrait-heteromethod discriminant validity, Imitation Pronunciation (.846) was clearly superior to the other traits. And Completion Grammar (.468) was clearly inferior to the other traits. These validities were higher overall than the heterotrait-monomethod dis-criminant validities of Table 7.3.

E. A final procedural step, which Campbell and Fiske (1959) advocate, is to inspect the pattern of the magnitudes of the correlation coefficients within trian-gles. If this final criterion of validity is met, the pattern of magnitude will be the same within triangles whether the same or different methods are being used. Since this criterion is almost never in practice realized, it seems unproductive to this author to give it serious consideration. It is mentioned here only as a matter of historical record.

F. One further matter of concern is that in situations where reliabilities are vastly different among the tests used for deriving the matrix, it may be necessary and desirable to correct for attenuation before the above procedures are followed for the comparison of correlation coefficients. In the present example all of the reliabilities were so high and so comparable that correction for attenuation was deemed unnecessary.

There is a sense in which the boundaries between reliability and validity may become blurred in this procedure. In fact, there is no theoretical reason why multitrait-multimethod validation could not be used in the comparison of reliability coefficients among independent raters of a variety of skills. Presumably such a study would reflect which raters were most reliable and valid in different skill rating situations. The heterotrait-monomethod coefficients would be inter-rater reliability coefficients, while the monotrait-heteromethod coefficients would be convergent validity coefficients.

7.5   Summary

This chapter has presented the notion of validity from a variety of conceptual and methodological viewpoints. Definitions of validity were offered. The relationships between reliability and validity were discussed. A series of possible threats to validity were considered along with possible remedies. The major kinds of validity were introduced including content or face validity, response validity, concurrent validity, predictive validity, and a variety of construct validities. A distinction was made between empirical and nonempirical validities and between criterion-related and noncriterion-related validities. Procedure was detailed for the computation of internal construct validity and multitrait-multimethod validity. A formal distinction was made among monotrait-heteromethod convergent validity, heterotrait-monomethod discriminant validity, and heterotrait-heteromethod discriminant validity. It was emphasized that validity implies a purpose for which the test is to be applied, and that the same tests may at the same time be valid for some purposes and invalid for others.

Exercises

1. List the five major types of validity described in the chapter and tell what each is used for.
2. Compare and contrast the content validities of norm-referenced proficiency tests and criterion-referenced achievement tests.
3. Content validity is related differently to reliability than is empirical validity. Explain.
4. List four ways one might seek to establish construct validity.
5. List four common threats to validity.
6. If reliability of a test of listening comprehension is 0.73, what is the maximum possible empirical validity this test could exhibit under ideal conditions?
7. If the correlation between a locally constructed test which we wish to validate and a reputable criterion measure is 0.75, what is the true concurrent validity if the criterion measure has a reliability of 0.90?
8. According to the following scoring matrix, what is the internal construct validity proportion for reading comprehension?

	Reading Comprehension					Grammar			
	1	2	3	T		1	2	3	T
1	0	1	1	2		0	1	1	2
2	0	0	0	0		1	1	0	2
3	1	1	1	3		0	0	1	1
4	1	1	1	3		1	1	1	3
5	0	1	0	1		0	0	1	1

9. Inspecting the multitrait-multimethod matrix of Table 7.2, what do you find to be the two convergent validity coefficients for variable 8, Completion Pronunciation?

10. Considering Table 7.2 again, what are the two convergent validity coefficients for variable 12, Interview Fluency? List the respective coefficients each of these convergent validities would have to exceed to exhibit heterotrait-mono-method discriminant validity. Then list the respective coefficients each would need to exceed to exhibit heterotrait-heteromethod discriminant validity.

Chapter Eight

Latent Trait Measurement

8.1   Classical vs. Latent Trait Measurement Theory

The focus in the preceding chapters was on a loosely defined body of knowledge that might be designated "classical" measurement theory. Classical theory is concerned with an approach to item and test analysis that relies heavily on the correlation coefficient as a statistical procedure. This is evident in estimation of item discriminability and test reliability and validity. Classical theory is further distinguishable by the mathematical interrelationships posited between true score, observed score, measurement error, reliability, and validity.

The point here is that classical measurement theory is not the only way to approach the analysis and interpretation of item and test data. Indeed, recent developments in measurement theory suggest that there may be profound advantages in approaching test development and analysis from other perspectives as well. *Item response theory* or *latent trait theory*, as it has been variously termed, is the most notable complementary perspective. One author has likened the advent of this new approach in measurement to the advent of nuclear physics in the world of physics (Warm, 1978). This analogy suggests that there may be some profound and powerful benefits from an awareness and an application of the more recent approaches.

Latent trait measurement or item response theory refers primarily, but not entirely, to three families of analytical procedures. These are identified as the *one-parameter* (or Rasch Model), the *two-parameter*, and the *three-parameter logistic models* (Rasch, 1960; Lord and Novick, 1968; Warm 1978; Hambleton and Swaminathan, 1985). What these models have in common is a systematic procedure for considering and quantifying the probability or improbability of individual item and person response patterns given the overall pattern of responses in a set of test data. They also offer new and improved ways for the estimation of item difficulty and person ability.

As the names suggest, these models differ in complexity depending on whether they incorporate one, two, or three parameters. The first parameter is a scale of person ability and item difficulty; the second parameter is a continuous estimate of discriminability; the third parameter is an index of guessing. More will be said about the comparative differences of these three models, but it is appropriate at this point to consider what advantages may accrue through the use of these models.

8.2 Advantages Offered by Latent Trait Theory

Advantages available through the application of latent trait theory have been discussed in detail elsewhere (Henning, 1984). The advantages that are listed here do not apply equally to each of the three models named above. In general, these benefits are universally available through the Rasch one-parameter model, but may or may not be available in the other models. In this text priority of perspective has been given to the Rasch Model because it appears to be more readily applicable at the level of the small program or school. It is also easier for analysis, computation, and interpretation purposes, and its use is not dependent on the availability of mainframe computers. Subsequent space will be devoted to further comparison of these alternative models.

Sample-Free Item Calibration

In classical measurement, the estimated difficulty of any given item will vary widely with the average ability of the particular sample of examinees observed. When we report a difficulty or p-value we are always constrained to include a full description of the examinees, knowing that the difficulty index will vary for samples of different ability. It is not possible to compare item difficulties of different tests unless the same original sample is retested with both tests. Item analysis is sample-bound.

In latent trait measurement we derive an item difficulty scale that is in one sense independent of ability differences of any particular sample of examinees drawn from the population of interest. This is a powerful advantage. It is analogous to stating that we can now carry a uniform measuring stick to measure person height without the need to bring along the last group of persons measured to determine whether standards are being maintained. In classical measurement, items that are analyzed or normed with one group of examinees are forever suspect with any other group of examinees. Sample-free item calibration allows us to overcome this problem.

Test-Free Person Measurement

Ability measurement according to classical theory is dependent on the unique clustering of items in any given measurement instrument. It is not possible to administer one test of reading comprehension to person A and a different test of reading comprehension to person B and then make direct comparisons of ability unless the tests are pre-equated in a way that would involve the administration of both tests to the same large group of persons. In latent trait measurement it is possible to compare abilities of persons using different tests by referring to a small *link* of common items or common persons. Once items have been calibrated and joined to a common bank of items, any cluster of these items may be used to measure ability that would be located on the same scale as ability measured by any other cluster of these items. It would no longer be important what the exact number of items used on a given instrument might be, nor what the unique clustering of those items with other items would be. This is intuitively satisfying, much the same as the belief that measurement of length should be independent of whether a one-meter stick is used or a ten-meter tape.

Multiple Reliability Estimation

In classical measurement theory, one global estimate of reliability is obtained by any appropriate method for any given test. While this is a useful procedure, it is not altogether satisfactory. Consider the fact that measurement of ability tends to be more reliable near the mean of the scoring distribution than at either end. This suggests that ability estimation varies in accuracy or reliability according to position along the scoring continuum. One global estimate of reliability should not be applied uniformly in evaluating the accuracy of scores for every individual examined. In latent trait measurement the standard error of measurement is determined for every possible point along the scoring continuum. This standard error measure may be derived for estimates of both person ability and item difficulty. Thus, with latent trait theory, reliability estimation goes beyond a global estimate for a given test, to a confidence estimate associated with every possible person and item score on that test.

Identification of Guessers and Other Deviant Respondents

Earlier in this same text we encountered the notion of correction for guessing. By use of the formulas provided it is possible to partially compensate for the guessing inherent in multiple-choice testing. These formulas penalize incorrect responses over and above the penalty for not attempting to respond. In some situations this procedure will improve test reliability. But, because every wrong response is penalized the same as every other wrong response, no attempt is made to differentiate between wrong responses that are truly blind guesses and wrong responses that are considered choices. It is not possible with classical measurement theory, therefore, to quantify the amount of guessing occurring for any given individual.

Latent trait theory allows us to quantify the improbability of any response given knowledge of the difficulty of the item and of the ability of the person responding. If a person of low ability repeatedly passes items of high calibrated difficulty, it may be inferred that guessing is taking place. The lower the person's ability is with regard to the difficulty of the item passed, the more improbable the successful response. Usually, guessing is noticeable when an examinee passes items that have known difficulty greater than his or her known ability. In the three-parameter latent trait model, this kind of guessing is quantified directly for each examinee as one of the parameters of the model. In the one- and two-parameter models, guessing is quantified along with other error sources as the index of person fit to the model. This index of fit, referred to as the person fit statistic, lumps together guessing with all other sources of improbable response patterns. Persons may be ranked in terms of the degree of their misfit to the model. If a person is identified as misfitting the expectations of the model, then the test may not be valid for that person. Such persons are not identified as showing invalid responses under classical measurement theory.

Misfitting the model might occur, by way of example, when there is much guessing taking place, when an examinee is not cooperating during the examination, when instructions are not clear, when the examinee copies the answers of someone with greater ability during some portion of the test, when there is some perceptive handicap in the examinee (e.g., hearing or visual deficiencies), and so on. If possible, it is advantageous to interview misfitting persons to determine some explanation for their improbable responses. Any test scores for such persons should be interpreted with caution.

Potential Ease of Administration and Scoring

Once items have been calibrated for difficulty it is possible to select items to match the known ability range of the examinees. Since only those items are used that are necessary to measure the ability of the examinees, many redundant or superfluous items can be deleted from the test. The result is a test that can be administered in less time, with less fatigue or boredom for the examinees, and with less expense for the examiners. And this can be accomplished without the sacrifice of test reliability and validity.

The scoring process can also be made more efficient. In classical measurement, first, the total raw score is computed as the sum of the correct items. Then, if indicated, some correction for guessing adjustment is applied. Finally, a scaled score conversion is made to enable reference across forms of the test. In latent trait measurement, since precalibrated item difficulties are used to define the variable, person ability inferences may be drawn directly from performance on any item task. This means that person ability can be determined without the need to compute a total score on the test. Figure 8.1 shows how this is possible.

Note from Figure 8.1 that the actual positioning of a person's ability level ($\backslash/$) on the ability continuum can be based on a consideration of success or failure with items positioned at intervals along the continuum. In this case an end-of-success point ($+$) is arbitrarily set as the point along the ability/difficulty continuum at

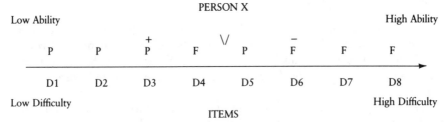

FIGURE 8.1   Potential latent trait scoring technique based on pattern of passing (P) and failing (F) calibrated items (D1–D8) arrayed for difficulty

which the examinee last succeeds with three successive items. A beginning-of-failure point $(-)$ is located where the examinee first begins to fail with three successive items. Person ability can then be located as the bisecting mid-point between the points $+$ and $-$. This process assumes that the items have been precalibrated and arranged for difficulty. Use of such a procedure is especially valuable in computer adaptive testing, where ability estimates must be generated in an ongoing, iterative fashion before it is possible for the examinee to respond to all of the machine-stored items.

Economy of Items

If only those items are used that approximate in difficulty the known ability region of the examinees, then fewer items will be required. If ability measurement can cease whenever examinee ability is estimated with predetermined levels of accuracy, then fewer items will be needed for any given individual. If items are precalibrated, banked, and randomly summoned for any given measurement task, then there is less risk of a security breakdown that would disqualify large numbers of items for future use. All of these advantages add up to greater economy of items over time and use.

Reconciliation of Norm-Referenced and Criterion-Referenced Testing

The distinctions between norm-referenced and criterion-referenced tests were discussed in chapter one. It was noted that the former approach references individual performance to that of a group or norm, while the latter procedure references individual performance to an objective-based standard of content knowledge or skill. In latent trait measurement, all of the benefits of both approaches can be reaped in one and the same test. Since both person ability and item or task difficulty are positioned along the same latent continuum, it is possible to draw inferences from examinee performance that are referenced to the performances of other individuals or to the standards imposed by other tasks. This is a powerful advantage over a classical test theory which was not able to reconcile these two approaches to measurement.

111

Test Equating Facility

In chapter six the notion of parallel forms of tests was introduced. There it was asserted that tests could be said to be statistically parallel or equivalent if they could demonstrate equal means, equal variances, and equal covariances. Satisfying these rigorous criteria is sufficiently difficult that most test developers settle for equated, as opposed to equivalent, forms of tests.

According to classical measurement theory, equated tests require that all test forms to be equated be administered in their entirety to the same large sample of examinees. Then, assuming that the test forms are highly intercorrelated, some procedure must be adopted (e.g., regression or equipercentile methods) for the generation of a common set of scaled scores that can serve as a translation of comparative performance on the various tests. This is usually an expensive and time-consuming activity. It is often difficult to find a sufficiently large sample of persons who have time to participate in the administration of two or more tests within a short period of time. Even if such persons are found, the fatigue associated with the administration of so many test items in such a short time can often invalidate the overall results.

Latent trait measurement theory can greatly facilitate equating of tests. By this approach, it is no longer necessary to administer all forms of tests in their entirety to the original, large sample of examinees. By means of a group of common linking items (perhaps only ten or more), scores on one test form can be equated with those on other forms, even though the other forms are administered to different samples of individuals drawn from the same general population at various times. This powerful advantage greatly reduces the testing time of any individual examinee, while it increases the likelihood that valid participation will be elicited from appropriate samples of examinees.

Test Tailoring Facility

Once items have been calibrated on a latent trait continuum, it is possible to use those items in the construction of tests appropriate to specific measurement needs. Consider Figure 8.2 as an illustration of how this might be possible.

Notice in this example we are considering cut-off scores for entrance into and exit from an English language institute prior to full university admission. For

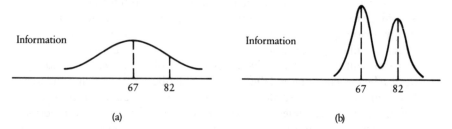

FIGURE 8.2   An illustration of the advantages of test tailoring (a) Information levels for cut-off scores with an untailored standardized test (b) Information levels for cut-off scores with a tailored test

112

purposes of illustration, a score of 67 is said to qualify a foreign student for entrance into the intensive English program of the institute, but not for full admission into university classes. Below 67, applicants are rejected from both the university and the language institute. A score of 82 is accepted as grounds for full admission into the university without remedial intensive English study.

In Figure 8.2(a) we see that a standardized proficiency exam has been administered with a corresponding normal distribution of the test information function (see page 54 for a discussion of information function). Maximum information about the examinees is available at the mean of the scoring distribution. The average respondent would have a 50 percent probability of success with items that have difficulty estimates falling near the mean of the scoring distribution. Comparatively less information is available at the critical decision cut-off points. We can see from this example that decision accuracy resulting from the application of this test will be low—especially at the 82-score university admission criterion.

In Figure 8.2(b) we see the information function of a test that has been tailored for this particular decision-making situation. This test has been purposely loaded with items with difficulty calibrations falling near the 67- and 82-score decision points. Notice that this test has the same total number of items as the test of Figure 8.2(a), and probably the same overall information is made available for the same time of test administration. The important point here, and the purpose for this illustration, is that the information in the tailored test has been concentrated at the decision-making cut-off points. The tailored test will provide much greater decision accuracy than the standardized test. Fewer students will be wrongly admitted to or wrongly rejected from university study or intensive English study by use of the tailored test. This advantage may easily be gained through use of latent trait measurement theory.

Item Banking Facility

Once items have been calibrated according to latent trait or item response theory, they can be stored in an item bank according to a common metric of difficulty. This is generally true regardless of the equality of the ability or size of the subsequent person samples tested. The item bank becomes more than just a catalog of used items with descriptions of their successes and failures. It becomes an ever-expanding test which spans the latent ability continuum beyond the measurement needs of any one individual, but which may be accessed to gather items appropriate to any group of persons from the same general population with respect to the ability measured. Latent trait theory facilitates item banking by allowing all of the items to be calibrated and positioned on the same latent continuum by means of a common metric. Also, it permits additional items to be added subsequently without the need to locate and retest the original sample of examinees. Furthermore, an item bank so maintained permits the construction of tests of known reliability and validity based on appropriate selection of item subsets from the bank without further need for trial in the field.

The Study of Item and Test Bias

Prior to the advent of latent trait testing theory it was uncommon to find bias studies that attempted to quantify the amount and direction of bias for any given item or person. Bias was usually studied with regard to a test as an entire unit or with respect to a group or class of persons. One exception to this assertion concerns the practice of relying on a panel of experts to rate individual items as biased for or against some group of persons. Unfortunately, expert opinion has not consistently been successful in identifying biased items.

Latent trait methodology has the advantage that it permits the quantification of the magnitude and direction of bias for individual items or persons. This enables the correction of test bias whether through removal, revision, or counterbalancing of biased items. Thus test bias may not only be neutralized through the removal of biased items, but also through the purposeful inclusion of items biased in the opposite direction.

Elimination of Boundary Effects in Program Evaluation

One of the persistent problems associated with the analysis of learning gain in any language teaching program is the problem of instrument boundary effect. As students acquire or achieve greater proficiency or skill, the group mean performance score increases along the effective range of the test. When, in classical measurement, the group mean approaches the highest or lowest extremes of the effective range, the score distribution becomes skewed. When students become capable of scoring beyond the highest possible score on the test, a ceiling effect becomes apparent. The net result of these phenomena is that measurement of group learning gains over time becomes obscured. The instrumentation is no longer capable of accurately registering the mean learning gains that have taken place.

With latent trait measurement boundary effects are removed. A logarithmic transformation is used to change the raw obtained scores to interval scores. The interval scores are adjusted to hold sample size, ability spread, test size, and test variance constant. Ability measurement may then be articulated from one test to another or from one sample of examinees to another, because the same scale is in use in all cases and because both item difficulty and person ability are calibrated on this same scale. If any person in the test sample gets zero items correct or manages to get all items correct, no estimate is made of that person's ability. This is because it is acknowledged from the start that such a person may be almost infinitely weaker or more capable than the test is able to measure. Similarly, if any item is missed by all persons or is gotten correct by all persons, no estimate is made of that item's difficulty. There is no way to gauge the item difficulty accurately since both success and failure were not experienced with the item. In the case of persons who fail to experience both success and failure with the items of a test, a search is made for items of greater or lesser difficulty as required so that ability estimation may occur. For the calibration of item difficulty when items are uniformly passed or failed by all persons in the sample, a search is made for persons of lesser or greater ability until at least one person passes and one person fails each item. When program evaluation is made only with persons and items that exhibit both success and failure in this manner, and when sample size, dispersion, and central tendency are transformed to articulate to the same interval scale, then boundary effects cease to exist.

Item and Person Fit Validity Measures

In classical measurement theory, criterion-related or construct validity of an item may be ascertained through correlational methods, given an appropriate criterion. The actual response validity associated with a person or an item is not estimated per se.

Latent trait measurement provides this valuable additional information. Due to the probabilistic nature of latent trait models, it is possible to quantify for any person or item the magnitude of the departure of the given pattern of responses from the pattern predicted by the model. This departure or unlikelihood statement is a kind of response validity or model fit validity estimate that is available for both persons and items without the need to go outside of the given sample of persons and items in search of a criterion.

Score Reporting Facility

Figure 8.3 illustrates how score reporting might be facilitated through latent trait measurement. This represents some of the possible content of a score reporting form for the teacher and/or the examinee who has completed a language test battery.

Figure 8.3 illustrates the potential value of latent trait theory in the area of diagnostic score reporting. Notice that this figure depicts a language test battery

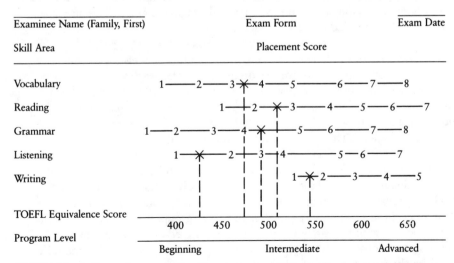

FIGURE 8.3 **A diagnostic reporting form for a test constructed according to latent trait measurement theory**

115

consisting of a total of 35 items calibrated within five different subscales (i.e., Vocabulary, Reading, Grammar, Listening, and Writing). This sample form reports the ability estimates for one examinee in each of the five skills measured. Since this particular student was placed into an intermediate level course on the basis of a 500 TOEFL score, it is immediately apparent that there is a need for remedial work in the areas of Listening and Vocabulary. Such forms are easily constructed, require a minimal number of precalibrated items, are easily interpreted, and provide a wealth of valuable information to students, teachers, and administrators.

8.3   Competing Latent Trait Models

The three primary models that are given focus here are the One-Parameter Logistic (Rasch) Model, the Two-Parameter Logistic Model, and the Three-Parameter Logistic Model. As the names imply, these models are graduated in complexity as each adds a parameter of investigation to the previous model. The models are interrelated in the sense that, when you suppress parameters of a more complex model, you revert to a less complex model. The One-Parameter Model may then be said to be a special case of the Three-Parameter Model with guessing and discriminability parameters suppressed. Many of the same assumptions underlie the application of each of these models; e.g., unidimensionality, non-speededness, local independence, and sample invariance (Henning et al., 1985).

Choice of a model has been the focus of much controversy in the literature. Accuracy, economic, and philosophical concerns have formed the basis of a polarization of advocacy of simple versus complex models. Advocates of more complex models are often motivated by the ideal of more thorough approximation of the complexities of the real world. Advocates of simpler models are concerned with the creation of latent continua which have maximal pragmatic and utilitarian value. Some of the important concerns in model selection are summarized in Table 8.1.

As Table 8.1 indicates, the Rasch One-Parameter Model is probably to be preferred by teachers and language testers over the other models for the majority of testing situations. Sample size constraints alone may dictate this choice since the Rasch Model is fully operative with a sample of from 100 to 200 persons; while the Two-Parameter Model requires 200–400, and the Three-Parameter Model depends on the availability of 1,000 to 2,000 persons for parameter estimation to proceed meaningfully. There is often also a fundamental philosophical difference underlying the selection of a simple versus a more complex model. The advocates of a Three-Parameter Model attempt to employ a model to approximate the real-world fluctuations of a large data set; whereas advocates of a One-Parameter Model are primarily concerned with the construction of a measurement scale for utilitarian decision-making purposes. For the latter group, it is a matter of small consequence if proportionately more items are rejected as misfitting during the process of scale construction. For one-parameter advocates, the fact that the scale defined by the model does not admit the full range of item discriminabilities or guessing behaviors does not outweigh the advantages of specific objectivity or

TABLE 8.1 Rank ordering of three latent trait models on five characteristics affecting selection (ranking, 1–3)

Characteristic	One Parameter	Two Parameter	Three Parameter
Accuracy of Estimation*	2	1	3
Economy of Computing Time	1	2	3
Minimal Sample Size Required	1	2	3
Information Provided	3	2	1
Ease of Interpretation	1	2	3
Total Rankings	8	9	13

*Accuracy preference is given to the Two-Parameter Model in that it explains more reliable variance than the One-Parameter Model through the inclusion of the discriminability parameter, but the added explanatory power of the third parameter is minimal and is achieved at the expense of building measurement error into the model, adding warps in multidimensional space (Waller, 1980).

reduced sample size constraints. For these reasons, the following discussion of models will focus on the Rasch Model.

Introduction to the Rasch, One-Parameter Model

Georg Rasch, a Danish mathematician, is credited with the formal development of the one-parameter logistic model known as the Rasch Model (Rasch, 1960). Because of the practical utility of this model it has been greatly expanded and applied in a variety of educational contexts, so that it is in fact a generic term for a family of models (Wright and Stone, 1979; Hashway, 1978; Ollerup and Sorber, 1977; Andrich, 1973; Choppin, 1968; Draba, 1978; Woodcock, 1974; Wright, Mead, and Draba, 1976).

Unlike classical test theory, the Rasch Model is probabilistic in nature in that the persons and items are not only graded for ability and difficulty, but are judged according to the probability or likelihood of their response patterns given the observed person ability and item difficulty. This relationship is summarized in Figure 8.4.

Notice in Figure 8.4 that two persons of varying ability and four items of varying difficulty have been calibrated and placed in their respective positions along

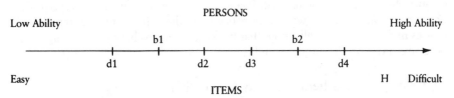

FIGURE 8.4 A representation of person ability (b) and item difficulty (d) along the latent continuum

117

the latent continuum. Person b2 is said to be more able than person b1, and person b2 is also "smarter" than items d1, d2, and d3. We would expect a person with the ability of person b2 to pass items d1, d2, and d3, and to fail item d4. The probability that person b2 will pass item d1 is greater, however, than the probability that she or he will pass item d3 or fail item d4 because the latter two items are closer to the actual ability of person b2. An item that has exactly the same difficulty as a given person's ability would have a 50–50 chance of being passed by that person. Expected outcomes can then be expressed as exact probabilities, and this is the key to understanding the model. It follows that guessers can be identified because their response patterns do not conform to expectation.

This model can be summarized in the expression,

$$P \{x_{\nu\iota}: B_{\nu}, \delta_{\nu}\} = \exp [x_{\nu\iota}(B_{\nu} - \delta_{\iota})] / [1 + \exp (B_{\nu} - \delta_{\iota})] \qquad (8.1)$$

This expression may be read as the probability P of a given response x of person ν on item ι, given the ability of person ν, B_{ν}, and given the difficulty of item ι, δ_{ι}, is equal to the difference between the person's ability and the item's difficulty, expressed as the logarithmic exponent of the natural constant e, divided by the quantity one-plus-(the-difference-between-the-person's-ability-and-the-item's-difficulty-expressed-as-the-logarithmic-exponent-of-the-natural-constant-e).

Computation of Item Difficulty and Person Ability

In practice this computation is usually done by computer with one of several available packages, such as BICAL (Mead, Wright, and Bell, 1979) or BILOG II (Mislevy and Bock, 1984), using a variety of maximum-likelihood estimation procedures, or by hand, using an approximation of that procedure called PROX (Wright and Stone, 1979). The PROX procedure can be done successfully with a calculator, according to the following five steps.

Edit the Binary Response Matrix

This is done in such a way that every person or item for which all responses are correct or all responses are incorrect, is eliminated. Be aware that this may be an iterative process, such that as an additional item is deleted, additional persons may need to be deleted, etc. Consider the hypothetical scoring matrix in Table 8.2.

Notice that persons 1, 9, and 10 have been edited out of the matrix because they have experienced either all failures or all successes with these items; therefore, it is concluded that their ability is either below or above the capacity of the test to measure. Notice also that items 1, 2, 9, and 10 have been eliminated because only successes or only failures were experienced for these items by the remaining persons in the sample. Finally, note that items and persons have been arranged in successive order of difficulty and ability.

Calculate Initial Item Difficulty Calibrations

This involves finding the logit incorrect value for each possible number correct, and setting the mean of the vector of logit difficulty values at zero.

TABLE 8.2 Hypothetical scoring matrix for a 10-item vocabulary test

					Items					
Persons	1	2	3	4	5	6	7	8	9	10
1	0	0	0	0	0	0	0	0	0	0
2	1	1	1	0	0	0	0	0	0	0
3	1	1	1	1	0	0	0	0	0	0
4	1	1	1	1	0	1	0	0	0	0
5	1	1	0	1	1	1	0	0	0	0
6	1	1	1	1	1	1	0	0	0	0
7	1	1	1	0	1	0	1	1	0	0
8	1	1	1	1	1	1	1	0	0	0
9	1	1	1	1	1	1	1	1	1	1
10	1	1	1	1	1	1	1	1	1	1

Table 8.3 illustrates steps in the hand calculation of initial item difficulty calibrations. Bear in mind that, while calibrations may be computed for very small groups of items and persons for illustrative purposes, the resultant standard errors of measurement with very small samples tend to be so large that they restrict the number and kinds of applications that can be made.

Notice that the logit incorrect value for each item was computed as the natural logarithm of the ratio of the proportion incorrect to the proportion correct. This procedure is facilitated by consulting Table F in Appendix A. This procedure places item difficulties on an interval scale and eliminates the boundaries inherent in the zero-to-unity range of classical p-values. Next note that the zero point, or origin, of the item difficulty calibrations is arbitrarily set at the mean of the logit incorrect values for all analyzable items. This is done by subtracting the mean adjustment

TABLE 8.3 Calculation of item difficulty calibrations

Item Name	Number Correct	Item Freq.	Prop. Corr.	Prop. Incor.	*Logit Incor.	Freq. × Logit	Freq. × Logit²	Item Diff.
3	6	1	6/7 = .86	.14	− 1.82	− 1.82	3.31	− 1.73
4	5	1	5/7 = .71	.29	− 0.90	− 0.90	.81	− 0.81
5,6	4	2	4/7 = .57	.43	− 0.28	− 0.56	.16	− 0.19
7	2	1	2/7 = .29	.71	0.90	0.90	.81	0.99
8	1	1	1/7 = .14	.86	1.82	1.82	3.31	1.91
		6				− 0.56	8.40	

*Logit Incorrect = Ln [Proportion Incorrect/Proportion Correct]
Mean Adjustment = [Sum of Frequency × Logit]/[Sum of Frequency]
Initial Item Difficulty = Logit Incorrect − Mean Adjustment

value, computed as the sum of the frequency times logit values divided by the sum of the frequencies, from the logit incorrect value for each item.

For purposes of item banking, all future calibrations of items will be adjusted to employ the same origin as that of this initial calibration. This adjustment is achieved simply by adding a "translation constant" to all future calibrations. The translation constant is equal to the mean difference of final calibrations of a group of common items or persons employed in both calibration runs (time one minus time two). These common items or persons are termed the "link," and most commonly consist of ten or more items that have been found to have good fit statistics, low standard errors, and stability of calibrated difficulty.

Calculate the Initial Person Measures

See Table 8.4. Notice that, with persons, unlike the case with items, calculations are done using logit correct values instead of logit incorrect values. This is because we are effectively subtracting item difficulties from person abilities in order to place both these estimates on the same single ability-difficulty continuum.

Calculate the Expansion Factors

This permits us to adjust the item calibrations for sample spread and the person measures for test width. The item difficulty expansion factor due to sample spread is calculated using the following formula:

$$Y = \left(\frac{1+V/2.89}{1-UV/8.35}\right)^{1/2} = \left(\frac{1+1.06/2.89}{1-1.67(1.06)/8.35}\right)^{1/2} = \left(\frac{1.37}{.79}\right)^{1/2} = 1.32 \qquad (8.2)$$

where, V = the variance of person measures = the sum of Frequency times Logit squared from Table 8.4 minus N times the mean adjustment squared, all divided by $(N - 1)$; i.e.,

$$\frac{6.45 - 7(.01)}{7-1} = \frac{6.38}{6} = 1.06$$

TABLE 8.4 Calculation of initial person ability measures

Person Number	Person Score	Person Freq.	Prop. Corr.	*Logit Corr.	Freq. × Logit	Freq. × Logit²	Person Measure
2	1	1	1/6 = .17	− 1.59	− 1.59	2.51	− 1.69
3	2	1	2/6 = .33	− 0.69	− 0.69	.48	− 0.79
4,5	3	2	3/6 = .50	0.00	0.00	.00	− 0.10
6,7	4	2	4/6 = .67	0.69	1.38	.95	0.59
8	5	1	5/6 = .83	1.59	1.59	2.51	1.49
		7			0.69	6.45	

*Logit Correct = Ln [Proportion Correct/Proportion Incorrect]
Mean Adjustment = [Sum of Frequency × Logit]/[Sum of Frequency]
Initial Person Measures = Logit Correct Values − Mean Adjustment

U = the variance of item calibrations = the sum of Frequency times Logit squared from Table 8.3 minus n times the mean adjustment squared, all divided by the quantity (n − 1); i.e.,

$$\frac{8.40 - 6(.01)}{6-1} = \frac{8.34}{5} = 1.67$$

The person ability expansion factor due to test width is calculated using the following formula:

$$X = \left(\frac{1+U/2.89}{1-UV/8.35}\right)^{1/2} = \left(\frac{1+1.67/2.89}{1-1.67(1.06)/8.35}\right)^{1/2} = \left(\frac{1.58}{.79}\right)^{1/2} = 1.41 \qquad (8.3)$$

These expansion factors are then multiplied by the initial difficulty calibrations or person measures to obtain the final estimates, as is summarized in Table 8.5.

Calculate the Standard Errors Associated with These Estimates

The formula for the calculation of the standard error for each of the final item difficulty calibrations is as follows:

$$SE(d) = Y \left(\frac{N}{\text{Number Correct } (N - \text{Number Correct})}\right)^{1/2} \qquad (8.4)$$

The formula for the calculation of the standard error of each of the final person ability measures is as follows:

$$SE(b) = X \left(\frac{n}{\text{Person Score } (n - \text{Person Score})}\right)^{1/2} \qquad (8.5)$$

TABLE 8.5 Final difficulty and ability estimates with associated standard errors

Item Number	Initial Calibration	Expansion Factor	Final Calibration	Standard Error (d)
1,2	All Correct Responses			
3	− 1.73	1.32	− 2.28	1.43
4	− 0.81	"	− 1.07	1.11
5,6	− 0.19	"	− 0.25	1.00
7	0.99	"	1.31	1.11
8	1.91	"	2.52	1.43
9,10	All Incorrect Responses			

Person Number	Initial Measure	Expansion Factor	Final Measure	Standard Error (b)
1	All Incorrect Responses			
2	− 1.69	1.41	− 2.38	1.55
3	− 0.79	"	− 1.11	1.23
4,5	− 0.10	"	− 0.14	1.16
6,7	0.59	"	0.83	1.23
8	1.49	"	2.10	1.55
9,10	All Correct Responses			

The final computation of item difficulty calibrations and person ability measures and their associated standard errors is illustrated in Table 8.5. It should be remembered that this hand calculation procedure provides a reasonably accurate estimation of the unconditional maximum likelihood estimation procedure that is employed with computer programs such as BICAL, BILOG, and MICROSCALE. With very small samples and small groups of items, the unconditional maximum likelihood estimation procedure is to be preferred over PROX for accuracy.

Note that the standard errors were predictably high due to the small numbers of persons and items in this example. Since the magnitude of the standard errors, also in logit units, is greater than the distances between calibrated item difficulty and person ability values, this hypothetical test would have little practical value in terms of defining a latent trait. Note also the normal tendency for standard error estimates to be higher at the extremes of ability and difficulty, and lower toward the means. This finding is intuitively satisfying, and constitutes an improvement over unitary, global reliability estimates made to apply to all possible scores. Kuder-Richardson Formula 20 reliability estimation for this same test would be at the magnitude of .91, due in part to the high variance of the score distribution. Rasch Model analysis would lead us to place somewhat less confidence in the test, due to the high standard errors and the presence of four items and three persons with invariant responses. Probably with an increase in the sample of examinees, the item difficulty estimates would increase in accuracy. In any event, it is now evident how Rasch Model ability and difficulty estimation can proceed, and how these estimates can be positioned on the same interval scale to define a given latent trait operationally.

Computation of Item and Person Fit to the Model

Now that items and persons have been placed on the same difficulty/ability continuum, it is possible to analyze item and person fit to the model. This is done with reliance on Formula 8.1 as a means of quantifying the unlikelihood of a given response pattern now that the abilities of the persons and the difficulties of the items are known. The unlikelihood of success or failure (degree of misfit) in responding to an item is a function of the distance of person ability from item difficulty, $(b - d)$. The farther person ability is below item difficulty, the more unlikely will be success in responding to the item. Similarly, the farther person ability is above item difficulty, the more unlikely will be failure in responding to the item. The probability of instances of response then may be estimated according to the following formula when item difficulty and person ability are known:

$$p = \frac{\exp(b-d)}{1+\exp(b-d)} \quad (8.6)$$

The difference between the observed item response, x, with values of zero or one, and the expected response, p, may be written as the expression, $x - p$. This expression refers to the amount of departure from expectation, or the residual, in a given response. The residual may be standardized in a manner analogous to the calculation of standard deviation units or z-scores. That involves simply dividing the residual, x − p, by the standard deviation of expected values as in the following formula:

$$z = \left(\frac{x-p}{p(1-p)}\right)^{1/2} \tag{8.7}$$

Combining with Formula 8.6, and squaring the standardized residual, z, the squared standardized residual for incorrect (zero) responses reduces to,

$$z_0^2 = \exp(b - d) \tag{8.8}$$

and for correct (one) responses to,

$$z_1^2 = \exp(d - b) \tag{8.9}$$

Combining both correct and incorrect possible outcomes, the formula may be written as follows:

$$z^2 = \exp[(2x - 1)(b - d)] \tag{8.10}$$

The sum of these squared standardized residuals for any item or person may be used to indicate the comparative degree of misfit to the model for that item or person. This measure of fit may be expressed as a t-value according to the following formula:

$$t = [\text{Ln} \frac{\Sigma z^2}{d.f.} + \frac{\Sigma z^2}{d.f.} - 1] \left(\frac{d.f.}{8}\right)^{1/2} \tag{8.11}$$

where d.f. equals the degrees of freedom associated with the particular standardized residual, which, for items, is equal to the number of items minus one $(n - 1)$, and for persons is equal to the number of persons minus one $(N - 1)$.

The establishment of a critical value of t for the rejection of persons or items as misfitting is somewhat arbitrary. Commonly the t-value of positive 2.00 is set as the critical value, so that items or persons with t-values of 2.00 or above are considered misfits to the model, lacking response validity. A negative t-value of −2.00 or below reflects overfit to the model and usually does not constitute grounds for the rejection of items or persons. There is some suspicion, however, that overfitting items or persons may exhibit less stable difficulty or ability estimates on recalibration. Table 8.6 illustrates the calculation of fit for items and persons in our sample vocabulary test.

Notice that person 7 exhibited a highly unlikely response pattern (sum of squared standardized residuals = 17.05). This is particularly because, with an estimated ability of 0.83, this person missed item 4 and got item 8 correct. Similarly, item 3 exhibited an unlikely response pattern (sum of squared standardized residuals = 10.13). This is primarily due to the fact that person 5, with an ability estimated at −0.14, was unable to pass item 3, with a difficulty of only −2.28. Item and person fit statistics are summarized in Table 8.7.

Notice that person 7 was the only item or person that exceeded the critical t-value of 2.00, and would therefore be rejected. Normally, rejection of items or persons should be an iterative process requiring that remaining persons and items be recalibrated. Often in practice, however, misfitting persons are removed,

TABLE 8.6 Calculation of fit from scoring matrix

Persons	3	4	5	Items 6	7	8	b	Σz²
2 ×	1	0	0	0	0	0	−2.38	1.65
d − b	0.10	1.31	2.13	2.13	3.69	5.90		
z²	1.11	0.27	0.12	0.12	0.02	0.01		
3 ×	1	1	0	0	0	0	−1.11	2.31
d − b	−1.17	0.04	0.86	0.86	2.42	3.63		
z²	0.31	1.04	0.42	0.42	0.09	0.03		
4	1	1	0	1	0	0	−0.14	2.83
d − b	−2.14	−0.93	−0.11	−0.11	1.45	2.66		
z²	0.12	0.39	1.12	0.90	0.23	0.07		
5	0	1	1	1	0	0	−0.14	10.99
d − b	−2.14	−0.93	−0.11	−0.11	1.45	2.66		
z²	8.50	0.39	0.90	0.90	0.23	0.07		
6	1	1	1	1	0	0	0.83	1.67
d − b	−3.11	−1.90	−1.08	−1.08	0.48	1.69		
z²	0.04	0.15	0.34	0.34	0.62	0.18		
7	1	0	1	0	1	1	0.83	17.05
d − b	−3.11	−1.90	−1.08	−1.08	0.48	1.69		
z²	0.04	6.69	0.34	2.94	1.62	5.42		
8	1	1	1	1	1	0	2.10	1.36
d − b	−4.38	−3.17	−2.35	−2.35	−0.79	0.42		
z²	0.01	0.04	0.10	0.10	0.45	0.66		
d	−2.28	−1.07	−0.25	−0.25	1.31	2.52		
Σz²	10.13	8.97	3.34	5.72	3.26	6.44		

and all items are recalibrated only one additional time. In the present example, it appears necessary to reject person 7. For person 7 this means that the obtained test score is probably invalid and should be interpreted with extreme caution. The pattern of responses for person 7 is typical of a person who is blindly guessing. It would probably be useful to interview person 7 if possible to determine whether test instructions were understood, whether there was lack of serious cooperation, whether there was some visual or other handicap present, or simply whether random guessing was taking place. Note that classical test theory makes no provision for the identification of such misfitting persons and, therefore, increases the possibility that invalid scores may be reported for certain persons in the sample of examinees.

TABLE 8.7   Item and person Rasch Model fit statistics

Item Number	Σz^2	t	Person Number	Σz^2	t
3	10.13	1.05	2	1.65	−1.41
4	8.97	0.78	3	2.31	−1.04
5	3.34	−0.89	4	2.83	−0.79
6	5.72	−0.08	5	10.99	1.57
7	3.26	−0.92	6	1.67	−1.39
8	6.44	0.12	7	17.05	2.88
			8	1.36	−1.60

8.4   Summary

This chapter has provided a comparison of classical and latent trait measurement theory. Certain advantages of item response theory have been discussed. A brief comparison was made of various latent trait models. A description was provided of the procedures necessary for the computation of Rasch Model item difficulty and person ability estimates and their associated standard errors. Computation of item and person fit statistics was explained with examples.

Exercises

1. List and explain five advantages of latent trait measurement theory over classical measurement theory.
2. List and describe the three most common latent trait models, including advantages and disadvantages of each.
3. Explain how test tailoring can improve the information value of tests at the decision cut-off points.
4. List and explain four assumptions underlying the application of latent trait models.
5. Explain the possible causes and consequences of person misfit in Rasch Model applications.
6. For the following sample scoring matrix for a test of communicative competence, calculate the Rasch item difficulty estimates and their associated standard errors, using either a hand calculator or a computer program:

			Items		
Persons	1	2	3	4	5
1	1	0	0	0	0
2	0	1	1	0	0
3	1	1	0	1	0
4	1	0	1	1	1
5	1	1	1	1	0

7. Using the same scoring matrix as in exercise 6, calculate Rasch person ability estimates and their associated standard errors.
8. Calculate item fit statistics, and indicate which, if any, items would be rejected with a 2.00 fit t criterion.
9. Calculate person fit statistics, and indicate which, if any, persons would be rejected with a 1.50 fit t criterion.
10. Calculate a matrix of standardized residuals for all responses.

Chapter Nine

Item Banking, Machine Construction of Tests, and Computer Adaptive Testing

In chapter eight, the underlying principles of latent trait theory or item response theory were introduced, with special focus on the one-parameter Rasch Model. There it was affirmed that item banking, machine construction of tests, and computer adaptive testing were facilitated by this comparatively new approach to item and test analysis. In the present chapter examples of these applications will be presented and discussed. Focus here will be pragmatic, with emphasis on how an operation may be done rather than on the important theoretical and philosophical ramifications of doing it. The examples are borrowed from a test development context at the University of California Los Angeles, where these procedures are operational in conjunction with the UCLA English As a Second Language Proficiency Examination (ESLPE), used in screening and placement of university students for ESL courses.

9.1   Item Banking

The development of an efficient item banking procedure is dependent on at least five factors. First, there must be an available population of examinees for regular test administration and analysis purposes. Samples from this population should exceed 100 persons for each analysis. Secondly, there should be a measurement model that permits the computation of item difficulty estimates and associated standard errors that can be made to generalize beyond a given test administration with a given sample of persons. The Rasch One-Parameter Logistic Model is advocated here for reasons given in chapter eight, including its feasibility with small samples, and its viability for computer adaptive testing with comparatively few items. Third, there must be a set of criteria for describing, classifying, accepting, and rejecting items. This will permit organization and efficiency in the use of the limited space available in the bank. Fourth, there is a need for a linking schema or plan for the systematic joining of future items to the bank with a minimum of resultant translation error. This plan will allow for cross-checking of translated difficulty calibrations to minimize error. And finally, there should be available computer hardware and software for appropriate storage and retrieval of items for specific purposes.

Sample Constraints

If there is no need to maintain a continuing testing program involving repetitive administrations of tests with samples of persons from a similar underlying population, then item banking is probably not a worthwhile undertaking. In situations where large-scale admissions, placement, or exit testing is required, and where there is a demand for locally developed tests, item banking is an appealing activity. For purposes of Rasch Model item calibration and item banking, exam administrations should involve a minimum of 100 examinees. Use of larger samples will help minimize the standard errors associated with difficulty estimates. It may be more direct, therefore, to speak of a minimum standard error estimate acceptable than to set a sample size constraint; however, the two are inversely related.

Beyond the sample size constraint, there is also the need to satisfy the population invariance assumption. This assumption is similar to the assumption of unidimensionality for items, but reflects person unidimensionality instead of item unidimensionality. It may be violated if populations of examinees change characteristics dramatically over time. The assumption may be tested using factor analysis of the person tetrachoric correlation matrix. To satisfy the assumption, there must be a primary, dominant person factor that explains at least 20 percent of the total matrix variance (Henning, Hudson, and Turner, 1985).

Finally, criteria must be set for person fit to the measurement model employed, so that procedures may be established for the treatment of misfitting persons. Use of misfitting persons in the derivation of item difficulty and fit statistics may contaminate these statisics. Rejection of such persons constitutes an admission that their response patterns were invalid, and that test scores derived for these persons do not have the same meaning and cannot be relied upon for the same decisions as test scores for "fitting" persons. Persons with an overall fit t-value equal to or exceeding 2.00 are usually excluded from the sample for purposes of item banking (chapter eight). More stringent criteria may be adopted for situations calling for greater accuracy — as with machine construction of tests with small numbers of items. Additionally, in the case of computer adaptive testing, where precalibrated items are used, but where person fit statistics may not be computed for each new examinee, rejection criteria for persons may be established on the basis of numbers of items encountered before "convergence" is reached. In other words, a person who encounters and responds to 50 items and still does not exhibit an ability estimate standard error below .50 may be assumed to misfit the model. The exact number of items set as the criterion will vary with the nature of the test and the level of error deemed acceptable.

The Measurement Model

Item response theory (IRT) latent trait procedure is probably the most suitable and powerful procedure for most item banking applications. This is because it readily permits expansion of the bank by inclusion of new items calibrated on the same difficulty continuum with the same scale and origin as for all items already existing in the bank. Also, latent trait procedure enables machine construction of tests from the bank with predetermined estimates of difficulty, dispersion, and reliability, even though the exact combination of items in the machine constructed test has never appeared before and has not yet been administered in its present form to any examinees. These and other advantages are discussed in chapter eight.

The choice of a particular latent trait model is also discussed in chapter eight. Consistent with the conclusions reached in that chapter, the Rasch one-parameter model is the model advocated here for item banking purposes. This is primarily because it permits the calibration of item difficulty and the linking of new items to the bank based on response patterns of as few as 100 persons (UCLA ESLPE calibrations are based on samples ranging in size from 300 to 900). The two- and three-parameter models require such large samples of examinees as would be prohibitive in the case of most language institutes where the need for item banking exists. Furthermore, in the use of item banking for computer adaptive testing, when the Rasch Model is employed, ability estimation is not tied to fluctuations in discriminability or guessing parameters, as it is with other models. It should be noted, however, that similar results can be achieved in computer adaptive testing with the two- and three-parameter models by suppressing discriminability and guessing parameters (Tung, 1985). This effectively reverts to a one-parameter model.

Item Classification

As information is gathered about the items to be placed in the bank, the decision must be made regarding what information should be retained in the bank itself. Minimally, there must be some item name or identification number, some indication of item difficulty and associated measurement error, and an index of fit to the model employed. Additionally, it may be desirable to include a printed copy of the item itself with any multiple-choice options attached, a record of the dates of item use, a classification of item content (e.g., grammatical feature tested), and additional item statistics (e.g., point-biserial correlation, error impact, susceptibility to test response strategies, bias statistics, and/or an additional discriminability index). Also it may be desirable to include repeated estimates of item statistics on subsequent test administrations.

While it may be useful to include as much information as possible, storage and retrieval constraints must also be considered. Item banks containing thousands of items with numerous large data fields are often slow and cumbersome for applications such as computer adaptive testing. A sample of the evolving structure of the data base BANKER.DBF, used to store language items in DBASEII/III format for ESL proficiency and achievement testing at the University of California is presented in Table 9.1.

Note that this particular item bank structure has frequently been modified, and it has probably not yet reached final form. As the table indicates, there are currently 19 fields ranging in size from one to 145 columns. Nine of these fields are character fields (C), and ten are numeric fields (N). Only numeric fields have entries to the right of a decimal point (002). Field number one (IDNO) contains an item identification number. Field number two (FORM) holds a test form number that is coded to indicate the date(s) of item use. Field number three (PASSAGE) contains passage identification so that items within listening, reading, or writing error detection passages may be accessed as a group. The CONTENT field (004) is used to label passage topics in accordance with the various academic specializations of the students who regularly sit for the examination. The numeric fields numbered 5 through 11 are used to store item statistics including adjusted (linked) Rasch difficulty calibrations, standard errors of measurement, overall fit t-values, between groups fit *t*-values, discriminability statistics, point-biserial correlations, and an index of error impact. Field number 12 (CLASS) contains coded item classification information such as grammatical feature tested. Fields 13–15 contain the actual

TABLE 9.1   Structure of item bank data base BANKER.DBF

Field	Name	Type	Width	Decimals
001	IDNO	C	005	000
002	FORM	C	040	000
003	PASSAGE	C	005	000
004	CONTENT	C	008	000
005	DIFCAL	N	006	002
006	SEM	N	004	002
007	TFIT	N	006	002
008	TFITB	N	006	002
009	DISC	N	005	002
010	PBIS	N	005	002
011	ERIM	N	004	002
012	CLASS	C	001	000
013	ITEM	C	065	000
014	ITEML	C	145	000
015	ITEMO	C	145	000
016	DIFCAL2	N	006	002
017	DIFCAL3	N	006	002
018	DIFCAL4	N	006	002
019	KEY	C	001	000

items according to a short (ITEM) or long (ITEML) format version, along with the multiple-choice options used (ITEMO). Fields 16–19 are employed to store information on subsequent difficulty calibrations as a check on stability of item difficulty calibrations. And, finally, field 19 holds the scoring key for the items. Additional information on bias for or against major language groups may be added as that information becomes available. Information on susceptibility to test wiseness strategies may also be incorporated.

This may serve as an example or model for storage of information in an item bank. The advantage of such a system is that items may be called from the bank according to a large combination of specifications, including difficulty range, skill area, fit to the model, and anticipated measurement error. Items may then be used for the construction of new exams according to specifications, or for purposes of computer adaptive testing.

Linking Schema

It was mentioned earlier that one of the many advantages of Rasch Model approaches to item banking is that new items can readily be joined to the same measurement scale and added to the bank. Typically, this is done through the use of a selected group of pre-analyzed items or persons called a "link." Items are more often used for this purpose than persons due to the maturation, learning, and forgetting factors that are inherent in persons. Usually, then, a group of ten or more items are carefully chosen for difficulty, fit, and stability, and these items are employed in two administrations of a test with persons from the same invariant population. The average difficulty estimates for the items at each administration are compared. The difference in mean item difficulty between time one and two is called a "translation constant." This constant is then applied to all items administered at time two in order to link them with all items administered at time one. An example of this linking procedure is illustrated in Table 9.2.

In this hypothetical linking example, a test of 15 items (Test 1) has been Rasch analyzed, and the calibrated items form the nucleus of the item bank. A subsequent test of 15 items (Test 2) was devised, administered, and Rasch analyzed. Ten items were common to both tests: these comprised the link, and consisted of items 6 through 15 on Test 1 and items 1 through 10 on Test 2. Notice that, although these ten items were identical, the calibrated difficulties were different for the two tests. This difference is due primarily to the fact that the origin or zero point of the item difficulty scale has arbitrarily been set to the mean of item difficulties in each calibration.

At the bottom of Table 9.2, the computation procedure is given for determining the translation constant, which is then added to the Test 2 difficulty estimates in order to link them to Test 1 difficulty estimates. Following this procedure, we can see that adjusted item difficulty estimates for Test 2 become equivalent to Test 1 item difficulty estimates for common items. In this way the estimates are said to be "linked" or joined to the same scale as that of the original item bank.

131

TABLE 9.2 Sample linking procedures

	Test 1		Test 2		Test 2 (Adj.)	
	Item No.	Diff.	Item No.	Diff.	Item No.	Adj. Diff.
	1	3.50				
	2	3.00				
	3	2.50				
	4	2.00				
	5	1.50				
C						
O	6	1.00	1	3.50	1	1.00
M	7	0.50	2	3.00	2	0.50
M	8	0.00	3	2.50	3	0.00
O	9	−0.50	4	2.00	4	−0.50
N	10	−1.00	5	1.50	5	−1.00
	11	−1.50	6	1.00	6	−1.50
I	12	−2.00	7	0.50	7	−2.00
T	13	−2.50	8	0.00	8	−2.50
E	14	−3.00	9	−0.50	9	−3.00
M	15	−3.50	10	−1.00	10	−3.50
S			11	−1.50	11	−4.00
			12	−2.00	12	−4.50
			13	−2.50	13	−5.00
			14	−3.00	14	−5.50
			15	−3.50	15	−6.00

Mean link Test 1 = −12.50/10 = −1.25
Mean link Test 2 = 12.50/10 = 1.25
Translation Constant = Test 1 mean link minus Test 2 mean link = −1.25 − (1.25) = −2.50
Adjusted Difficulty = Test 2 Calibrated Difficulty plus Translation Constant

If this same procedure were followed over a period of years, employing different linking items each time, it is to be expected that an ever-increasing error factor would be introduced to the translation constant. This error would be inversely related to the accuracy and stability of difficulty estimates of linking items. The standard error associated with a translation constant may be expressed in logits as in Formula 9.1 below:

$$G_e = \left(\frac{3.5}{NK}\right)^{1/2} \tag{9.1}$$

where, N = the number of persons in the linking sample
K = the number of items in the link

The approximate fit of the link can be evaluated with the chi-square statistic with K degrees of freedom according to Formula 9.2:

$$\sum_{i}^{k} (d_{iA} - d_{iB} - G_{AB})^2 \frac{N}{12} \frac{K}{K-1} \sim \chi_K^2 \tag{9.2}$$

where, G_{AB} = the translation constant = $(d_{iA} - d_{iB})/K$
d_{iA} = the difficulty estimate for a given link item from test A
d_{iB} = the difficulty estimate for the same link item as estimated for test B

N   = the number of persons in the linking sample (B)
K   = the number of items in the link

The fit of any one item in the link may be estimated using Formula 9.3.

$$(d_{iA} - d_{iB} - G_{AB})^2 \frac{N}{12} \frac{K}{(K-1)} \sim \chi_1^2 \tag{9.3}$$

As a further check on the consistency and cohesion of the linking process, it is possible to construct a loop with three links, as in the example of Figure 9.1. In such a loop, the sum of the translation constants should approximately equal zero, as stated in Formula 9.4.

$$G_{AB} + G_{BC} + G_{AC} \sim 0 \tag{9.4}$$

In the University of California (UCLA) experience, the procedure has been to develop one additional test form each academic quarter. Each test form contains a minimum of 80 pre-analyzed items which serve as links to other test forms and to the item bank. Since each new test form has the same length, format, and approximately the same difficulty as all preceding forms, and since no items are either failed or passed by every person in any sample of examinees, the translation constants tend to be small in magnitude and easily derived. Figure 9.2 shows approximately how this cycle is repeated each year.

Note from this example that each form of the test has approximately 80 items in common with preceding forms. These common linking items are distributed about equally across the subtests of the ESLPE battery. The summer version is linked with both the spring and fall versions as indicated in Figure 9.2. This kind of a network provides both quarterly and annual links with the item bank with the possibility of a loop to check on linking accuracy. One of the practical reasons for linking with immediately preceding forms is that in some subtest formats items are

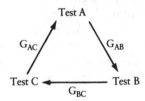

FIGURE 9.1   A loop involving three links

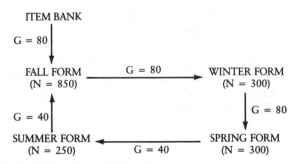

FIGURE 9.2   The UCLA ESLPE annual linking loop

bound in groups to a common comprehension passage. When one item in a group of new experimental, passage-bound items is found to misfit the model or is otherwise rejected on analysis, it is necessary to revise that one item and readminister it in conjunction with the other items and their common passage before the entire set of items can be received into the item bank. The pre-analyzed, acceptable items of the set can be included among the items of the link; whereas the revised, readministered item is treated as a new experimental item.

Computer Hardware and Software

Choosing or developing a computer system for item banking involves several decision steps.

Purpose

There must be a thorough conceptualization of the exact item banking functions desired. Is the purpose of the item bank to be merely the conservation and secure maintenance of a set of items for future use? Is there also the intention to maintain a capability for machine construction of tests? Is there a need to develop a computer adaptive test in conjunction with the item bank; i.e., is the item bank to serve as a data base from which the computer adaptive test will draw in presenting and processing responses from the examinees?

Process

Given the purposes that have been determined for the item bank, what is the storage capacity needed and what are the speed-of-processing constraints to be imposed? How many items, test formats, item descriptors, and other information fields are to be created for the purposes envisioned? If a computer adaptive test is planned, is it intended for ease of marketing or private use that the items for each test all be resident on one storage diskette (as if there were no more than approximately 500 items and their accompanying information fields)? If larger item banks are needed, along with implied need for increased speed of processing, perhaps a fixed or "hard" disk system or a mainframe computer is needed.

Software

Once specific purposes and processing needs have been specified, there needs to be a review of existing software. It may be the case that available software packages can be located at appropriate costs to handle all of the functions envisioned within all of the storage and processing constraints intended. On the other hand, it may be necessary to develop customized software with features not commercially available. Software development projects will depend on existence and availability of programming skills.

Hardware

The identification of appropriate software may, in combination with other previously mentioned considerations, help in the choice of suitable computer hardware. Hardware often represents the greatest resource expenditure; therefore, selection should not be made before consideration of all of the above matters. Also, thought must be given to hardware maintenance and repair, compatibility with preexisting or planned systems, and availability of appropriate storage facilities for the hardware. Hardware portability may also be a consideration. These general remarks are intended to reflect the likelihood that suitable item banking computer systems will vary widely from situation to situation.

The ESLPE item bank makes use of the popular data base management microcomputer software, DBASE II and DBASE III. This particular choice afforded the advantages of large data capacity (more than 50,000 items), flexibility in the choice of microcomputer operating systems (both DOS and CP/M), and accompanying programming language capability for development of customized features of machine construction of tests, computer adaptive testing, and reporting of test scores. DBASE compiler programs are beginning to appear on the market, and they also bring the possibility of enhancing processing speed as the actual DBASE programs are converted to machine language. These few remarks are intended not to promote any particular hardware or software system, but to provide the encouraging information that many suitable systems are readily available at the present time and that, while hardware and software are constantly improving, existing low-cost systems are more than adequate for most applications.

9.2   Machine Construction of Tests

Once items have been appropriately entered and indexed into an item bank or series of banks, it is readily possible to access the items via computer for the assembling of tests according to specifications. In the example of the UCLA ESLPE mentioned above, since items in the bank have been pre-analyzed and calibrated for difficulty and fit to a latent trait model, it is easily possible to match item difficulties along the latent continuum to course levels in the existing program of instruction. The DBASE program commands make it possible to access, display, and print all banked items within specified difficulty ranges in a matter of seconds. Since prior global estimates of reliability have been made for combinations of these items in use with the same target population of examinees, it is readily possible through use of the Spearman-Brown Prophecy Formula (see chapter six) to determine numbers of similar items needed to achieve prespecified levels of reliability. Thus, it is possible to determine in advance the level of reliability that the test will exhibit (within close approximation), even before the exact group of items in the test has ever appeared in the same combination in any previous test administration. Since items can be almost perfectly matched to level of instruction, the capability of constructing achievement tests that are directly related to proficiency/placement tests is also afforded. It is possible through the use of DBASE command files to construct (at the

135

press of a button) a series of tests that exhibit in a prespecified manner the desired number of items, category of content, format selection, mean difficulty, range of difficulty, global reliability, and proportion or precise designation of overlapping or linking items.

9.3   Computer Adaptive Testing

Computer adaptive testing is a variation of tailored testing which permits the determination of the sequence of items encountered to be based on the ongoing pattern of success and failure experienced by the examinee. Most commonly, such an approach would, for an examinee who experienced success with a given item, result in the purposeful presentation of an item of greater difficulty. The examinee who experienced failure with a given item would next encounter an item of lower difficulty. Some variation of this process would continue in an iterative fashion until it was determined that sufficient information had been gathered about the ability of the examinee to permit the termination of the test.

Advantages and Disadvantages of Computer Adaptive Testing

Profound advantages accrue through the use of such an approach. Some of these advantages may be described as follows:

1. *Individual testing time may be reduced.* Since the test program is developed so that a given examinee is most likely to encounter only items matched to his or her ability, it is usually true that fewer items need be encountered than in the standard paper-and-pencil testing situation where every item in the test is presented, regardless of whether or not these items are matched to the ability of any given student.
2. *Frustration and fatigue are minimized* in the case of students who would otherwise be forced to respond to quantities of items that would be beyond their ability levels.
3. *Boredom is reduced* for those examinees who would otherwise be asked to encounter numbers of items that would be too easy for them.
4. *Test scores may be provided immediately* since scoring is performed by the computer as the exam is in progress.
5. *Diagnostic feedback may be given immediately* to examinees, teachers, and/or administrators.
6. *Test security may be enhanced* since it is highly unlikely that any two examinees would encounter the exact same set of items in exactly the same sequence.
7. *Record-keeping functions are improved* so that it is more feasible to maintain longitudinal records of the progress of individual students than is usually the case with other kinds of programs.
8. *Reporting, research, and evaluation capabilities are expanded* since detailed information is stored concerning the performance of each student and may be considered in relation to other demographic information about the student.

It is only fair to note that there may also be some subtle disadvantages to computer adaptive tests, and methods may need to be found to overcome or compensate for these disadvantages.

1. *Unfamiliarity, anxiety, or hostility* with regard to the computer as a testing medium may produce invalid test performance on the part of some examinees. Such an argument could be advanced equally with regard to almost any testing format or medium.
2. *CAT items may be limited to objective, recognition format.* While some more creative format varieties are being developed slowly, the operational formats are currently limited. It must be recognized, however, that objective, recognition formats are still highly reliable and valid for many purposes.
3. *In some language skills there may be warm-up effects* that CAT approaches fail to recognize. The thought here is that an examinee beginning at a low level of item difficulty and progressing sequentially up the difficulty scale may, in some cases, reach a higher point of success than an examinee who enters a test at a median level of difficulty and who is confined to items at difficulty levels matching his or her performance. While this warm-up phenomenon is recognized in tests of speech production, and may exist in other kinds of tests as well, it is likely that many CAT approaches permit a kind of upward shift in ability estimation that would at least partially admit the process.
4. *There may be legal objections* to the promulgations of scores for different students based on different combinations of items which are used for the identical academic decisions. An examinee might argue that he or she was refused admission or held for an unwanted course, when other examinees encountering different items, in differing total numbers, experienced more desirable testing outcomes. It may be necessary systematically to inform the public and the legal system that it is more desirable to hold measurement error constant for different examinees than to hold constant the number and exact examples of items encountered.

Varieties of Computer Adaptive Tests

Four basic categories of computer adaptive tests are considered here. While these categories allow for considerable intracategory variation, there will certainly be many other creative developments in computer adaptive testing that transcend these particular categories.

Decision Point Tests

This kind of test preserves the capability of shaping the information function of the test. Essentially what happens with this kind of test is that items in the bank are limited to difficulty points where decisions of admission, exemption, etc. must be made. If a certain cut-off point of ability has been predetermined for admission to or exemption from a program of instruction, then the computer presents the candidate only with items at the corresponding difficulty levels, rather than with items at all points along the difficulty continuum. After success and failure patterns for a given examinee are considered for a specified number of items at a designated decision point, the decision algorithm programmed into the computer may move the item selection and presentation process to another, more appropriate, decision point along the continuum. Eventually the cut-off decision is made by the computer algorithm at some prespecified level of acceptable error. This kind of program tends to be highly efficient for decision-making purposes in that highly accurate decisions may be made on the basis of responses to very few items.

Step Ladder Tests

This kind of test is constructed so that a specified number of items are held in the bank at each of a specified number of proficiency or achievement steps. This also presupposes that all items have been pre-analyzed, calibrated, and arranged in rank order on a difficulty continuum. Imagine a computer adaptive test with 500 items arranged so that ten items appear at each of 50 difficulty steps. The computer algorithm would select some entry level for a given examinee. Based on the experience of success or failure with a given item, a more appropriate item would be selected at a specified number of steps above or below the first item. After a series of such items are presented in an iterative fashion, it would be possible to "hone in" on the appropriate step reflective of the ability of the examinee. The algorithm could limit the iteration distance after an initial set of items were encountered. As a check, the total score for all items at the appropriate step should approximately match a pre-set percentage—say, 50 percent. This is the kind of test developed for Spanish and ESL at Brigham Young University (Jones, 1986; Larsen, 1986; Madsen, 1986).

Error-Controlled Tests

These tests differ from the preceding approaches in that, following exposure to a specified set of introductory items, they employ a procedure such as unconditional maximum likelihood estimation in order to estimate examinee ability on the ability continuum. They then access and present the item in the bank that is nearest in difficulty to the estimated person ability—provided the item was not previously encountered. After each new item is encountered, a revised estimate of person ability is provided with an associated estimate of measurement standard error. The process continues in an iterative manner until the estimate of measurement error drops to a prespecified level of acceptability. The total number of items encountered will vary with the level of error that has been specified in advance. This is the current procedure in use with the ESLPE computer adaptive test at UCLA, applying Rasch latent trait modeling (Henning, 1985). A similar approach was described with simulated data by Tung (1985) using the three-parameter model, but suppressing the discrimination and guessing parameters.

The actual algorithm programmed into the computer adaptive test developed by the author for use at UCLA may be summarized in the following steps:

1. The examinee selects the subtest of interest after the program has been accessed.
2. The examinee responds to the item of median difficulty which is displayed by the program.
3. The program chooses an appropriate second item. The item will be one logit of difficulty above the first item if the examinee succeeded with the first item. The item will be one logit of difficulty below the first item if the examinee experienced failure with the first item.
4. Items three and four are selected and presented in the same manner as item two.
5. Once four items have been encountered, the program routinely estimates ability (b_f) and associated error of estimate (s_f) after each item encountered. To do this, use is made of the following approximation formulas:

$$b_f = h + w(f - .5) + \ln\left(\frac{A}{B}\right) \qquad (9.5)$$

where, h = test height or mean difficulty of items encountered at each point, considered cumulatively — the sum of the difficulty estimates divided by the number of items encountered so far, or

$$\frac{\Sigma d}{L} \qquad (9.6)$$

w = test width or the span of item difficulties encountered, represented as the following quantity:

$$\frac{d_L + d_{L-1} - d_2 - d_1}{2}\left(\frac{L}{L-2}\right) \qquad (9.7)$$

This formula averages the two highest and two lowest difficulties encountered in deriving test width, in order to provide greater accuracy.

$$f = \text{proportion correct, or } r/L \qquad (9.8)$$

$$A = 1 - \exp(-wf) \qquad (9.9)$$

$$B = 1 - \exp[-w(1-f)] \qquad (9.10)$$

$$C = 1 - \exp(-w) \qquad (9.11)$$

$$s_f = \left(\frac{w}{L}\cdot\frac{C}{AB}\right)^{1/2} \qquad (9.12)$$

6. An acceptable level of error of estimation is determined in advance by consideration of the precise needs for accuracy of ability estimation with a given test. Once the error of estimate (s_f) diminishes to the prespecified level, the test is terminated. With this particular computer adaptive test, a standard error of estimate of 0.5 logits can be achieved with as few as 18 items encountered. If this level of accuracy is not attained within 30 items (which has not yet happened), the program can be terminated on the grounds that the respondent is misfitting the measurement model by responding arbitrarily.

Multi-Stage Tests

A variation of two-stage and three-stage testing that has long been reported in the literature on test tailoring is also applicable to computer adaptive testing. In multi-stage tests, a decision is made on the basis of performance on the first-stage test that determines which of several tests of varying difficulty will be administered during the second stage. Still further levels of tests may be assigned in subsequent stages. The purpose is to maximize the information function of the multi-stage test at the same time that the total number of items encountered by any individual is minimized somewhat (although not so much as in the computer adaptive approaches already described above). The computer adaptive variation of multi-staging described here relates to the use of passage-bound items, as in tests of reading or listening comprehension. Passages may be rated for reading complexity and associated items are calibrated for difficulty. In this way the range of ability tapped by each passage may be compared with that of every other passage. The first stage of the computer adaptive test presents a passage with a very broad range of item difficulty. On the basis of performance on the first passage, the program algorithm calls for branching to a second passage the items of which may be at one of several narrower ranges of difficulty. In this way, very accurate estimates of reading or listening comprehension can be made with as few as three passages, depending on the numbers of items attached to each passage and the statistical characteristics of each item. This approach provides one of the several possible solutions to the problems associated with the presentation of passages in computer adaptive format.

9.4 Summary

In this chapter we have reviewed practical requirements for the establishment of a program of item banking. Possible extensions of item banking into the applications of machine construction of tests and computer adaptive testing have been presented along with a description of the features of such programs. Four general types of computer adaptive tests have been described, including decision point tests, step ladder tests, error-controlled tests, and multi-stage tests.

Exercises

1. List and describe five general considerations for the establishment of an item bank. These are concerns and requirements to review in the process of item bank development.
2. Prepare an item bank file structure that you would propose for a specified stated measurement purpose. List and describe the fields in the file structure.
3. List and explain three advantageous features of a system for the machine construction of tests.
4. Argue in favor of and against the use of computer adaptive testing by advancing at least three advantages and three disadvantages of this approach.
5. Describe with illustrations three general types of computer adaptive tests.
6. If a link is established using ten linking items, and the difficulty calibrations of these same items are as follows for Test 1 and Test 2,

					Items					
	1	2	3	4	5	6	7	8	9	10
Test 1	3.1	2.7	2.4	1.3	0.8	−0.6	−1.1	−1.9	−2.3	−2.6
Test 2	2.4	2.1	1.3	0.9	−0.3	−1.2	−1.8	−2.8	−3.0	−3.7

then compute the translation constant for linking Test 2 item difficulty calibrations to Test 1 item difficulty calibrations.

7. Explain how the translation constant in exercise 6 would be applied to Test 2 items for linking purposes, and report the corrected Test 2 linking item difficulties.

8. Assuming that 500 persons were administered Test 1 above and 200 persons were administered Test 2, and assuming that both tests consist of 150 items, compute the standard error of the link.

9. For the same data employed in exercise 8 above, perform a chi-square test of link fit.

10. What should the sum of translation constants approximate when they are used in the same linking loop?

Chapter Ten

Evaluation of Language Instruction Programs

One of the most obvious applications of language test development is in the evaluation of programs of language instruction. This chapter is intended to provide an overview of various methods of evaluation. Ultimately such evaluation can only be as good as the quality of the instrumentation used, but evaluation procedure is also a matter deserving consideration. Use of the finest instrumentation is not in itself a guarantee of quality evaluation unless due regard is given to planning and procedures, design, and methodology.

Evaluation may be viewed from several perspectives: prior-to-program implementation, during-program delivery, and following-program execution. Focus may be directed to affective and/or cognitive program impact. Concern may be with learning gains, instructional delivery, needs responsiveness, materials quality, cost effectiveness, continuing motivation, and/or the degree of realization of a variety of explicit or implicit objectives. Evaluation may be longitudinal or cross-sectional, formative or summative, criterion-referenced or norm-referenced. Good evaluation is a highly creative activity which may be either formal and structured or informal and unstructured. Whatever form it takes, good evaluation will provide reliable and relevant information about the quality of the instructional program and how it may be improved.

10.1   Affective Evaluation

Affective evaluation is usually conducted by means of an affective questionnaire or an interview. Likert-type questionnaires (see chapter two) are particularly effective in that they elicit information in a manner that permits quantification and comparison with other programs or with other features of the same program. Such questionnaires may be administered to students, to teachers in the program(s), or to potential or actual employers. They may provide feedback about the usefulness of materials, the popularity of either the teaching methodology or the teachers, the comparative perceived value of course offerings in the curriculum, the level of continuing motivation following exposure to the program, and many other program concerns.

An affective index of this sort permits valuable correlational research. It becomes possible to relate overall program affect to class size, monetary expenditure, teacher experience, and a host of other manipulatable program variables. Affective evaluation is particularly valuable in comparing language teaching methodologies, since the comparison of cognitive outcome historically has not been very fruitful. In the few cases where systematic, rigorous research was conducted to compare language teaching methodologies on cognitive outcomes such as learning gain, little if any advantage was found for any one over any other. A preferred methodology can be determined if, for example, affective evaluation indicates, that one method is more likely than others to promote continuing motivation.

10.2   Cognitive Evaluation

Ultimately it is of value to determine how effective a program of instruction is in the promotion of learning. There are many ways to conduct this kind of evaluation. Only a few are mentioned here.

Pretest/Posttest Comparisons — Norm-Referenced

Learning for any group of students may be assessed as the difference between entry-level and exit-level performance. This is usually measured by means of a pretest and a posttest administered at the beginning and at the end of a period of instruction. The difference between the scores on these two tests is referred to as a *gain score*. The judgment as to whether a gain score for a group of students is sufficiently large that one may conclude that learning was taking place at the desired rate depends on several important considerations:

1. How long was the period of instruction? For very short periods it is not customary to observe large learning gains.
2. Was the instrumentation appropriate? Were the tests sensitive to the kind of instruction taking place? Were they too difficult or too easy, so that the distribution of scores was skewed and not normal? Instrumental ceiling effect may lead to the wrong conclusion that sufficient learning was not taking place. Invalid instrumentation may cause one to draw inferences about rate of learning that are related to the wrong kinds of learning.
3. Was there a practice effect associated with a posttest that was the same as the pretest? If so, and there usually is with short tests over a short period of instruction, there are several techniques to control or eliminate such a practice effect. Use may be made of equated or equivalent forms of tests, as mentioned in chapter six. Alternatively, the pretest may be administered several times in a quasi-experimental approach that permits an estimate of the amount of improvement expected in subsequent administrations of the test — improvement

that is related to practice and not to instruction. If appropriate assumptions are met, use may be made of analysis of covariance procedure, with pretest scores serving as a concomitant variable and gain scores or posttest scores as a dependent variable.

4. If group comparisons are being made, is there evidence for the comparability of the groups prior to instruction? Were the groups drawn from the same general population and assigned randomly to the different instructional programs or treatments? If aptitude or pretest measures are available immediately prior to instruction, is there group comparability demonstrated by the absence of significant mean differences on test scores between the groups?

5. If group comparisons are being made with pretest-posttest measures, it may also be useful to administer a second posttest after an extended period—say, from several months to a year. The purpose of this delayed measure is to compare groups on retention of course content. Care must be exercised to ensure that the program exposures for the two groups during the extended period are similar.

Criterion-Referenced Evaluation

It may be that the focus of evaluation is not group or individual comparison, but rather determination of the extent to which prespecified program objectives have been met. This approach may also involve pretest-posttest comparison. Commonly, however, when there is reason to assume that the learners have no prior exposure to the content of instruction, or have not already mastered the course objectives, only a posttest is employed. By this method, a program is judged to have been successful if the posttest results support the conclusion that instructional objectives were met. Several concerns arise with this approach:

1. *Are the objectives appropriate?* If the objectives are too easy or too difficult, or if they are not relevant to the needs of the students or the society at large, attainment or failure to attain the objectives may not reveal whether the program was worthwhile or not.

2. *Are the objectives measurable?* If the objectives are worded so that it is not possible to determine precisely whether they have been met or not, then criterion-referenced evaluation will not be successful. Consider an objective that is worded, "Students will have a good knowledge of vocabulary." This objective fails to specify what "a good knowledge" is, both in quality and in quantity. On the other hand, a more clearly stated objective would be, "Students will identify the appropriate synonym for 90 percent of the given sentence-contextualized lexical items, when items are randomly sampled from the specified list of 500 words, and when synonyms are presented as options along with three multiple-choice distractors." Its advantage is that it is measurable.

3. *Does the test actually measure the objectives?* The objectives may be appropriate, relevant, and measurable; but, if the test fails to be sensitive to those objectives, then the test results will not be useful for this kind of evaluation. Of course, this assumes that the teaching has also been sensitive to the objectives and that the test is sensitive to the content of instruction. Such tests should not require knowledge of information or skills that are not presented in the

145

instructional sequence. A system of drawing items from pools of objective-sensitive items may be adopted. If a course has five measurable objectives, then a test may be designed to have as many as ten items relating to each objective. Mastery of a given objective may be reflected in achieving nine out of ten correct responses to the items measuring that objective.

4. *Is the criterion cut-off appropriate?* In setting a cut-off score on the test, did the evaluator take care to ensure that scoring above the cut-off score is a true reflection of mastery and that scoring below the cut-off score is a true reflection of nonmastery? Arbitrary selection of cut-off scores may result in a wrong conclusion about the success or failure of the instructional program. Consideration of previous group performance or latent trait indexes of person ability and task difficulty can assist in the establishment of appropriate evaluation criteria.

5. *Is both formative and summative evaluation conducted?* Rather than limiting the evaluation to a posttest, summative measure only, it may be desirable to evaluate the program in an ongoing, iterative fashion that measures attainment of objectives from lesson to lesson or from unit to unit. An advantage of this formative approach is that it allows for the adjustment of the program during the course of instruction. Formative evaluation holds promise for the establishment of courses and programs that are sensitive to the needs of the students and that provide appropriate sequencing and presentation of the content of instruction.

Growth-Referenced Evaluation

Growth-referenced evaluation is a comparatively recent approach in the literature (Henning, 1982). This technique purports to provide comparative information on rates of learning of component skills. Thus, it avoids some of the pitfalls associated with using absolute levels of performance for decision-making purposes (Glass, 1978: 259).

Growth-referenced evaluation has six distinguishing characteristics:

1. An attempt is made to analyze the teaching objective into component skills. If the goal of the program is to promote "communicative competence," then a variety of kinds of communicative competence are identified and measured at several key points in the program. If the program has reasonably unchanging, concurrently offered ascending levels of instruction, then testing can be done cross-sectionally with the same comprehensive instruments applied to all levels at the same time.

2. Each component skill is weighted for comparative importance. "Importance" is determined empirically as the magnitude of the correlation or discriminant function coefficient with some important global criterion. In this case the component skill exhibiting the highest correlation with the best global measure of communicative competence (possibly the total score of the battery of component skills tests) is said to be the most "important" component skill. It would be necessary to correct for attenuation (see chapter 6) and for part-whole overlap (see chapter 5) to ensure that the coefficients for comparison do not

146

cloud the investigation of importance with factors such as disparate reliabilities of component skills tests or differential additive contribution to total score.

3. The rate of program learning is determined for each component skill. This is usually accomplished by correlating scores on the component skills test with ascending numbers corresponding to interval level of attainment in the academic program. Once again, correction for attenuation is indicated for the same reasons mentioned above. High correlation of skills with program level suggests that the comparative rate of program-related learning was high for those skills. A comparatively low correlation here suggests that the program was less effective in the promotion of learning for that skill. This, in itself, is not a criticism of the program, since some skills are naturally easier to promote than others.

4. A commensurate growth ratio (CGR) is computed to determine the ratio of program rate of learning (PRL) to component skill importance (CSI).

$$CGR = \frac{PRL}{CSI} \tag{10.1}$$

Fisher Z transformations are used when correlation coefficients are manipulated arithmetically in this way. The resultant coefficient (CGR) reflects the comparative extent to which rate of learning of the component skill is commensurate with the importance of the skill. It is assumed that it is more critical to exhibit a high rate of learning of more important skills than of skills of lesser importance.

5. A remedial potential index (RPI) is calculated to indicate the comparative extent that each component skill is amenable to instruction.

$$RPI = \frac{r^2_{sl(z)}}{r^2_{tt(s)}} \tag{10.2}$$

In this computation, following the Fisher Z transformation, the squared correlation of skill with level is divided by the squared reliability estimate associated with the respective component skill instrument. A high remedial potential index would indicate that the portion of variance (in test scores) associated with participation in the program is high with respect to the total variance in test scores that exists irrespective of program participation. Variation in test scores for that skill can be said to be comparatively more a function of participation in the program than would be the case for skills with lower remedial potential indexes.

6. A final critical intervention index (CII) is promulgated as the ratio of remedial potential (RPI) to commensurate growth (CGR).

$$CII = \frac{RPI}{CGR} \tag{10.3}$$

This index permits identification of component skills that are underpromoted by the program but that are important to the program goals, and which are amenable to instruction. Thus, allocation of resources for curricular reform is restricted to those parts of the instructional program that are lagging behind other parts, but which are most critical to program goals and most likely to benefit from instructional intervention.

Application of this procedure to one four-year university EFL program served to identify listening comprehension and reading comprehension as the skills most critical for intervention, while ability to complete cloze tests and discrete-point grammar tests were found to be the least critical skills (Henning, 1982).

10.3   Evaluation of Delivery Systems

Programs may also be evaluated with regard to the quality of the delivery system, independent of considerations of cognitive or affective outcomes. Teaching quality, curricular sequencing, mode of content presentation, responsiveness to student needs, and suitability of teaching materials are some of the concerns of a delivery system. The following techniques are sometimes used to evaluate the program delivery system.

Portfolio Evaluation

This technique is not usually quantitative, but rather qualitative in nature. It calls for the cooperative maintaining of a set of files on the instructional program. Each teacher or teacher's aide writes notes or keeps an informal log as the program progresses. Relevant comments are inserted into a common file case or "portfolio" on a daily or weekly basis. All teachers and administrators have access to the portfolio to share or gather information about the effectiveness of particular segments of the curriculum. If several teachers are teaching the same levels and units in different sections of the same course, they can readily compare experiences and share information that is of common value. This approach has several advantages.

1. It promotes cooperation rather than competition among teachers. To be effective, this method requires a willingness on the part of teachers to share ideas and to note problems as well as successes.
2. It enhances professional communication. It is often difficult to gather all teachers regularly for discussion. If the teachers can regularly send notes to the portfolio and consult the comments of their colleagues, some of these communication problems can be reduced.
3. It more nearly ensures that needed reforms will take place. It is never so difficult to evaluate a program as it is to implement the changes called for by the evaluation, unless the teachers themselves are actively participating in the evaluation process.
4. It requires no technical knowledge of quantitative evaluation procedures. Very helpful information can be gathered and shared by teachers and administrators with no formal training in research design or statistics. Formal tests or questionnaires are not needed.
5. Ideas are conserved for future application in other classes. Often many good ideas are lost or forgotten with the change of teachers or students in a program unless some similar technique is adopted to preserve and promote the most successful ideas.

The portfolio itself usually consists of a set of file folders labeled so as to correspond with the lesson or unit numbers. Additionally, folders may be prepared for student problems, textbook ideas, procedural suggestions, and other program concerns. The portfolio is maintained in a central place, such as a teachers' lounge, where easy access is ensured. The folders may hold blank pieces of paper for random comments, or they may have pages with topical prompts for general areas of evaluative focus. At the end or in the course of a sequence of instruction, the comments are reviewed and worthwhile suggestions are adopted for implementation.

Need/Press Interaction Analysis

This technique serves as a valuable tool for assessing the extent to which students or teachers perceive that a program satisfies instructional needs. A Likert-type questionnaire is designed to elicit opinions about the importance of instructional components, and the same questionnaire items are repeated to elicit opinions about the emphasis given in the program to the various instructional components. It is then possible to measure and identify components of the program that are underemphasized or overemphasized in the curriculum. This kind of evaluation usually takes place in the final week of an instructional term. Students or teachers then can be expected to know what the focus and emphases of the program have been.

Table 10.1 illustrates the possible format of a questionnaire for need/press evaluation.

The questionnaire may alternatively employ separate pages to elicit need and press. That way it is less confusing for the respondent than in the present example where importance and help are rated on the same page. Once responses have been elicited, comparisons may be made between self-reported "need" and "press" (amount of help provided) for each skill considered for each class and for each type of student. Informative graphs may be used to display skill areas where greatest disparities are present between need and press. Statistical tests such as Student's t and Analysis of Variance may be used to test whether reported differences between need and press are generalized beyond a given sample of persons to other samples drawn from the same population. Most importantly, this technique allows the evaluator to identify skill areas that the students consider to be underemphasized or overemphasized in a particular class or program.

Teacher Ratings and Observations

Most instructional programs employ questionnaires for students to rate teaching effectiveness. Similarly, observation forms are often used by program administrators to rate teaching quality or to identify teaching problems for remediation. These also provide means to evaluate the quality of the delivery system of an instructional program.

TABLE 10.1 Sample need/press interaction questionnaire for evaluation of a language teaching program

Course Number _____   Section Number _____
Academic Major _____   Status: M F Grad Undergrad

Directions: Circle the number opposite each skill below that best shows the importance of that skill for your learning goals. Then circle the number that shows how much help you were given in class for each skill.

SKILL	IMPORTANCE		HELP	
	Not Important	Very Important	No Help	Much Help
Listening				
1. Understanding lectures	1 2 3 4 5		1 2 3 4 5	
2. Taking notes for lectures	1 2 3 4 5		1 2 3 4 5	
3. Writing dictations	1 2 3 4 5		1 2 3 4 5	
4. Using the language lab	1 2 3 4 5		1 2 3 4 5	
Speaking				
5. Pronouncing accurately	1 2 3 4 5		1 2 3 4 5	
6. Speaking fluently	1 2 3 4 5		1 2 3 4 5	
7. Public speaking	1 2 3 4 5		1 2 3 4 5	
8. Conversing	1 2 3 4 5		1 2 3 4 5	
Reading				
9. Reading comprehension	1 2 3 4 5		1 2 3 4 5	
10. Reading speed	1 2 3 4 5		1 2 3 4 5	
11. Understanding vocabulary	1 2 3 4 5		1 2 3 4 5	
12. Skimming for information	1 2 3 4 5		1 2 3 4 5	
Writing				
13. Organizing content	1 2 3 4 5		1 2 3 4 5	
14. Avoiding grammar errors	1 2 3 4 5		1 2 3 4 5	
15. Choosing appropriate words	1 2 3 4 5		1 2 3 4 5	
16. Avoiding spelling and punctuation errors	1 2 3 4 5		1 2 3 4 5	

Student Ratings

While it is not usually possible to avoid some student rating of teaching effectiveness, it is often true that such ratings leave much to be desired. Positive composite teacher ratings by students frequently load highly on factors such as sense of humor, dramatic activity, generous grading, manageable class size, and teacher enthusiasm. While these are important considerations, they may have minimal or even negative correlation with ability to promote learning. Sometimes student ratings of teachers are more indicative of student needs or desires than they are of teaching quality. But in spite of all of these problems, it is important to understand student reactions to particular teaching instances.

Due to the tendency for teacher ratings by students to become a kind of popularity poll when use is made of composite ratings, it is usually best to construct an evaluative questionnaire that requests opinions about specific components of the teaching process. Some of the most common questionnaire items seek to elicit information about the following performance areas:

    I. Lesson Quality
        A. Organization
        B. Appropriateness of content and materials
        C. Sequencing and pacing of material
        D. Use of illustrations and examples

E. Clarity of objectives
F. Opportunity for student practice
G. Fairness and adequacy of evaluation
H. Appropriate use of media
II. Teacher Characteristics
A. Prompt and regular attendance
B. Accessibility for consultation
C. Knowledge of subject material
D. Ability to communicate
E. Respect for student opinions
F. Ability to arouse interest in subject
G. Concern for student success

Note that all of these evaluative areas are amenable to improvement if a low rating is received. The object of such evaluation should be the improvement of teaching. For this reason teachers must be apprised of their ratings in a confidential, constructive atmosphere of professional development, not in a threatening, punitive way.

Since the object of student evaluations of teaching is the improvement of teaching, in the long run, course-specific evaluations may have more beneficial impact. Such evaluations would elicit student ratings of the comparative value of a variety of class activities. For example, an ESL writing teacher may try several techniques to improve student writing and then request students to rate the techniques for usefulness. Such techniques might include the following:

Dictation
Dicto-comp
Summaries
Editing
Free Composition
Guided Composition
Peer Correction
Computer Assisted Instruction
Speeded Writing
Take-home Writing
Paraphrasing

Following such an evaluation process, the teacher may then limit classroom activities to those that were found to be most beneficial for the students.

Teacher Observations

For hiring and promotion purposes, administrators are frequently called upon to observe teaching performance and to make qualitative judgments on the basis of the observation. It is important that administrators have some objective bases for such judgments. It is also important that teachers know what the bases are. If, for example, the observation focuses on lesson preparation, teacher presentation, and allowance for student participation, then the teacher should be advised that these are the critical concerns. It is also important that more than one observation, preferably by more than one observer, be used to form the basis of important decisions. Conference with the teacher soon after each observation is the appropriate procedure.

10.4   Statistical Procedures

Often when group comparisons are being made with regard to cognitive gains, use is made of statistical procedures to determine whether differences in mean gain are significant and generalizable beyond the given situation to other similar instructional contexts. Common statistical procedures used for program evaluative purposes include the following: Student's t-test (for both matched and unmatched groups), analysis of variance, Pearson product-moment correlation, analysis of covariance, chi-square analysis, multiple regression analysis, and path analysis. While it is beyond the intention of this book to offer detailed introductions to the application of these procedures, since many references are available (e.g., Guilford, 1973; Ferguson, 1981; Kirk, 1968; Kerlinger and Pedhazur, 1973; Namboodiri, Carter, and Blalock, 1975; Hatch and Farhady, 1982), it is useful to provide some indication of the kinds of evaluative contexts that call for specific statistical procedures.

Comparisons of Group Means

If only two groups are being compared with regard to mean posttest or mean gain score, it may be possible to apply the unmatched groups t-test. This procedure assumes that persons have been randomly assigned to groups or that treatments have been randomly assigned to persons. It assumes that there is a somewhat normal distribution of scores in the population(s) from which the samples have been drawn. Random assignment ensures the independence of error; i.e., it eliminates experimental bias. If students cannot be randomly assigned to classes, or if the instructional treatment cannot be randomly varied for the students within a class, then the unit of analysis may become the classroom rather than the student. This is important since it is usually easier to find 100 students for a study than to find 100 classes. Failure to randomly assign students to treatments or treatments to students may dramatically reduce the degrees of freedom and the power of generalization in an experiment.

If the comparison is being made for the same group before and after instruction, then the matched or correlated groups procedure is called for. Be sure to select the appropriate t-test procedure for the appropriate evaluative context.

If there are more than two groups in the study, or if comparisons are being made for outcome related to a variety of potential effects, such as method, sex, teacher experience, textbook, etc., it may be desirable to apply one of the many forms of analysis of variance (ANOVA). This procedure has the same underlying assumptions as the t-test, but it has the advantage that it allows for the consideration of many effects or groups simultaneously. Of particular importance is the advantage offered by the testing of the significance of interaction effects. This would tell us, for example, that while method of instruction makes a significant difference in achievement, the difference is such that girls do better with one method and boys do better with another. The t-test is not sophisticated enough to provide this important information.

As one multiplies variables of interest to the study, one must also increase the sample size. This is another way of saying that the size of the groups considered imposes certain limitations on how many variables may be analyzed at the same time. If there are two groups for whom five methods are used for both boys and girls by teachers with two levels of experience, this calls for a $2 \times 5 \times 2 \times 2$ factorial design. Such a design would have 40 cells. If we insisted on a minimum of five subjects per cell (which is a convention), the design would call for at least 200 persons. Adding still more variables would require still more persons.

Comparing Means with Concomitant Influences Removed

When it is suspected or known that group differences exist at the time of the pretest, or any time before the instructional treatment is given, it may be possible to control for these differences statistically after the study has been completed. Admittedly, randomization is the best procedure to control for or nullify group differences, but sometimes group differences persist even after random sampling or random assignment has been employed. Imagine comparing the growth in foreign language vocabulary recognition on the part of two groups of students learning by two different methods. If it became apparent, after instruction and testing was completed, that one group had a much higher mean verbal aptitude score than the other group, and if the higher-aptitude group also achieved more under instruction than the low-aptitude group, then it would not be known whether the greater learning by the high-aptitude group was the result of its particular instructional exposure or the result of its possessing greater aptitude.

If reliable and valid aptitude or pretest scores are available for the two groups from before the instructional treatment, it may be possible to adjust or control for the effect of greater aptitude on the part of one of the groups. To do this, use is made of a procedure called analysis of covariance, or ANCOVA. ANCOVA combines ANOVA and regression procedures. It is a powerful and useful procedure. Unfortunately it has very rigid assumptions. In addition to all of the assumptions of ANOVA, ANCOVA adds the assumption of homoscedasticity. This assumption requires that the slopes of the regression lines within each of the cells of the design are reasonably equivalent. This assumption should be tested; although, often ANCOVA is applied without adequate testing of the assumptions. Kirk (1968) provides a statistical test of the homogeneity of the regression coefficients.

Tests of Relatedness

Program effectiveness may sometimes be studied through correlational procedures as explained in chapter five. If a high negative correlation is found between class size and achievement, or between class size and positive program affect, this may provide evidence concerning optimal class size for program effectiveness. Similarly, a high positive correlation between years of teacher experience and positive student affect may, when combined with regression analysis, provide guidelines for the minimal amount of teaching experience to be required of new teachers.

Care must be taken in correlational studies to determine whether the relationships between variables are linear or curvilinear. Eyeballing the bivariate scatterplot can often help in the determination of the nature of the underlying relationships. When it is suspected that relationships are curvilinear rather than linear, it may be appropriate to use eta coefficients rather than product-moment coefficients to establish the magnitude of the relationships. Eta coefficients and their derivations are discussed in Nie et al. (1975).

It should also be reaffirmed that correlation does not imply causation. When two variables are highly related, it is not immediately clear from correlational analysis whether one of the variables causes the other, or whether some third variable causes the other two. A high correlation between attendance and positive attitude toward a program does not necessarily mean that attendance "causes" the positive attitude. Nor does it necessarily follow that positive attitude "causes" attendance. It may be that some third variable such as a prize incentive or a teacher's personality was the underlying cause of both attendance and positive affect.

Tests of Independence or Fit

Sometimes we can overcome parametric constraints of normality of distribution by means of the chi-square procedure. Chi-square is a test of independence or fit. If we were to classify students as "those who attained mastery" and "those who did not attain mastery," and if we examined two or more methods for their independence of mastery attainment, we could use the chi-square statistic for evaluation. We might set up a contingency table similar to that in Figure 10.1.

As Figure 10.1 illustrates, the numbers of students in the various cells reveal that, in this example, there is a greater likelihood that students randomly assigned to Method A will achieve mastery than those assigned to Method B. The chi-square procedure provides a mathematical test of departure from the pattern of frequencies in the cells which would be expected under a condition of independence of the column and row variables. If we were actually to compute a chi-square value in this case, it would be 29.46. This value exceeds the critical value for the test of independence ($p < 0.05$; 1 d.f.). Our conclusion in this example would be

	Mastery	Non-Mastery
Method A	35	5
Method B	20	20

FIGURE 10.1 Chi-square contingency table for testing independence of mastery and method

154

that mastery and method are not independent; therefore, whether or not a student achieves mastery may depend on which method of instruction is employed. Method A has a greater probability of success in promoting mastery than Method B. Ferguson (1981) provides a fuller explanation of actual chi-square computation procedures.

Multiple Correlation and Multiple Regression

When more than two (independent) variables are examined at one time to determine the strength of their combined relationship with a single (dependent) variable, multiple correlation procedure is used. This procedure is especially valuable because of its power to account for the overlapping variance or covariance between independent variables. Consider the application exemplified in Figure 10.2.

In this hypothetical example, five independent variables are shown to exhibit varying magnitudes of correlation with the dependent variables, as shown by the lowercase r's. Suppose, for purposes of example, that motivation was measured as total score on a questionnaire reflecting positive attitude toward learning the language, which was French. Suppose also that aptitude was measured as a verbal Scholastic Aptitude Test (SAT) score. Imagine that time on task was an accurate record of the number of hours in class and in private spent in the study of the French language during the academic semester considered. Let us operationalize experience as the number of months spent in study of other foreign languages. And, finally, let us identify nutrition as a rating on a scale of one to ten accurately reflecting the adequacy of the nutrients in the diet of each student during the program of study.

The dependent variable, language learning, is measured as final exam total score with an extensive, standardized French achievement test. Notice that the dependent variable shows a multiple correlation ($R = .90$) that is greater than any one of the bivariate correlations listed, but that is less than the sum of the bivariate correlations. The multiple correlation combines the predictive power of each one of the bivariate correlations, so that it is greater in magnitude than any of them; but, since there is considerable overlap in what is measured by each of the independent variables, the multiple correlation coefficient removes any redundancy and is no longer equal to the sum of the parts. We could readily imagine that motivation and time on task are highly related. They may be said to covary. When they are combined in the multiple correlation coefficient this redundant variance is eliminated.

Independent Variables		Dependent Variable
Motivation	(r = 0.35)	
Aptitude	(r = 0.65)	Language Learning
Time on Task	(r = 0.75)	(R = 0.90)
Experience	(r = 0.30)	
Nutrition	(r = 0.25)	

FIGURE 10.2 Five independent variables and their hypothetical relationships to the dependent variable, "Language Learning"

155

When we move from multiple correlation to multiple regression, we are actually able to predict (within quantifiable limits of accuracy) the dependent variable for any of the students, given the knowledge of the scores on the independent variables. This is a useful procedure for estimating for whom the program will be successful or unsuccessful, and for determining which variables account for the success and failure, and to estimate the comparative extent program variables may be related to desirable or undesirable outcomes. Kerlinger and Pedhazur (1973) provide a thorough explanation of multiple regression procedure.

Causal Models in Program Evaluation

A further application of multiple correlation and regression known as path analysis allows us to test the parsimony of competing causal models. This approach not only permits us to model and test sequential program effects, but it also serves as a superb technique for debunking theories that lack sufficient empirical basis. Consider the competing causal models in Figure 10.3 employing the same variables introduced in Figure 10.2.

In the example in Figure 10.3 we are shown two hypothetical models promulgated to account for language learning as measured. One model (A) holds aptitude to be the ultimate cause (the exogenous variable) with direct impact on (paths to) motivation and experience. Experience is said to impact nutrition, while motivation is shown to influence both nutrition and time on task. Nutrition has a direct path to time on task. Time on task is the only variable with direct effect on language learning.

Model B posits nutrition as the exogenous variable, impacting both motivation and aptitude. Aptitude has a path to experience, and motivation and experience both determine time on task to some extent, which in turn is the most direct determinant of language learning.

These two models are said to be recursive in that there is unidirectional flow of causation. Some models are nonrecursive because they permit mutual causation or bidirectional flow. Path analysis offers a test of these two models to determine which one provides the best (most parsimonious) explanation of the variance in language learning. If we were to find that Model B was the most parsimonious (and

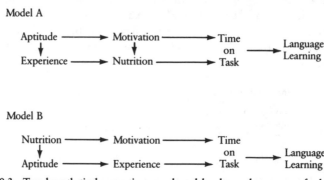

FIGURE 10.3 Two hypothetical competing causal models advanced to account for language learning

156

note that it has one less path than A), this would provide valuable information. First, we could eliminate Model A as a viable theoretical explanation. Then, we could find the indirect influence of nutrition on language learning to be highly important. In the multiple correlation study illustrated in Figure 10.2 it did not appear that nutrition was an important correlate of language learning. Path analysis, however, allows us to examine higher-order, indirect causes. If our findings were actually to support the hypothetical outcome posted in Model B, we would take far greater care to attend to the nutritional needs of our students. Namboodiri et al. (1975) provide a thorough discussion of path analysis.

These are a few of the common statistical techniques applied in program evaluation. For a thorough computational explanation of these statistics, the reader is encouraged to consult the texts cited earlier in this chapter. An awareness of computer packages such as SPSS, SPSSX, and SAS and available microprocessor statistical software described in their respective manuals will facilitate computation.

10.5 Summary

This chapter has reviewed a variety of evaluation methodologies that might be appropriate in the evaluation of aspects of programs of language instruction. Suggestions have been included for the evaluation of program affect, cognitive gains, and program delivery systems. Relevant statistical procedures have been introduced along with comments about their appropriate applications.

Exercises

1. Name five aspects of an instructional program that can appropriately become the focus of evaluation.
2. Develop a questionnaire that could be used to elicit student reactions to a variety of classroom activities that may be used in some class with which you are familiar.
3. Describe one qualitative and one quantitative procedure that may be used to evaluate the effectiveness of a series of language lessons.
4. Name three dangers to be avoided in the evaluation of teacher effectiveness, and explain how you would overcome them.
5. Identify at least three potential problems with pretest/posttest designs, and explain how they may be overcome.
6. Describe an evaluative context where a matched group t-test would be an appropriate statistical procedure to apply.
7. Describe an evaluative context where an unmatched group t-test would be appropriate.
8. List at least one advantage and one disadvantage of each of the following statistical procedures:
   A. t-test
   B. ANOVA

C. ANCOVA

D. Chi-square

9. Name and describe a statistical procedure that may be used to compare the efficacy of two or more empirical models used to explain the causal relationships underlying language learning for a group of students in an instructional program.

10. Give at least three reasons why random assignment of students to instructional treatments or instructional treatments to students is a preferred procedure in evaluative research.

Bibliography

Alderson, J. C. 1979. The cloze procedure as a measure of proficiency in English as a foreign language. *TESOL Quarterly.* 13: 219–227.

Alderson, J. C. 1980. Native and non-native speaker performance on cloze tests. *Language Learning.* 30: 59–76.

Alderson, J. C., and A. Hughes. (eds.) 1982. *Issues in Language Testing. ELT Documents No. 111.* London: British Council.

Bachman, L. F., and A. S. Palmer. 1981. The construct validation of the FSI oral interview. *Language Learning.* 31: 67–86.

Bachman, L. F., and A. S. Palmer. 1981. A multitrait-multimethod investigation into the construct validity of six tests of speaking and reading. *Construct Validation of Tests of Communicative Competence.* A. Palmer, P. Groot, and G. Trosper (eds.) Washington, DC: Teachers of English to Speakers of Other Languages.

Bock, R. D. 1975. *Multivariate Statistical Methods in Behavioral Research.* NY: McGraw-Hill.

Briere, E. J., and F. B. Hinofotis. (eds.) 1979. *Concepts in Language Testing: Some Recent Studies:* Washington, DC: Teachers of English to Speakers of Other Languages.

Bruner, J. S. 1966. *Toward a Theory of Instruction.* Cambridge, MA: Belknap Press of Harvard University.

Buros, O. K. 1965. *The Sixth Mental Measurements Yearbook.* Highland Park, NJ: Gryphon Press.

Campbell, D. T., and D. W. Fiske. 1959. Convergent and discriminant validation by the multitrait-multimethod matrix. *Psychological Bulletin.* 56: 81–105.

Campbell, D. T., and J. C. Stanley. 1963. *Experimental and Quasi-experimental Designs for Research.* Washington, DC: AERA.

Canale, M., 1986. The promise and threat of computerized adaptive assessment of reading comprehension. *Technology and Language Testing.* Stansfield, C. W. Washington, DC: Teachers of English to Speakers of Other Languages.

Canale, M., and M. Swain. 1980. Theoretical bases of communicative approaches to second language teaching and testing. *Applied Linguistics.* 1: 1–47.

Carroll, B. C. 1980. *Testing Communicative Performance: An Interim Study.* Oxford: Pergamon Press.

Carroll, J. B. 1972. Fundamental considerations in testing for English language proficiency of foreign students. *Teaching English as a Second Language: A Book of Readings.* Allen, H. B. and Campbell, R. N. (eds.) NY: McGraw-Hill.

Carroll, J. B., 1964. *Language and Thought.* Englewood Cliffs, NJ: Prentice-Hall.

Carroll, J. B., and S. M. Sapon. 1958. *Modern Language Aptitude Test.* NY: The Psychological Corporation.

Chen, Z., and G. Henning. 1985. Linguistic and cultural bias in language proficiency tests. *Language Testing.* 2(2): 155–163.

Choppin, B. 1968. An item bank using sample-free calibration. *Nature*. 219: 870–972.

Clark, J. L. D. 1977. The performance of native speakers of English on the test of English as a foreign language. *TOEFL Research Report No. 1*. (Nov.) Princeton, NJ: Educational Testing Service.

Clark, J. L. D., and S. S. Swinton. 1980. The test of spoken English as a measure of communicative ability in English-medium instructional settings. *TOEFL Research Report No. 7*. (Dec.) Princeton, NJ: Educational Testing Service.

Cohen, A. D. 1980. *Testing Language Ability in the Classroom*. Rowley, MA: Newbury House Publishers.

Cronbach, L. J. 1970. *Essentials of Psychological Testing*. (third edition) NY: Harper and Row.

Cronbach, L. J., and P. E. Meehl. 1955. Construct validity in psychological tests. *Psychological Bulletin*. 52: 281–302.

Cronbach, L. J., P. Schonemann, and T. D. McKie. 1965. Alpha coefficients for stratified-parallel tests. *Educational and Psychological Measurement*. 25: 129–312.

Cziko, G. A. 1980. Psychometric and edumetric approaches to language testing: Implications and applications. *Applied Linguistics*. 1: 27–44.

Davidson, F., and G. Henning. 1985. A self-rating scale of English difficulty: Rasch scalar analysis of items and rating categories. *Language Testing*. 2(2): 164–177.

De Jong, J. H. A. L. 1986. Item selection from pretests in mixed ability groups. *Technology and Language Testing*. C. W. Stansfield. Washington, DC: Teachers of English to Speakers of Other Languages.

Draba, R. E. 1978. The Rasch model and legal criteria of a "reasonable" classification. Doctoral Dissertation. Chicago: University of Chicago.

Ebel, R. L. 1971. Criterion-referenced measurement: Limitations. *School Review*. 79: 282–288.

Ebel, R. L. 1976. The paradox of educational testing. *NCME: Measurement in Education*. (Fall) Washington, DC: National Council on Measurement in Education.

Farhady, H. 1979. The disjunctive fallacy between discrete-point and integrative tests. *TESOL Quarterly*. 13(3): 347–357.

Ferguson, G. A. 1981. *Statistical Analysis in Psychology and Education*. (fifth edition) NY: McGraw-Hill.

Fisher, T. H. 1980. The courts and your minimum competency testing program: A guide to survival. *NCME Newsletter: Measurement in Education*. 11(1).

Flanders, N. S. 1970. *Analyzing Teacher Behavior*. Reading, MA: Addison-Wesley.

Guilford, J. P., and B. Fruchter. 1973. *Fundamental Statistics in Psychology and Education*. (fifth edition) NY: McGraw-Hill.

Gustafson, J. E. 1981. An introduction to Rasch's measurement model. *ERIC/TM Report No. 79*. (Sept.) Princeton, NJ: ERIC/Educational Testing Service.

Hale, G.A., P. J. Angelis, and L. A. Thibodean. 1980. Effects of item disclosure on TOEFL performance. *TOEFL Research Report No. 8*. (Dec.) Princeton, NJ: Educational Testing Service.

Hale, G. A., C. W. Stansfield, and R. P. Duran. 1984. Summaries of studies involving the test of English as a foreign language. *TOEFL Research Report No. 16.* (Feb.) Princeton, NJ: Educational Testing Service.

Hambleton, R. K., J. Algina, and D. B. Coulson. 1978. Criterion-referenced testing and measurement: A review of technical issues and developments. *Review of Educational Research.* 48(1): 1–47.

Hambleton, R. K., and H. Swaminathan. 1985. *Item Response Theory: Principles and Applications.* Boston: Kluwer-Nijhoff.

Harris, D. P. 1969. *Testing English as a Second Language.* NY: McGraw-Hill.

Hatch, E., and H. Farhady. 1982. *Research Design and Statistics for Applied Linguistics.* Rowley, MA: Newbury House Publishers.

Hattie, J. 1985. Methodology review: Assessing uni-dimensionality of tests and items. *Applied Psychological Measurement.* 9(2): 139–164.

Hays, W. L. 1973. *Statistics for the Social Sciences.* (second edition) NY: Holt, Rinehart and Winston.

Henning, G. 1973. Remembering foreign language vocabulary: Acoustic and semantic parameters. *Language Learning.* 23(2): 185–196.

Henning, G. 1975. Measuring foreign language reading comprehension. *Language Learning.* 25(1): 109–114.

Henning, G. 1977. Measurement of psychological differentiation and linguistic variation. Doctoral Dissertation. Los Angeles: University of California.

Henning, G. 1978. Developing English language proficiency measures for native speakers of Arabic. *UCLA Workpapers in Teaching English as a Second Language.* Vol. 12. Los Angeles: ESL Division, University of California Los Angeles.

Henning, G. 1978. Ego permeability and the acquisition of English as a foreign language. *Indian Journal of Applied Linguistics.* 4: 37–44.

Henning, G. 1982. Growth-referenced evaluation of foreign language instructional programs. *TESOL Quarterly.* 16(4): 467–477.

Henning, G. 1982. Twenty common testing mistakes for EFL teachers to avoid. *English Teaching Forum.* 20(3): 33–37.

Henning, G. 1983. Interest factors in second language acquisition. *Indian Journal of Applied Linguistics.* Vol. 9.

Henning, G. 1983. Oral proficiency testing: Comparative validities of interview, imitation and completion methods. *Language Learning.* 33: 3.

Henning, G. 1984. Advantages of latent trait measurement in language testing. *Language Testing.* 1(2): 123–133.

Henning, G. 1986. Item banking via DBASE II: The UCLA ESL proficiency exam experience. *Technology and Language Testing.* C. W. Stansfield. Washington, DC: Teachers of English to Speakers of Other Languages.

Henning, G., S. El Ghawaby, W. Saadalla, M. El Rifai, R. Kamel, and S. Matar. 1981. Assessment of language proficiency and achievement among learners of English as a foreign language. *TESOL Quarterly.* 15(4).

Henning, G., N. Gary, and J. Gary. 1983. Listening recall: A listening comprehension test for low proficiency learners. *System.* 11(3): 287–293.

Henning, G., T. Hudson, and J. Turner. 1985. Item response theory and the assumption of unidimensionality for language tests. *Language Testing*. 2(2): 141–154.

Hinofotis, F. 1981. A personal communication.

Hudson, T., and B. Lynch. 1984. A criterion-referenced measurement approach to ESLL achievement testing. *Language Testing*. 2(1): 171–201.

Hughes, A., and D. Porter. (eds.) 1983. *Current Developments in Language Testing*. London: Academic Press.

Ilyin, D. 1972. *Ilyin Oral Interview*. Rowley, MA: Newbury House Publishers.

Jacobs, H. L., D. R. Zingraf, D. R. Wormuth, V. F. Hartfiel, and J. B. Hughey. 1981. *Testing ESL composition: A practical approach*. Rowley, MA: Newbury House Publishers.

Kerlinger, F. N., and E. J. Pedhazur. 1973. *Multiple Regression in Behavioral Research*. NY: Holt, Rinehart and Winston.

Kirk, R. E. 1968. *Experimental Design: Procedures for the Behavioral Sciences*. Belmont, CA: Wadsworth.

Laine, J., G. Henning, C. Staez, et al. 1976. *Measures of Children's Language Performance*. Los Angeles: University of California.

Lennon, R. T. 1980. The anatomy of a scholastic aptitude test. *NCME: Measurement in Education*. Washington, DC: National Council on Measurement in Education. 11(2): 1–8.

Linn, R. L., D. A. Rock, and T. A. Cleary. 1969. The development and evaluation of several programmed testing methods. *Educational and Psychological Measurement*. 29: 129–146.

Lord, F. M., and M. R. Novick. 1968. *Statistical Theories of Mental Test Scores*. NY: Addison-Wesley.

Lowe, P., Jr., and R. T. Clifford. 1980. Developing an indirect measure of overall oral proficiency. *Measuring Spoken Language Proficiency*. J. R. Frith (ed.) Washington, DC: Georgetown University Press.

Madsen, H. S., and J. W. Larson. 1986. Computerized Rasch analysis of item bias in ESL tests. *Technology and Language Testing*. C. W. Stansfield (ed.) Washington, DC: Teachers of English to Speakers of Other Languages.

Magnusson, D. 1967. *Test Theory*. Reading, MA: Addison-Wesley.

Mansour, G. 1978. Objective versus subjective tests of EFL reading comprehension. Unpublished M.A. thesis. Cairo, Egypt: American University in Cairo.

Mead, R. J., B. D. Wright, and S. R. Bell. 1979. *BICAL: Version 3*. Chicago: Dept. of Education, University of Chicago.

Mehrens, W. A., and I. J. Lehman. 1975. *Standardized Tests in Education*. (second edition) NY: Holt, Rinehart and Winston.

Mislevy, R. J., and R. D. Bock. 1984. *Bilog II: Item Analysis and Test Scoring with Binary Logistic Models*. Mooresville, IN: Scientific Software.

Morcos, T. 1979. Psychological and sociological correlations related to the teaching and learning of English as a foreign language. Unpublished M.A. thesis. Cairo, Egypt: CDELT, Ain Shams University.

Naiman, N., M. Frohlich, and H. Stern. 1975. *The Good Language Learner*. Ontario, Canada: Ontario Institute for Studies in Education.

Namboodiri, N. K., L. F. Carter, and H. M. Blalock, Jr. 1975. *Applied Multivariate Analysis and Experimental Designs*. NY: McGraw-Hill.

Nedelsky, L. 1954. Absolute grading standards for objective tests. *Educational and Psychological Measurement*. 14: 3–19.

Nie, N. H., C. H. Hull, J. G. Jenkins, K. Steinbrenner, and D. H. Bent. 1975. *Statistical Package for the Social Sciences (SPSS)*. NY: McGraw-Hill.

Oller, J. W., Jr. 1973. Discrete-point tests versus tests of integrative skills. *Focus on the Learner*. J. W. Oller and J. C. Richards (eds.) Rowley, MA: Newbury House Publishers.

Oller, J. W., Jr. 1979. *Language Tests at School*. London: Longman.

Oller, J. W., and K. Perkins. 1980. *Research in Language Testing*. Rowley, MA: Newbury House Publishers.

Osgood, C. E., G. J. Suci, and P. H. Tannenbaum. 1957. *The Measurement of Meaning*. Urbana, IL: University of Illinois Press.

Pearson, K. 1901. Editorial. *Biometrika*. Vol. 1.

Pike, L. W. 1979. An evaluation of alternative item formats for testing English as a foreign language. *TOEFL Research Report No. 2*. (June) Princeton, NJ: Educational Testing Service.

Popham, W. J. 1978. *Criterion-referenced Measurement*. Englewood Cliffs, NJ: Prentice-Hall.

Popham, W. J., and E. Lindheim. 1980. The practical side of criterion referenced test development. *NCME: Measurement in Education*. (Spring) Washington, DC: National Council on Measurement in Education. 10(4).

Porter, D. 1983. Assessing communicative proficiency: The search for validity. *Perspectives in Communicative Language Teaching*. K. Johnson and D. Porter, (eds.) London: Academic Press.

Rasch, G. 1980. *Probabilistic Models for Some Intelligence and Attainment Tests*. Chicago: University of Chicago Press.

Ray, A. A., J. P. Sall, and M. Saffer. (eds.) 1982. *SAS Users Guide: Statistics*. Cary, NC: SAS Institute, Inc.

Reid, J. 1986. Using the writer's workbench in composition teaching and testing. *Technology and Language Testing*. C. W. Stansfield. Washington, DC: Teachers of English to Speakers of Other Languages.

Resnick, D. P. 1980. Minimum competency testing historically considered. *Review of Research in Education: No. 8*. D. C. Berliner, (ed.) Washington, DC: AERA.

Saadalla, W. Z. 1979. Social and psychological factors characterizing the poor language learner studying English in the secondary stage. Unpublished M.A. thesis. Cairo, Egypt: CDELT, Ain Shams University.

Scheuneman, J. 1984. Exploration of causes of bias in test items. Paper presentation. New Orleans: Annual American Educational Research Assn. Meeting.

Schumann, J. H. 1975. Affective factors and the problem of age in second language acquisition. *Language Learning*. 25: 209–235.

Shephard, L. 1980. Technical issues in minimum competency testing. *Review of Research in Education: No. 8*. D. C. Berliner. (ed.) Washington, DC: AERA.

Shereaf, M. 1981. A comparison of methods of scoring dictation. Unpublished M.A. thesis. Cairo, Egypt: CDELT, Faculty of Education, Ain Shams University.

Shohamy, E. 1984. Does the testing method make a difference? The case of reading comprehension. *Language Testing.* 1(2): 147–170.

Stansfield, C. W. (ed.) 1986. *Technology and Language Testing.* Washington, DC: Teachers of English to Speakers of Other Languages.

Stansfield, C. W. (ed.) 1986. Toward communicative competence testing: Proceedings of the second TOEFL invitational conference. *TOEFL Research Report No. 21.* (May) Princeton, NJ: Educational Testing Service.

Swinton, S. S. 1983. A manual for assessing language growth in instructional settings. *TOEFL Research Report No. 14.* (Feb.) Princeton, NJ: Educational Testing Service.

Thorndike, R. L., and E. Hagen. 1969. *Measurement and Evaluation in Psychology and Education.* (third edition) NY: Wiley and Sons.

Tuckman, B. W. 1972, 1978. *Conducting Educational Research.* (second edition) NY: Harcourt Brace Jovanovich.

Tung, P. 1986. Computerized adaptive testing: Implications for language test developers. *Technology and Language Testing.* C. W. Stansfield. (ed.) Washington, DC: Teachers of English to Speakers of Other Languages.

Upshur, J. A., and T. J. Homburg. 1983. Some relations among language tests at successive ability levels. *Issues in Language Testing Research.* J. W. Oller, Jr. Rowley, MA: Newbury House Publishers.

Valette, R. M. 1967. *Modern Language Testing: A Handbook.* NY: Harcourt, Brace and World.

Vollmer, H. J., and F. Sang. 1983. Competing hypotheses about second language ability: A plea for caution. *Issues in Language Testing Research.* J. W. Oller, Jr. (ed.) Rowley, MA: Newbury House Publishers.

Warm, T. A. 1978. *A Primer of Item Response Theory.* Oklahoma City, OK: U. S. Coast Guard Institute.

Williams, P. L., and E. J. Slawski. 1980. Application of the Rasch model for the development of equivalent forms of criterion referenced tests. Paper presented at the April annual meeting of AERA. Boston.

Witkin, H. A., C. A. Moore, D. R. Goodenough, and P. W. Cox. 1977. Field-dependent and field-independent cognitive styles and their educational implications. *Review of Educational Research.* 47(1): 1–64.

Woodcock, R. W. 1974. *Woodcock Reading Mastery Tests.* Circle Pines, MN: American Guidance Service.

Wright, B. D., and G. N. Masters. 1982. *Rating Scale Analysis.* Chicago: MESA Press.

Wright, B. D., R. J. Mead, and R. E. Draba. 1976. Detecting and correcting test item bias with a logistic response model. *Research Memorandum No. 22.* Chicago: University of Chicago, Statistical Laboratory, Dept. of Education.

Wright, B. D., and M. H. Stone. 1979. *Best Test Design.* Chicago: MESA Press.

Appendix A: Tables

Table A Random Numbers

Table B z-Scores Corresponding to Cumulative Area Proportions of the Normal Distribution

Table C Fisher Z Transformations of Correlations

Table D Standard Scores, Area Proportions, and Ordinates of the Unit Normal Curve

Table E Critical Values of the Pearson Product-Moment Correlation Coefficient

Table F Logit Correct and Logit Incorrect Values Corresponding to Proportion Correct Values

TABLE A Random Numbers*

22 17 68 65 84	68 95 23 92 35	87 02 22 57 51	61 09 43 95 06	58 24 82 03 47
19 36 27 59 46	13 79 93 37 55	39 77 32 77 09	85 52 05 30 62	47 83 51 62 74
16 77 23 02 77	09 61 87 25 21	28 06 24 25 93	16 71 13 59 78	23 05 47 47 25
78 43 76 71 61	20 44 90 32 64	97 67 63 99 61	46 38 03 93 22	69 81 21 99 21
03 28 28 26 08	73 37 32 04 05	69 30 16 09 05	88 69 58 28 99	35 07 44 75 47
93 22 53 64 39	07 10 63 76 35	87 03 04 79 88	08 13 13 85 51	55 34 57 72 69
78 76 58 54 74	92 38 70 96 92	52 06 79 79 45	82 63 18 27 44	69 66 92 19 09
23 68 35 26 00	99 53 93 61 28	52 70 05 48 34	56 65 05 61 86	90 92 10 70 80
15 39 25 70 99	93 86 52 77 65	15 33 59 05 28	22 87 26 07 47	86 96 98 29 06
58 71 96 30 24	18 46 23 34 27	85 13 99 24 44	49 18 09 79 49	74 16 32 23 02
57 35 27 33 72	24 53 63 94 09	41 10 76 47 91	44 04 95 49 66	39 60 04 59 81
48 50 86 54 48	22 06 34 72 52	82 21 15 65 20	33 29 94 71 11	15 91 29 12 03
61 96 48 95 03	07 16 39 33 66	98 56 10 56 79	77 21 30 27 12	90 49 22 23 62
36 93 89 41 26	29 70 83 63 51	99 74 20 52 36	87 09 41 15 09	98 60 16 03 03
18 87 00 42 31	57 90 12 02 07	23 47 37 17 31	54 08 01 88 63	39 41 88 92 10
88 56 53 27 59	33 35 72 67 47	77 34 55 45 70	08 18 27 38 90	16 95 86 70 75
09 72 95 84 29	49 41 31 06 70	42 38 06 45 18	64 84 73 31 65	52 53 37 97 15
12 96 88 17 31	65 19 69 02 83	60 75 86 90 68	24 64 19 35 51	56 61 87 39 12
85 94 57 24 16	92 09 84 38 76	22 00 27 69 85	29 81 94 78 70	21 94 47 90 12
38 64 43 59 98	98 77 87 68 07	91 51 67 62 44	40 98 05 93 78	23 32 65 41 18
53 44 09 42 72	00 41 86 79 79	68 47 22 00 20	35 55 31 51 51	00 83 63 22 55
40 76 66 26 84	57 99 99 90 37	36 63 32 08 58	37 40 13 68 97	87 64 81 07 83
02 17 79 18 05	12 59 52 57 02	22 07 90 47 03	28 14 11 30 79	20 69 22 40 98
95 17 82 06 53	31 51 10 96 46	92 06 88 07 77	56 11 50 81 69	40 23 72 51 39
35 76 22 42 92	96 11 83 44 80	34 68 35 48 77	33 42 40 90 60	73 96 53 97 86
26 29 13 56 41	85 47 04 66 08	34 72 57 59 13	82 43 80 46 15	38 26 61 70 04
77 80 20 75 82	72 82 32 99 90	63 95 73 76 63	89 73 44 99 05	48 67 26 43 18
46 40 66 44 52	91 36 74 43 53	30 82 13 54 00	78 45 63 98 35	55 03 36 67 68
37 56 08 18 09	77 53 84 46 47	31 91 18 95 58	24 16 74 11 53	44 10 13 85 57
61 65 61 68 66	37 27 47 39 19	84 83 70 07 48	53 21 40 06 71	95 06 79 88 54
93 43 69 64 07	34 18 04 52 35	56 27 09 24 86	61 85 53 83 45	19 90 70 99 00
21 96 60 12 99	11 20 99 45 18	48 13 93 55 34	18 37 79 49 90	65 97 38 20 46
95 20 47 97 97	27 37 83 28 71	00 06 41 41 74	45 89 09 39 84	51 67 11 52 49
97 86 21 78 73	10 65 81 92 59	58 76 17 14 97	04 76 62 16 17	17 95 70 45 80
69 92 06 34 13	59 71 74 17 32	27 55 10 24 19	23 71 82 13 74	63 52 52 01 41
04 31 17 21 56	33 73 99 19 87	26 72 39 27 67	53 77 57 68 93	60 61 97 22 61
61 06 98 03 91	87 14 77 43 96	43 00 65 98 50	45 60 33 01 07	98 99 46 50 47
85 93 85 86 88	72 87 08 62 40	16 06 10 89 20	23 21 34 74 97	76 38 03 29 63
21 74 32 47 45	73 96 07 94 52	09 65 90 77 47	25 76 16 19 33	53 05 70 53 30
15 69 53 82 80	79 96 23 53 10	65 39 07 16 29	45 33 02 43 70	02 87 40 41 45
02 89 08 04 49	20 21 14 68 86	87 63 93 95 17	11 29 01 95 80	35 14 97 35 33
87 18 15 89 79	85 43 01 72 73	08 61 74 51 69	89 74 39 82 15	94 51 33 41 67
98 83 71 94 232	59 97 50 99 52	08 52 85 08 40	87 80 61 65 31	91 51 80 32 44
10 08 58 21 66	72 68 49 29 31	89 85 84 46 06	59 73 19 85 23	65 09 29 75 63
47 90 56 10 08	88 02 84 27 83	42 29 72 23 19	66 56 45 65 79	20 71 53 20 25
22 85 61 68 90	49 64 92 85 44	16 40 12 89 88	50 14 49 81 06	01 82 77 45 12
67 80 43 79 33	12 83 11 41 16	25 58 19 68 70	77 02 54 00 52	53 43 37 15 26
27 62 50 96 72	79 44 61 40 15	14 53 40 65 39	27 31 58 50 28	11 39 03 34 25
33 78 80 87 15	38 30 06 38 21	14 47 47 07 26	54 96 87 53 32	40 36 40 96 76
13 13 92 66 99	47 24 49 57 74	32 25 43 62 17	10 97 11 69 84	99 63 22 32 98

*Table A is taken from Table XXXIII of Fisher, *Statistical Methods for Research Workers*, published by Oliver and Boyd, Ltd., Edinburgh, and by permission of the author and the publisher.

166

TABLE B z-Scores Corresponding to Cumulative Area Proportions of the Normal Distribution

z	Area	z	Area	z	Area	z	Area
−4.0	.0000	−1.9	0.287	0.1	.5398	2.1	.9821
−3.9	.0001	−1.8	.0359	0.2	.5793	2.2	.9861
−3.8	.0001	−1.7	.0446	0.3	.6179	2.3	.9893
−3.7	.0001	−1.6	.0548	0.4	.6554	2.4	.9918
−3.6	.0002	−1.5	.0668	0.5	.6915	2.5	.9938
−3.5	.0002	−1.4	.0808	0.6	.7257	2.6	.9953
−3.4	.0003	−1.3	.0968	0.7	.7580	2.7	.9965
−3.3	.0005	−1.2	.1151	0.8	.7881	2.8	.9974
−3.2	.0007	−1.1	.1357	0.9	.8159	2.9	.9981
−3.1	.0010	−1.0	.1587	1.0	.8413	3.0	.9987
−3.0	.0013	−0.9	.1841	1.1	.8643	3.1	.9990
−2.9	.0019	−0.8	.2119	1.2	.8849	3.2	.9993
−2.8	.0026	−0.7	.2420	1.3	.9032	3.3	.9995
−2.7	.0035	−0.6	.2743	1.4	.9192	3.4	.9997
−2.6	.0047	−0.5	.3085	1.5	.9332	3.5	.9998
−2.5	.0062	−0.4	.3446	1.6	.9452	3.6	.9998
−2.4	.0082	−0.3	.3821	1.7	.9554	3.7	.9999
−2.3	.0107	−0.2	.4207	1.8	.9641	3.8	.9999
−2.2	.0139	−0.1	.4602	1.9	.9713	3.9	.9999
−2.1	.0179	0.0	.5000	2.0	.9772	4.0	1.0000
−2.0	.0228						

For values between the listed points, you may interpolate according to the following example:

Problem: Find the area proportion for a z-score of 1.473.

Solution:
z interval	area interval	observed z interval
1.5	.9332	1.473
−1.4	−.9192	−1.4
.1	.0140	.073

.073 is to .1 as X is to .0140

$\frac{.073}{.1} = \frac{X}{.0140}$, $X = \frac{.073 \times .0140}{.1} = .0102$

.0102 + .9192 = .9294, corresponds to z-score of 1.473

TABLE C Fisher Z Transformations of Correlations

r	Z		r	Z		r	Z
.00	.000		.34	.354		.67	.811
.01	.010		.35	.365		.68	.829
.02	.020		.36	.377		.69	.848
.03	.030		.37	.388		.70	.867
.04	.040		.38	.400		.71	.887
.05	.050		.39	.412		.72	.908
.06	.060		.40	.424		.73	.929
.07	.070		.41	.436		.74	.950
.08	.080		.42	.448		.75	.973
.09	.090		.43	.460		.76	.996
.10	.100		.44	.472		.77	1.020
.11	.110		.45	.485		.78	1.045
.12	.121		.46	.497		.79	1.071
.13	.131		.47	.510		.80	1.099
.14	.141		.48	.523		.81	1.127
.15	.151		.49	.536		.82	1.157
.16	.161		.50	.549		.83	1.188
.17	.172		.51	.563		.84	1.221
.18	.182		.52	.576		.85	1.256
.19	.192		.53	.590		.86	1.293
.20	.203		.54	.604		.87	1.333
.21	.213		.55	.618		.88	1.376
.22	.224		.56	.633		.89	1.422
.23	.234		.57	.648		.90	1.472
.24	.245		.58	.662		.91	1.528
.25	.255		.59	.678		.92	1.589
.26	.266		.60	.693		.93	1.658
.27	.277		.61	.709		.94	1.738
.28	.288		.62	.725		.95	1.832
.29	.299		.63	.741		.96	1.946
.30	.310		.64	.758		.97	2.092
.31	.321		.65	.775		.98	2.298
.32	.332		.66	.793		.99	2.647
.33	.343					1.00	11.859

TABLE D Standard Scores, Area Proportions, and Ordinates of the Unit Normal Curve

z-score	Larger Area	Y-ordinate	z-score	Larger Area	Y-ordinate	z-score	Larger Area	Y-ordinate
.000	.500	.3989	.454	.675	.3599	1.036	.850	.2332
.013	.505	.3989	.468	.680	.3576	1.058	.855	.2279
.025	.510	.3988	.482	.685	.3552	1.080	.860	.2226
.038	.515	.3987	.496	.690	.3528	1.103	.865	.2171
.050	.520	.3984	.510	.695	.3503	1.126	.870	.2115
.063	.525	.3982	.524	.700	.3477	1.150	.875	.2059
.075	.530	.3978	.539	.705	.3450	1.175	.880	.2000
.088	.535	.3974	.553	.710	.3423	1.200	.885	.1941
.100	.540	.3969	.568	.715	.3395	1.227	.890	.1880
.113	.545	.3964	.583	.720	.3366	1.254	.895	.1818
.126	.550	.3958	.598	.725	.3337	1.282	.900	.1755
.138	.555	.3951	.613	.730	.3306	1.311	.905	.1690
.151	.560	.3944	.628	.735	.3275	1.341	.910	.1624
.164	.565	.3936	.643	.740	.3244	1.372	.915	.1556
.176	.570	.3928	.659	.745	.3211	1.405	.920	.1487
.189	.575	.3919	.675	.750	.3178	1.440	.925	.1416
.202	.580	.3909	.690	.755	.3144	1.476	.930	.1343
.215	.585	.3899	.706	.760	.3109	1.514	.935	.1268
.228	.590	.3887	.723	.765	.3073	1.555	.940	.1191
.240	.595	.3876	.739	.770	.3036	1.598	.945	.1112
.253	.600	.3863	.755	.775	.2999	1.645	.950	.1031
.266	.605	.3850	.772	.780	.2961	1.695	.955	.0948
.279	.610	.3837	.789	.785	.2922	1.751	.960	.0862
.292	.615	.3822	.806	.790	.2882	1.812	.965	.0773
.306	.620	.3808	.824	.795	.2841	1.881	.970	.0680
.319	.625	.3792	.842	.800	.2800	1.960	.975	.0584
.332	.630	.3776	.860	.805	.2757	2.054	.980	.0484
.345	.635	.3759	.878	.810	.2714	2.170	.985	.0379
.359	.640	.3741	.897	.815	.2669	2.326	.990	.0267
.372	.645	.3723	.915	.820	.2624	2.576	.995	.0145
.385	.650	.3704	.935	.825	.2578	2.652	.996	.0118
.399	.655	.3684	.954	.830	.2531	2.748	.997	.0091
.413	.660	.3664	.974	.835	.2482	2.878	.998	.0063
.426	.665	.3643	.995	.840	.2433	3.090	.999	.0034
.440	.670	.3621	1.015	.845	.2383	3.291	.9995	.0018

TABLE E   Critical Values of the Pearson Product-Moment Correlation Coefficient*

	Level of significance for one-tailed test				
	.05	.025	.01	.005	.0005
	Level of significance for two-tailed test				
$df = N - 2$	.10	.05	.02	.01	.001
1	.9877	.9969	.9995	.9999	1.0000
2	.9000	.9500	.9800	.9900	.9990
3	.8054	.8783	.9343	.9587	.9912
4	.7293	.8114	.8822	.9172	.9741
5	.6694	.7545	.8329	.8745	.9507
6	.6215	.7067	.7887	.8343	.9249
7	.5822	.6664	.7498	.7977	.8982
8	.5494	.6319	.7155	.7646	.8721
9	.5214	.6021	.6851	.7348	.8471
10	.4973	.5760	.6581	.7079	.8233
11	.4762	.5529	.6339	.6835	.8010
12	.4575	.5324	.6120	.6614	.7800
13	.4409	.5139	.5923	.6411	.7603
14	.4259	.4973	.5742	.6226	.7420
15	.4124	.4821	.5577	.6055	.7246
16	.4000	.4683	.5425	.5897	.7084
17	.3887	.4555	.5285	.5751	.6932
18	.3783	.4438	.5155	.5614	.6787
19	.3687	.4329	.5034	.5487	.6652
20	.3598	.4227	.4921	.5368	.6524
25	.3233	.3809	.4451	.4869	.5974
30	.2960	.3494	.4093	.4487	.5541
35	.2746	.3246	.3810	.4182	.5189
40	.2573	.3044	.3578	.3932	.4896
45	.2428	.2875	.3384	.3721	.4648
50	.2306	.2732	.3218	.3541	.4433
60	.2108	.2500	.2948	.3248	.4078
70	.1954	.2319	.2737	.3017	.3799
80	.1829	.2172	.2565	.2830	.3568
90	.1726	.2050	.2422	.2673	.3375
100	.1638	.1946	.2301	.2540	.3211

*Table E is taken from Table VII of Fisher, *Statistical Methods for Research Workers*, published by Oliver and Boyd, Ltd., Edinburgh, and by permission of the author and the publisher.

TABLE F Logit Correct and Logit Incorrect Values Corresponding to Proportion Correct Values

Proportion Correct	Logit Incorrect	Logit Correct	Proportion Correct	Logit Incorrect	Logit Correct
.01	4.595	−4.595	.51	−.040	.040
.02	3.892	−3.892	.52	−.080	.080
.03	3.476	−3.476	.53	−.120	.120
.04	3.178	−3.178	.54	−.160	.160
.05	2.944	−2.944	.55	−.201	.201
.06	2.752	−2.752	.56	−.241	.241
.07	2.587	−2.587	.57	−.282	.282
.08	2.442	−2.442	.58	−.323	.323
.09	2.314	−2.314	.59	−.364	.364
.10	2.197	−2.197	.60	−.405	.405
.11	2.091	−2.091	.61	−.447	.447
.12	1.992	−1.992	.62	−.490	.490
.13	1.901	−1.901	.63	−.532	.532
.14	1.815	−1.815	.64	−.575	.575
.15	1.735	−1.735	.65	−.619	.619
.16	1.658	−1.658	.66	−.663	.663
.17	1.586	−1.586	.67	−.708	.708
.18	1.516	−1.516	.68	−.754	.754
.19	1.450	−1.450	.69	−.800	.800
.20	1.386	−1.386	.70	−.847	.847
.21	1.325	−1.325	.71	−.895	.895
.22	1.266	−1.266	.72	−.944	.944
.23	1.208	−1.208	.73	−.995	.995
.24	1.153	−1.153	.74	−1.046	1.046
.25	1.099	−1.099	.75	−1.099	1.099
.26	1.046	−1.046	.76	−1.153	1.153
.27	.995	−.995	.77	−1.208	1.208
.28	.944	−.944	.78	−1.266	1.266
.29	.895	−.895	.79	−1.325	1.325
.30	.847	−.847	.80	−1.386	1.386
.31	.800	−.800	.81	−1.450	1.450
.32	.754	−.754	.82	−1.516	1.516
.33	.708	−.708	.83	−1.586	1.586
.34	.663	−.663	.84	−1.658	1.658
.35	.619	−.619	.85	−1.735	1.735
.36	.575	−.575	.86	−1.815	1.815
.37	.532	−.532	.87	−1.901	1.901
.38	.490	−.490	.88	−1.992	1.992
.39	.447	−.447	.89	−2.091	2.091
.40	.405	−.405	.90	−2.197	2.197
.41	.364	−.364	.91	−2.314	2.314
.42	.323	−.323	.92	−2.442	2.442
.43	.282	−.282	.93	−2.587	2.587
.44	.241	−.241	.94	−2.752	2.752
.45	.201	−.201	.95	−2.944	2.944
.46	.160	−.160	.96	−3.178	3.178
.47	.120	−.120	.97	−3.476	3.476
.48	.080	−.080	.98	−3.892	3.892
.49	.040	−.040	.99	−4.595	4.595
.50	.000	−.000	.995	−5.293	5.293

Appendix B: Answers to Questions[*]

Chapter 1

1. Reliable: Obtaining the same estimates of weight for the same object(s) on repeated use of a scale, getting approximately the same test scores on repeated application of the same test to the same individuals.

   Valid: Measuring only the substance or quality intended with nothing else mixed in.

2. Diagnosis and Feedback, Screening and Selection, Placement, Program Evaluation, Providing Research Criteria, Assessing Attitudes and Socio-Psychological Differences. Most recent use will vary with personal experience.

3. Indirect, objective, integrative, norm-referenced, proficiency.

4. Writing Error Detection Tests: tests which require identification of errors in written context.

   Short Answer Tests: tests which require brief, fragmental answers to questions about a given passage or content area.

   Translation Tests: tests which require translation of words, sentences or passages either from or into the target language.

5. Objective Tests: tests which may be scored by machine or by persons using a scoring key who have no particular expertise in the area tested.

   Subjective Tests: tests which rely for scoring on the critical judgments and opinions of persons considered to be authorities.

6. Direct Tests: tests which observe and measure the exact targeted (language) behavior in a natural manner and in an authentic context.

   Indirect Tests: tests which elicit and measure (language) behavior deemed to reflect the targeted behavior, in a contrived manner and in an artificial context.

7. Norm-Referenced Tests: tests which evaluate person performance with reference to the mean or average score of all persons tested in the test development sample.

   Criterion-Referenced Tests: tests which evaluate person performance with reference to an arbitrary standard of mastery of instructional objectives.

8. Discrete-Point Tests: tests, usually in multiple-choice item format, which purport to measure a distinct component of grammatical structure or language skill.

   Integrative Tests: tests, usually not in multiple-choice item format, which purport to measure a combination of language abilities or competencies.

9. Speed Tests: tests which employ content of a sufficiently low difficulty level that the majority of persons for whom the tests are intended would be expected to perform perfectly, given enough time. But the majority of persons do not have sufficient time to finish the test, thus rate of responding is of primary importance in determining success.

   Power Tests: tests which allow sufficient time for responding, so that nearly all persons

---

[*]In the answers to the computational exercises, errors of rounding have been minimized in most cases by delaying the rounding of numbers until after the final step of the calculations. Due to the possibility of errors of rounding, readers should not be concerned about minute differences in calculations from those in the answers to the exercises.

may attempt every item; but items are of such a high difficulty level that no person is expected to get every item correct.

10. Employ Table 1.1 to obtain a rating on a scale of zero to 100.

Chapter 2

1.

Nominal	Counting Frequency	Finding the number of native speakers of a given language in an ESL class.
Ordinal	Rank Ordering	Ranking students according to frequency of spelling errors.
Interval	Measuring with Equal Intervals	Determining z-scores or standard scores on a grammar test.
Ratio	Measuring Intervals from a Real Zero	Measuring height, weight, speed or absolute temperature.

2. With interval scales, measurement is conducted using equal size units along the scale, thus distances between measurements represent uniform comparative differences in measured ability.

3. ordinal, nominal, ordinal, ratio, interval, interval, ratio.

4. The Likert scale is usually a five-point scale on which the respondent registers extent of agreement/disagreement with statements provided; whereas, the semantic differential is often a seven-point scale ranging between opposing descriptors, such as good/bad, intelligent/stupid, rich/poor, etc.

5. Linear transformations: An example is the transformation of raw scores to percentage scores using total score possible as a divisor and raw score as dividend, and multiplying the quotient by 100.

Normalization transformations: An example is z-score transformation used to transform ordinal scales to interval scales.

6.

Raw Scores:	6,	9,	11,	12,	12,	13,	15,	17,	17,	21
(a) ordinal rating	8th	7th	6th	5th	5th	4th	3rd	2nd	2nd	1st
(also acceptable)	10th	9th	8th	6th	6th	5th	4th	2nd	2nd	1st
(b) percentage	24	36	44	48	48	52	60	68	68	84
(c) percentile	5	15	25	40	40	55	65	80	80	95

7.

Raw Scores:	11,	13,	16,	16,	18,	20,	20,	25,	27,	29
(a) z-scores	−1.60	−1.09	−.59	−.59	−.25	.08	.08	.92	1.26	1.93
(b) T-scores	34	39.1	44.1	44.1	47.5	50.8	50.8	59.2	62.6	69.3
(c) area proportions	.05	.14	.28	.28	.40	.53	.53	.82	.90	.97

8.

Raw	10,	12,	15,	20,	21,	21,	21,	23,	26,	29,	32,	37,	38,	41,	42
Stan.	2	2	3	4	4	4	4	4	5	6	6	7	7	8	8
I.Q.	77	80	84	91	93	93	93	96	100	105	109	116	118	122	124

9. $\frac{36}{50} \times 100 = 72$ percent

10. The program provides insufficient emphasis on vocabulary expansion.

Chapter 3

1. $S_{cg} = N_r - \frac{N_{wa}}{N_o - 1} = 72 - \frac{13}{2} = 65.5$

2. Use of a rating schedule, use of thoroughly trained raters, use of multiple independent raters.

3. Test data can be summarized in minimal space. Computation of person and item statistics such as row and column means and totals is facilitated. Manual input of test data to computers is facilitated.

4. The *possible range* refers to the entire range of possible raw scores obtainable on the test, from zero to all correct items. The *actual range* refers to the actual range of raw scores obtained by a given sample of examinees, from the lowest to the highest obtained score. The *effective range* of the test refers to region of the distribution of possible scores where meaningful discrimination takes place. Thus scores expected by guessing alone are excluded from this range. A 20-item True/False test would have a 50 percent expected rate of successful guessing, or ten items would be expected to be answered correctly by guessing alone; therefore, such a test would have an effective range of 11–20.

5. Positive skew tells us that the test was probably too hard. Negative skew tells us that the test was probably too easy (unless it was a criterion-referenced test).

6. mean = 12.07; median = 12; mode = 14

7. symmetry; mean = mode = median; asymptotic tails of the curve.

8. $s = 3.45$; $s^2 = 11.92$

9. A population parameter is based on every observation in the entire population of interest and, as such, is seldom available. Parameters are characterized by letters of the Greek alphabet. A sample statistic is based on a limited sample of observations drawn from the population of interest and is used to estimate the population parameter. Statistics are characterized by letters of the Latin alphabet.

10. 0.34 between plus and minus one standard deviation; 0.96 between plus and minus two standard deviations. (Obtainable through the known relationship between z-scores and normal distribution area proportions summarized in Table B of Appendix A, since one standard deviation is associated with the same area proportion as one z-score. In this example we are considering z-scores immediately below and above the mean.)

Chapter 4

1. Mixed response, option cues (length, convergence, inconsistent distractor cues, nonsense distractors), inappropriate number of options, trick questions, common knowledge responses, etc. (examples provided in text).

2. Time of testing may be determined in advance, appropriateness of test difficulty may be predetermined, item analysis may be conducted and weak items may be edited or removed, reliability and validity estimates may be calculated.

3. In general, reliability increases as the number of items is increased, up to a point of asymptote, where little is gained through the addition of new items.

4. Use may be made of cloze test procedure to elicit the most appealing alternatives from respondents. These alternatives may then become distractors on a multiple choice test. Distractors are functioning as desired when they attract selection to a reasonable extent on the part of examinees who are uncertain about the correct option.

5. The need to include specific content, the need to provide an easy introduction, the need to shape the test information curve, and the availability of items.

6.
Item number	1	2	3	4	5
Item difficulty ($p = C_r/N$)	.86	.71	.43	.29	.57
Proportion incorrect ($q = 1 - p$)	.14	.29	.57	.71	.43

We may reject item 1 as too easy, and item 4 as too difficult.

7. Item number   1   2   3   4   5

Item number	1	2	3	4	5
Item discriminability	.67	.33	1.00	1.00	1.00

We may reject item 2 as having weak discriminability by the method of sample separation.

$$D = \frac{H_c}{H_c + L_c}$$

Item number	1	2	3	4	5
8. Item discriminability	.70	−.38	.66	.68	.43

We may reject item 2 as having weak discriminability by the method of point biserial correlation. Note that the result is the same in this case regardless of which of the two methods (i.e., sample separation or point biserial correlation) is employed.

Item number	1	2	3	4	5
9. Item variability $s_i^2 = pq$	.12	.21	.25	.21	.25

Items 3 and 5 provide the most information about these examinees since the item variance or variability means the same as the item information index.

10. Assuming that the test was not speeded (so that item difficulty was not a function of item sequence order), difficulty, discriminability, and information indices are reported below for each of the 15 items of Table 3.4. Note that discriminability was computed by the point biserial method since the sample separation technique may produce a variety of discriminability estimates for each item, depending on which examinees are assigned to the high and low scoring groups.

Items	1	2	3	4	5	6	7	8	9	10	11	12	13	14	15
Diff.	.67	.77[a]	.60	.60	.77[a]	.50	.47	.57	.63	.60	.63	.63	.27[b]	.43	.13[b]
Disc.	.41	.29[c]	.37	.45	.17[b]	.40	.55	.49	.54	.62	.50	.50	.63	.56	.24[b]
Info.	.22	.18[b]	.24	.24	.18[b]	.25	.25	.25	.23	.24	.23	.23	.20	.25	.11[b]

a = index too high (low difficulty); b = index too low (high difficulty, low discriminability, low information); c = index nearly too low

According to these results, item 2 would be rejected for being too easy, providing little information, and being comparatively non-discriminating. Item 5 would be rejected on the same grounds as item 2. While item 13 appears to be overly difficult, it may still be maintained because of its high discriminability. Item 15 would be rejected for being too difficult, non-discriminating, and providing little information. It is apparent that, since the information index is derived from the difficulty index, the two indices agree in their indication of item quality.

Chapter 5

1. Negative (inverse)

2. Low correlated variables tend to have amorphous, circular scatterplots; whereas, highly correlated variables tend to have narrow, elongated, elliptical scatterplots.

3. All the information available on one variable is perfectly revealed or predicted in the other. The variables are redundant.

4. It means that the probability of error of generalization about the existence of the observed relationship is less than five in 100. It also means that if similar samples were drawn at random from the same underlying population, it would be expected that the same kind of relationship would be observed in more than 95 out of 100 replications.

5. A one-tailed test occurs when it is hypothesized that one specific directional relationship exists and it is specified in advance which direction (positive or negative). A two-tailed test occurs when it is hypothesized that a relationship exists but it is not specified in which direction (i.e., it is not specified whether the correlation will be positive or negative). A

one-tailed test is usually preferable where possible because it permits greater power of generalization and more sensitive hypothesis testing. In other words, with one-tailed hypotheses, statistical significance can be obtained with smaller coefficients than is the case with two-tailed hypotheses, all else being equal.

6. The correlation coefficient, r_{xy}, equals 0.72, derived as follows:

$$r_{xy} = \frac{N\Sigma XY - \Sigma X\Sigma Y}{\sqrt{[N\Sigma X^2 - (\Sigma X)^2][N\Sigma Y^2 - (\Sigma Y)^2]}}$$

$$= \frac{10(5277) - 193(268)}{\sqrt{[10(3867) - (193)^2][10(7330) - (268)^2]}} = 0.72$$

The coefficient of determination equals $r_{xy}^2 = 0.52$

7. The regression equation, $\hat{Y} = a_{yx} + b_{yx} X$, may be derived for the data set in problem six as follows:

$$b_{yx} = \frac{r_{xy}s_y}{s_x} = .72\frac{4.05}{3.97} = 0.74$$

$$a_{yx} = \bar{Y} - b_{yx}\bar{X} = 26.80 - .74(19.30) = 12.59$$

Therefore, the regression equation becomes $\hat{Y} = 12.59 + .74X$ and the general proficiency $(\hat{Y})$ for a person with a listening comprehension score (X) of 23 would be estimated as follows:

$$\hat{Y} = 12.59 + .74(23) = 29.52$$

8. The 95 percent confidence interval is the predicted score plus and minus 1.96 standard error scores. In this case it will be 29.52 plus and minus 1.96 times the standard error of estimate. The standard error of estimate is computed as follows:

$$s_{y \cdot x} = s_y \sqrt{1 - r_{xy}^2} = 4.05(.69) = 2.80$$

Therefore the confidence interval is 29.52 plus and minus 1.96 times 2.80 (that is, plus and minus 5.49). In other words, we are 95 percent confident that the general proficiency score will fall in the range 24.03 to 35.01 if the listening comprehension score obtained is 23, given the nature of the relationship between the two sets of scores in problem six.

9. The phi coefficient may be computed using one of the standard Pearson product-moment formula variations, or by using the following short-cut variation possible because of the binary nature of the item scores for this problem:

$$r_{phi} = \frac{p_{ik} - p_i p_k}{\sqrt{p_i q_i p_k q_k}} = \frac{.4 - .6(.6)}{[.6(.4)(.6)(.4)]^{1/2}} = \frac{.04}{.24} = 0.17$$

10. Using the formula for point biserial correlation given in chapter 4, we arrive at the following correlation between item 3 and total score:

$$r_{pbi} = \left[\frac{\bar{X}_p - \bar{X}_q}{s_x}\right]\sqrt{pq} = \left[\frac{4 - 1.5}{1.58}\right](.49) = 0.78$$

Note that use of a standard variation of the Pearson product-moment formula would yield a correlation value of 0.87 instead of the value 0.78 obtained above. This slight difference is due to the fact that the Pearson formula uses a population parameter in place of the standard deviation statistic used above (i.e., 1.41 in place of 1.58 above). In more common applications where the sample size is much larger than the five persons considered in the simplified example above, the two formulas will produce equivalent results.

Chapter 6

1. If observed score variance increases and error of measurement remains constant, the increase in observed score variance would have to be due to a corresponding increase in true score variance. Any increase in true score variance in relation to error variance will result in an increase in reliability of measurement because of the relationships between reliability, true score variance and error variance summarized in the following formula:

$$r_{tt} = \frac{s_T^2}{s_T^2 + s_e^2}$$

2. Removal of all error of measurement from a person's observed score leaves only that person's true score.

3. Threats to reliability or consistency of measurement with this kind of an oral interview would include the following:

(a) Fluctuations in the interviewee including changes in true score brought about by practice, learning, or forgetting taking place in the interval between the two successive interviews. Also included would be changes in performance brought about by varying levels of fatigue, anxiety, hostility or mental awareness on the part of the interviewee.

(b) Fluctuations in the rater, termed intra-rater error variance, that result in altered ratings of unchanged interviewee performance. These fluctuations could be caused by fatigue, boredom, experience accrued during or between ratings, changing attitudes towards the interviewee, or other changes in the subjective mood of the rater.

(c) Fluctuations in the administration of the interview. These could include changes in the length of the interview, changes in the topical focus of the interview, changes in the nature of the interaction between the interviewer and the interviewee, or changes in the introductory instructions or warm-up activities provided to the interviewee. These could also include changes in the time or place of the interview, in the physical setting, or in the nature of distractions or interruptions present during the two successive interviews.

4. The Kuder-Richardson Formula 20 (or the Cronbach's alpha) method for estimating test reliability has the primary advantage over the split-half method that it results in an estimate of reliability that is based on an average of the estimates from every possible split-half test division. This is especially important since split-half method reliability estimates may vary widely according to the arbitrary method in which the test is divided. KR-20 avoids this problem inasmuch as it represents the value that would be obtained if every possible test division were employed and the mean of all resulting estimates were calculated.

The KR-20 method is also to be preferred over the KR-21 method since the latter method is only a short-cut conservative estimation procedure that tends slightly to underestimate actual reliability. KR-21 also assumes binary item format and a reasonable number of items to provide stable estimates (say, more than five).

5. The Spearman-Brown Prophecy Formula may be used (a) to provide adjusted estimates of test reliability given changes in the number of items or the number of performance raters, or (b) to estimate the number of additional items or raters required to increase a given reliability estimate to a pre-specified level.

6. The standard error of measurement would be 11.18, derived as follows:

$$s_e = s_t \sqrt{1 - r_{tt}} = 25[(1 - .80)^{1/2}] = 11.18$$

7. Split half reliability by the odd-even method would be 0.14. This would be obtained in the following manner:

(a) Two columns of total scores would be calculated — one for the odd numbered items and one for the even numbered items.

	Odd	Even
1	2	1
2	1	3
3	3	2
4	2	0
5	2	2
6	1	0

(b) Obtain the Pearson product-moment correlation for these two halves of the test. In this case the correlation coefficient is 0.07.

(c) Adjust this correlation coefficient using the Spearman-Brown Prophecy Formula to allow for the fact that the test is twice as long as either of its halves. This procedure is as follows:

$$r_{tt} = \frac{2r_{xy}}{1+r_{xy}} = 2\frac{.07}{1+.07} = 0.14$$

8. Four (or eight) independent raters similar to the present raters would be needed to obtain a composite rating reliability estimate of 0.85. This was determined by using the Spearman-Brown Prophecy Formula in the following manner:

$$n = \frac{r_{ttd}(1-r)}{r_{tt}(1-r_{ttd})}$$

$$= \frac{.85(1-.60)}{.60(1-.85)} = 3.78$$

The quantity 3.78 represents the number of times we must increase the number of raters used to derive the original reliability estimate (0.60). Since a partial rater cannot be used, it is necessary to round off this quantity to the whole number four. Note that, if the original reliability was determined for the ratings of either one of the two raters, then the number of raters needed would be 3.78 × 1, rounding to four raters, to achieve 0.85 reliability. If, on the other hand, the reliability estimate (0.60) were based on the composite ratings of the two raters, then the number of raters needed would be 3.78 × 2, rounding to eight.

9. The disattenuated correlation would be 0.81. This is derived as follows:

$$\frac{.65}{(.75 \times .85)^{1/2}} = 0.81$$

10. The KR-20 reliability estimate from the matrix of problem 7 is 0.54. The KR-20 reliability estimate from the same matrix is 0.37. These estimates were derived as follows:

$$KR\text{-}20 = \left(\frac{n}{n-1}\right)\left(\frac{s_t^2 - s_i^2}{s_t^2}\right)$$

$$= \left(\frac{6}{5}\right)\left(\frac{2.17 - 1.19}{2.17}\right) = 0.54$$

$$KR\text{-}21 = \left(\frac{n}{n-1}\right)\left[1 - \frac{(\bar{X} - \bar{X}^2/n)}{s_t^2}\right]$$

$$= \left(\frac{6}{5}\right)\left[1 - \frac{(3.17 - 3.17^2/6)}{2.17}\right] = 0.37$$

Chapter 7

1. (a) Content or Face Validity: Used to determine whether the test content (or format) is sufficiently representative and comprehensive to measure adequately what the test is supposed to measure.

(b) Response Validity: Used to indicate the extent to which the manner in which the examinee(s) responded to the exam resulted in scores that reflected the true ability said to be measured by the test.

(c) Concurrent Validity: Used to indicate how well performance on the exam in question correlated with performance on another exam that can serve as a suitable criterion for the intended skill or ability being measured.

(d) Predictive Validity: Used to show how well scores on the exam in question correlate with a subsequent measure of future performance in the target behavioral domain. Ratings of academic or job performance usually serve as criterion measures in determining predictive validity.

(e) Construct Validity: Used to determine whether hypothetical constructs are truly measured by given tests. For example, if we designed a test to measure "personal success" and it consisted solely of items measuring financial independence, someone who was not wealthy but who made a significant contribution to the well-being of the community might well object if he got a low score on our test and was pronounced "unsuccessful." Construct validation procedures could be used to determine whether our "personal success" construct was valid as measured.

2. Norm-referenced proficiency tests differ from criterion-referenced achievement tests in the ways in which they arrive at representative and comprehensive content. A content-valid proficiency test will include content that is broadly representative of general use — not bound to the specific content of any particular course of instruciton, but comprehensive of the skills needed to demonstrate proficiency. Due to the norm-referenced characteristic of the test, there may also be a tendency for content to be limited to those skills, features and items that are found to be of median difficulty for the target population. Such a language proficiency test will not include items over every obscure feature of grammar, for example, but may well sample widely from among those median difficulty features that serve to discriminate well between testees who are proficient and those who are not. Content-valid criterion-referenced achievement tests will restrict content to items or other behavior indicators that are reflective of the objectives and syllabi of particular courses of instruction. Thus these tests will be valid to the extent that content is representative and comprehensive of what has been taught.

3. Content validity calls for heterogeneous content on a test in order for the test to be comprehensive and, thus, valid. Internal consistency estimates of reliability call for homogeneity of test content in order for the test to be consistent and, thus, reliable. So there is a dynamic tension between the opposing needs for reliability and content validity. On the other hand, empirical estimates of validity depend on the reliability of the measures, and are thus positively related to reliability. Unlike the case with content validity, reliability is a necessary but not sufficient condition for empirical validity to exist.

4. Construct validity may be established by studying (a) group differences predicted by theory, (b) the influence of environmental changes on test results, predicted by theory, (c) correlations among tests measuring the same variable, or (d) correlations among items or subscales of a test.

5. Threats to validity could include any of the following: invalid application of tests, inappropriate selection of content, imperfect cooperation of the examinees, inappropriate referent or norming population, poor criterion selection, sample truncation, or use of invalid constructs. ·

6. The maximum possible validity under ideal conditions is equal to the square root of the reliability estimate. In this case maximum possible validity would be 0.85, the square root of the reliability estimate (0.73).

7. The true concurrent validity would be 0.79. This is determined by dividing the square root of the criterion variable reliability estimate ($0.90^{1/2} = 0.95$) into the validity coefficient (0.75).

8. The internal construct validity proportion is 1.00. It is obtained as follows:

(a) Reading comprehension item scores are correlated with reading comprehension total to obtain the coefficients (item 1, 0.84; item 2, 0.77; item 3, 0.91).

(b) Reading comprehension item scores are correlated with grammar total to obtain the coefficients (item 1, 0.22; item 2, −0.13; item 3, 0.33).

(c) Reading comprehension item correlations with reading comprehension total are corrected for part-whole overlap to allow for the fact that reading items contribute to reading total. This results in corrected reading item-total coefficients (item 1, 0.50; item 2, 0.39; item 3, 0.50).

(d) Corrected reading item-total correlations are compared with reading item-grammar total correlations to determine the proportion of invalid items (i.e., items that show a higher correlation with grammar than with reading). In this case there were no invalid items by this method since all of the reading items showed a higher correlation with their own subtest total than with the grammar total, and it is concluded that the proportion of valid items is 1.00.

9. The two convergent validity coefficients in Table 7.3 for Completion Pronunciation are .540 and .691. These are located horizontally and vertically opposite the marginal number eight in the diagonal between the broken lines.

10. The two convergent validity coefficients in Table 7.3 for Interview Fluency are .762 and .542. These are located beneath the marginal number 12 in the diagonals between the broken lines.

To exhibit heterotrait-monomethod discriminant validity these coefficients would need to exceed the coefficients in the adjacent rows and columns enclosed within the solid triangles. Before locating adjacent coefficients, it will help if you extend the matrix to include its mirror image in the blank region of the lower left-hand corner of Table 7.3. Thus the coefficients .762 and .542 would need to exceed .957, .968, .969, and .940 in the leftmost solid triangle; .873, .671, .923, and .567 in the centermost solid triangle; and .760, .844, .954, and .892 in the rightmost solid triangle. Only three of these 12 coefficients were exceeded, and these only by one of the two convergent validity coefficients (.762). Therefore it can be asserted that the underlying constructs failed to exhibit heterotrait-monomethod discriminant validity.

To exhibit heterotrait-heteromethod discriminant validity the convergent validity coefficients .762 and .542 would need to exceed the adjacent row and column coefficients enclosed within the triangles with broken lines. Again, it is helpful to extend the matrix to locate adjacent coefficients more easily. Thus the coefficients to be exceeded are .712, .416, .630, and .535 in the topmost left-hand broken triangle; .721, .614, .761, and .678 in the topmost right-hand broken triangle; .690, .611, .603, and .615 in the left-hand broken triangle second from the top; .590, .457, .356, and .496 in the right-hand broken triangle that is third from the top; and .589, .514, .185, and .442 in the bottom right-hand broken triangle. Since the convergent validity coefficients did not exceed every adjacent heterotrait-heteromethod coefficient, we conclude that the underlying constructs do not exhibit heterotrait-heteromethod discriminant validity.

Chapter 8

1. Latent trait measurement theory exhibits the following advantages over classical measurement theory:

(a) The possibility of sample-free item difficulty calibration. This means that with latent trait theory, unlike the case with classical theory, the estimation of item difficulty is independent of the group size and unique combination of persons in the particular sample from which the difficulty estimates are derived. The difficulty estimate can be generalized beyond the examinee sample.

(b) The possibility of test-free person ability measurement. This means that with latent trait theory, unlike the case with classical theory, estimates of person ability are independent of the particular number and combination of items used on the test applied. The ability estimate can be generalized beyond a given test.

(c) The possibility of multiple reliability estimation. With latent trait theory an estimate of standard error can be derived for every attainable score. With classical theory dependence is placed upon a global estimate of reliability that is interpreted equally for all scores regardless of their comparative distances from the mean of the distribution.

(d) The identification of guessers and other deviant respondents. Latent trait theory allows us to quantify the amount of deviation of response patterns from the predictions of the models (i.e., fit or response validity). The three parameter model even includes a guessing parameter that is purported to quantify the extent of guessing on the part of each examinee. While classical theory permits a correction for guessing procedure with multiple-choice type items, this does not differentiate between considered and casual responses and, thus, fails to quantify guessing for each person.

(e) Reconciliation of Norm-referenced and Criterion-referenced testing. With latent trait theory, because of its capacity for placing task (item) difficulty and person ability on the same scalar continuum, it is possible to derive and report test results of a single given test from both a norm-referenced and a criterion-referenced perspective.

2. The most commonly applied latent trait models are (a) the (Rasch) one-parameter logistic model, (b) the two-parameter logistic model, and (c) the three-parameter logistic model. While the two- and three-parameter models provide successively more information parameters on each item and person than the one-parameter model, they have the disadvantages of requiring substantially larger sample sizes and more computational time in analysis. They are less amenable to computer adaptive testing applications than the one-parameter model and are more difficult to explain to the test score user. Nevertheless, it is probably wisest to choose a respective model on the basis of the resources, needs and applications in any given situation.

3. Test tailoring permits us to load the test with items that have highest variance for persons with ability levels near the decision cut-off points. In this way we can maximize the test information value at those decision points.

4. The application of latent trait models assumes (a) unidimensionality of the test, (b) that the test is non-speeded, (c) that the test items exhibit local independence, and (d) that the population of persons from which the examinees are drawn is invariant.

Unidimensionality is demonstrated when the test shows homogeneity of content and focus as would be indicated, for example, if there is high internal consistency reliability or if the test items load on only one dominant factor. A number of additional techniques exist for the testing of unidimensionality (Hattie, 1985).

Speededness is avoided when it can be affirmed that reasonably sufficient time was provided for examinees to complete the test. In practice there may always be a few stragglers or persons who consume every minute allowed in order that they might review their responses. The presence of such persons does not necessarily violate the assumption of non-speededness.

Local independence is ensured when the response to any given item is not dependent on the responses to adjacent items or to the sequential positioning of the item among other items on the test. In a sense, speededness causes items at the end of a test to appear more difficult because examinees may not have time to respond to them. In this sense, getting the item correct is dependent on the sequential position of the item in the test, and thus speededness leads to a violation of local independence. More common violations occur with sequential mathematics problems when getting the correct answer to one question depends on a correct response to the preceding question.

Population invariance is assured when it can be affirmed that the population from which the sample of examinees is being drawn has not changed qualitatively with regard to the abilities measured from one application of the theory to the next. An example of a violation might be a case in which second language test items are calibrated for difficulty and tested for fit with adult second language learners and subsequent items to be joined to the same item bank are calibrated with native language speaking children.

5. Person misfit to the Rasch Model might be caused by a variety of factors including the following: random guessing on the part of an examinee, cheating on some portion of the exam (while cheating on the exam as a whole would be unlikely to cause misfit), physical handicap related to some portion of the exam (e.g., hearing deficiency for a listening comprehension component), improper use of an answer sheet, temporary loss of attention while responding to items, etc. These factors cause response patterns to be improbable (e.g., a low ability examinee may succeed with a high difficulty item) and result in obtained scores that lack response validity. Scores for such misfitting persons must be rejected or interpreted with caution, and the persons themselves may be interviewed, asked to repeat the exam, or referred to some other more appropriate exam.

6. Rasch Model item difficulty estimates and their associated standard errors calculated manually are as follows:

Item 1: Difficulty is -1.54; Standard Error is 1.50
Items 2, 3, 4: Difficulty is -0.23; Standard Error is 1.22
Item 5: Difficulty is 2.18; Standard Error is 1.50

The following tabled steps were used in these calculations:

Item	No. Cor.	Frq.	Prp. Cor.	Prp. Inc.	Lgt. Inc.	Frq.x Lgt.	Frq.x L^2	Init. Diff.	Exp. Fct.	Fnl. Diff.	S.E.
1	4	1	.80	.20	-1.39	-1.39	1.92	-1.15	1.34	-1.54	1.50
2, 3, 4	3	3	.60	.40	-0.41	-1.22	.49	-0.17	1.34	-0.23	1.22
5	1	1	.20	.80	1.39	1.39	1.92	1.63	1.34	2.18	1.50

7. Rasch Model person ability estimates and their associated standard errors calculated manually are as follows:

Person 1: Ability is -2.14; Standard Error is 1.60
Person 2: Ability is -0.88; Standard Error is 1.17
Person 3: Ability is 0.17; Standard Error is 1.17
Persons 4 and 5: Ability is 1.42; Standard Error is 1.60

Procedural steps in calculation are summarized in the following table.

Pers.	Pers. Score	Frq.	Prp. Cor.	Lgt. Cor.	Frq.x Lgt.	Frq.x L^2	Pers. Meas.	Exp. Fct.	Fnl. Ablty.	S.E.
1	1	1	.20	-1.39	-1.39	1.92	-1.67	1.28	-2.14	1.60
2	2	1	.40	-0.41	-0.41	.16	-0.69	1.28	-0.88	1.17
3	3	1	.60	0.41	0.41	.16	0.13	1.28	0.17	1.17
4, 5	4	2	.80	1.39	2.77	3.84	1.11	1.28	1.42	1.60

8. Item fit statistics are calculated, including the sum of squared standardized residuals and the associated t values, with reference to the matrix reported in problem 10 below, and according to the formula for calculating t (i.e., $t = [Ln(\Sigma z^2/d.f.) + \Sigma z^2/d.f. - 1](d.f./8)^{1/2})$. Mean squared standardized residuals and fit t-values for each item are as follows:

Item	Σz^2	t
1	4.03	0.01
2	8.14	1.23
3	3.94	−0.02
4	1.72	−1.00
5	2.79	−0.47

Note that no items would be rejected as misfitting by the conventional criterion of fit t surpassing 2.00.

9. Person fit statistics, calculated in the same way as item fit statistics above except that z^2 residuals are summed across items instead of across persons and that the associated degrees of freedom are determined as the number of items minus one instead of the number of persons minus one, are reported as follows:

Person	Σz^2	t
1	2.28	−0.70
2	6.34	0.74
3	3.13	−0.33
4	7.78	1.14
5	1.09	−1.43

Note that since none of the t-values exceeded the criterion 2.00, we can conclude that there was no person misfit in this example.

10. A full matrix of standardized residuals and item responses as employed in the calculation of fit statistics would appear as follows:

Persons	Items					b	Σz^2	t
	1	2	3	4	5			
1	1	0	0	0	0	−2.14		
(d − b)	.60	1.91	1.91	1.91	4.32			
z^2	1.82	.15	.15	.15	.01		2.28	−.70
2	0	1	1	0	0	−.88		
(d − b)	−.66	.65	.65	.65	3.06			
z^2	1.93	1.92	1.92	.52	.05		6.34	.74
3	1	1	0	1	0	.17		
(d − b)	−1.71	−.40	−.40	−.40	2.11			
z^2	.18	.67	1.49	.67	.12		3.13	−.33
4	1	0	1	1	1	1.42		
(d − b)	−2.96	−1.65	−1.65	−1.65	.76			
z^2	.05	5.21	.19	.19	2.14		7.78	1.14
5	1	1	1	1	0	1.42		
(d − b)	−2.96	−1.65	−1.65	−1.65	.76			
z^2	.05	.19	.19	.19	.47		1.09	−1.43
Σz^2	4.03	8.14	3.94	1.72	2.79			
t	.01	1.23	−.02	−1.00	−.47			

Note that such a table provides information about the points of deviation from expected performance both for persons and for items.

Chapter 9

1. General concerns for item bank development are as follows:

(a) Availability of examinees for regular test administration and analysis purposes.

(b) Familiarity with and employment of an appropriate latent trait measurement model such as the Rasch Model.

(c) Establishment of item classification and rejection criteria.

(d) Development of an item linking scheme.

(e) Availability of computer hardware and software for analysis, storage, and retrieval of items and item descriptors.

2. A sample file structure is provided in Table 9.1. Minimally such a file structure would need to contain item identification and item difficulty information. Other details may vary according to intended application.

3. Advantages of a system for machine construction of tests would include the following:

(a) Item difficulty and content range could be specified in advance so as to match the ability and exposure range of the intended examinees.

(b) By consideration of the number of items employed and the precalibrated standard errors associated with item difficulty estimates, test reliability could be estimated in advance of the actual administration of the particular test being assembled.

(c) Since the items are being assembled by machine from a large item bank, security is maintained in that it is unlikely that anyone would be able to predict which items will appear on the test.

4. Three advantages of computer adaptive testing would be:

(a) Reduction of individual testing time since accurate measurement is achievable with fewer items than is the case with paper and pencil tests.

(b) Boredom and frustration are reduced in that the items encountered by the testees are only those items that are appropriate in difficulty level.

(c) Feedback can be immediate, both in terms of test scores and in terms of diagnosis of weaknesses and provision of remedial suggestions.

Three potential disadvantages would be the following:

(a) Anxiety or hostility in the testing situation may be promoted for some persons through the use of computers if these persons are unfamiliar with or feel threatened by computers.

(b) Formats available for testing may be more limited in variety with computer adaptive testing than is the case with paper and pencil testing.

(c) There may be legal objections raised by testees who are unsuccessful with computer adaptive tests who maintain that their test differed in length and content from the tests of other students who may have succeeded.

5. Three examples of computer adaptive tests are as follows:

(a) Decision point tests. These tests are constructed with items of difficulty limited to the task difficulty at the decision cut-off points. Thus an admissions test may be limited to items with difficulty matching the entry and exit levels of performance. Examinees who succeed with the entry-level items are then referred to the exit-level items by the machine algorithm.

(b) Step ladder tests. On these tests precalibrated items are clustered at a series of graduated difficulty steps. Success or failure with a prespecified number of items at one step signals the machine algorithm to present items at a more appropriate step. Test score becomes the same as the number of the assigned step which is found to present the best match to examinee ability.

(c) Error-controlled tests. These tests are distinguishable in that, with them, examinee ability is re-estimated using an appropriate ability estimation algorithm after each item is encountered. The ability estimation procedure includes the calculation of a standard error associated with each successive ability estimate. An acceptable criterion level of error is specified in advance. The testing process is terminated when the size of the standard error has diminished to the pre-specified criterion level, indicating that sufficient confidence may be placed in the accuracy of the ability estimate.

6. The translation constant for linking Test Two to Test One is 0.79. This is derived as the mean linking-item difficulty for Test One minus the mean linking-item difficulty for Test Two. In the present example this reduces to $0.18 - (-0.61) = 0.79$.

7. Applying the translation constant from problem 6 in order to link the two tests requires the addition of the constant to all of the item difficulties of Test Two so that they will be on the same continuum as those of Test One. The corrected Test Two linking-item difficulties would then become:

Item number	1	2	3	4	5	6	7	8	9	10
Corrected Difficulty	3.19	2.89	2.09	1.69	.49	.41	−1.01	−2.01	−2.21	−2.91

8. The approximate standard error of the link would be 0.08. This is determined approximately by the following formula:

$$\text{S.E.} = \frac{3.5}{(NK)^{1/2}} = \frac{3.5}{(200 \times 10)^{1/2}} = 0.08.$$

9. The approximate chi square value for this test of link fit is 10.56. This value was obtained using the chi square formula below:

$$\Sigma (d_A - d_B - G_{AB})^2 \left(\frac{K}{K-1}\right) = 0.57 \left(\frac{200}{12}\right)\left(\frac{10}{9}\right) = 10.56.$$

Since this value does not exceed the critical value for chi square with 10 degrees of freedom (i.e., $18.31, p < 0.05$), we can conclude that the link is not flawed and can safely be applied in the joining of the two tests.

10. The sum of the translation constants should always approximate zero when they are used in the same linking loop. In an example of linking three tests (e.g., A, B, and C) the AB, BC, and AC translation constants should add up to zero if it is truly to be concluded that the test items have been joined to the same difficulty continuum, using the same metric and the same origin for all tests.

Chapter 10

1. The following five aspects, and no doubt many other aspects, of an instructional program could become the focus of evaluation: (a) learning gains, (b) instructional delivery, (c) needs responsiveness, (d) cost effectiveness, (e) continuing motivation.

2. Evaluative questionnaires will vary widely in form from one class or program to another. They will probably have in common only that they provide a list of class activities and a procedure, such as a Likert scale, for rating the usefulness of each activity.

3. A qualitative evaluation procedure might be Portfolio Evaluation. By this procedure a series of files might be centrally maintained for access by all teachers and supervisors concerned with the implementation of the language lesson. File folders might be organized according to lesson number, day or week of instruction, class sections, skill area, etc. Teachers or teacher aides might regularly record information such as student reactions to the lesson, appropriateness of length of materials, appropriateness of difficulty, interestingness of content, adequacy of organization and sequencing, sufficiency of student opportunity for practice, problems in implementation, and suggestions for lesson improvement.

A quantitative evaluation procedure might be the unmatched groups t-test. By this procedure students are randomly assigned to one of two different instructional groups. Each group receives a different instructional treatment. This treatment may be a method of instruction, a set of course materials, an incentive for achievement, and so on. Achievement or achievement gain is measured using the same instrument(s) for both groups. Test score means and standard deviations are computed separately for each group. A t-value is computed and examined as an indication of the significance of the difference between the means for the two groups.

4. Three dangers to be avoided in the evaluation of teacher effectiveness are:

(a) Student ratings of teacher effectiveness can be biased by the comparative presence or absence of humor, dramatic activity, generous grading, and so on in the teacher(s). If such effects cannot be eliminated, then ratings should be interpreted with caution.

(b) Ratings of teacher effectiveness may wrongly be elicited in areas that are not subject to improvement, such as teacher personality. In designing a rating scale care should be taken to include only items that might have implications for improvement of teacher effectiveness.

(c) Teachers may not be adequately and constructively advised about the focus of evaluation nor about the results of evaluation. Teachers should be consulted privately before and after the evaluation to maximize the positive benefits of such a process.

5. Pretest/posttest designs in evaluation have at least the following potential problems:

(a) The period of instruction might not have been long enough nor the instrumentation sensitive enough to show learning gains. Care should be taken to allow enough time for expected measurable learning to take place, and the tests used must first be examined for reliability and sensitivity.

(b) There might be a practice effect associated with the use of the same test as both pretest and posttest. This can be avoided by the use of alternate or equated forms of the test or by using multiple administrations of the test as pretest and posttest in order to measure the size of the practice effect.

(c) If groups are being compared on gains from a pretest/posttest design, then there should be evidence to indicate that the groups were comparable at the time of the pretest. Usually this comparability is ensured through random assignment of students to treatments or treatments to students. A nonsignificant difference between the mean scores for groups would support the assertion of group comparability. It may also be supported in a post hoc manner by the use of analysis of covariance procedure, providing the rigid assumptions of that procedure are met.

6. A matched group t-test would apply in a situation where a group is randomly drawn from a population with a normal distribution of the ability to be measured. The group is then administered some reliable and valid measure of the target performance before and after some treatment that is hypothesized to affect that performance. The purpose of the t-test would be to establish whether the group mean change in performance from pretest to posttest is sufficient in magnitude to permit the generalization that the treatment brought about change.

7. An unmatched group t-test might be applied in a situation where two different groups of students are drawn from the same underlying population having a normal distribution of the target ability. The groups are randomly assigned to two different instructional treatments. A t-value is computed to test the research hypothesis that there will be a significantly higher mean posttest or gain score for one group or the other.

8. Some advantages and disadvantages of statistical procedures are as follows:

(a) t-Test. This has the advantage of simplicity, both in computation and in meeting underlying assumptions. It has the disadvantage that it does not permit simultaneous comparison of more than two groups or effects nor the testing of interaction effects.

(b) ANOVA. This has the advantage that in most variations it permits the comparison of multiple groups and effects and the testing of interaction effects. It has the disadvantage that it may require large sample size and computer access in order to test multiple effects simultaneously.

(c) ANCOVA. This has the advantages of ANOVA with the added capacity to control for pre-treatment group differences in a post hoc manner. Unfortunately it has the disadvantage that the underlying assumptions are very rigid and difficult to satisfy in most applications.

(d) CHI SQUARE. This has the advantage of simplicity of computation and, since it is a nonparametric statistic, it has the added advantage of not requiring a normal distribution in the population. If there is a disadvantage it might be that its requirement of nominal data may necessitate the reduction of continuous data from ordinal or interval scales to nominal scales with a corresponding loss of information. For this and other reasons chi square tends to be slightly less sensitive and less likely to yield significant results than t-test, ANOVA, or ANCOVA.

9. Path analysis may be used to compare the efficacy of two or more empirical models used to explain the causal relationships underlying language learning for a group of students in an instructional program. By this procedure an array of program (independent) variables are arranged according to alternative orders of impact on an outcome (dependent) variable. Each alternative ordering of program variables constitutes a model for testing. The most logical and effective models are those found to be most parsimonious; i.e., requiring the least paths in order to fully account for the variance in the prediction of the dependent variable.

10. Random assignment of students to treatments or treatments to students is a preferred approach in quantitative evaluation research for the following reasons:

(a) Randomization can nullify group differences that might impact treatment effect. By distributing these error sources randomly across all groups, randomization neutralizes experimental bias.

(b) Randomization is a requirement for the use of statistical inference both with parametric and nonparametric statistical techniques. This is because use of those techniques is intended to enable quantification of the likelihood or probability of error in generalization of findings from the sample to the population.

(c) Randomization in the assignment of students to treatments can ensure more degrees of freedom and thus more power in a statistical test. Without randomization the classroom itself may become the unit of measurement rather than the students in the classroom(s). This would require a much larger sample size to permit statistical generalization than would be the case if randomization is used.

Appendix C: Glossary

Achievement Test   An achievement test measures the extent of learning of the material presented in a particular course, textbook, or program of instruction.

Alternate Forms   Alternate forms are the same as equivalent forms of a test. Their scoring distributions must exhibit equal means, variances, and covariances (i.e., equal correlations with an external criterion) in order for them to be classified as equivalent.

Analysis of Covariance   Analysis of covariance or ANCOVA is a variation of analysis of variance that permits the removal of effects associated with concomitant variables that might otherwise contaminate the results and lead to faulty conclusions.

Analysis of Variance   This refers to a family of statistical procedures used to test the strength of main effects and interaction effects by determining the partition of overall variance attributable to each effect and relating that to associated error variance.

Aptitude Test   An aptitude test is designed to measure capability or potential, whether it is capability to succeed with an academic program, to learn a foreign language, to acquire a specific vocation, or some other capability.

Bias   Bias in testing refers to the nonrandom distribution of measurement error. It usually results in an unfair advantage for one or more groups or categories of individuals over other groups taking the same test.

Biserial Correlation   Biserial correlation is an improvement of the point biserial correlation such that the derived coefficient can extend the full length of the continuum from zero to unity.

Boundary Effects   These effects appear when a test is too easy or too difficult and there is a tendency for scores to accumulate at the top of the distribution (ceiling effects) or at the bottom (floor effects). Such effects promote unreliable measurement.

Chi Square   Chi square is a powerful non-parametric statistical procedure that is used to test independence of categorical variables or goodness of fit to mathematical expectancy models. Part of its value stems from its not assuming a normal distribution.

Cloze Test   A cloze test is one that requires filling in the blanks in a passage from which there have been systematic or random deletions. Usually every fifth or seventh word has been removed from the passage beginning at a randomized starting point.

Coefficient of Alienation   The coefficient of alienation is the proportion of variance in one variable not accounted for by the variance in another variable. It is calculated as one minus the square of the correlation between the two variables.

Coefficient of Determination   The coefficient of determination is the proportion of the variance in one variable accounted for by variance in the other variable. It is computed as the square of the coefficient of correlation between the two variables.

Coefficient of Equivalence   The coefficient of equivalence is the product-moment correlation coefficient between the scores of two parallel or random parallel forms of a test when the forms are administered to the same group of persons within an appropriate time interval.

Coefficient of Precision   The coefficient of precision is the product-moment correlation coefficient between two truly equivalent forms of a test, both administered to the same group of persons within an appropriate time interval. It is expected to be high, approaching 1.00.

189

Computer Adaptive Testing This is a procedure using computer hardware and software to present test content to examinees in ways that allow for iterative consideration of ability demonstrated in the ongoing testing process. Items are chosen to match individual testee ability.

Concurrent Validity Concurrent validity is shown by the magnitude of correlation between scores for a given test and some recognized criterion measure. The test is said to have concurrent validity if it correlates highly with the established criterion.

Confidence Interval A confidence interval is the range around an estimated value within which a specified level of estimation accuracy holds. Commonly 95 and 99 percent levels are used to delimit ranges within which corresponding confidence in an estimate exists.

Construct Validity Construct validity means the validity of the constructs measured by a test. This may be established by confirmatory factor analysis or by comparing the same constructs measured via a variety of methods, as in multitrait-multimethod validation, etc.

Content Validity This is usually a non-empirical expert judgment of the extent to which the content of a test is comprehensive and representative of the content domain purported to be measured by the test. Some authors do not distinguish between content and face validity.

Convergence Cues Convergence cues in multiple-choice options can lead an examinee to guess the correct answer without knowledge of the information tested. These cues occur when distractors focus on domains, and only the correct option is associated with all domains.

Convergent Validity This is a kind of empirical validity akin to concurrent validity, indicated as a monotrait-monomethod coefficient on a multitrait-multimethod correlation matrix. It is used to establish the validity of measurement constructs.

Correction for Attenuation Correction for attenuation or disattenuation is a way of holding reliability constant when making comparisons among correlation coefficients. It is made by dividing the correlation coefficient by the square root of the cross-product of reliabilities.

Correlation This represents a family of computational procedures used to determine the extent to which variables may be said to covary. The most common parametric version is known as Pearson product-moment correlation and is the mean cross-product of z-scores.

Criterion-Referenced Test A criterion-referenced test is one that assesses achievement or performance against a cut-off score that is determined as a reflection of mastery or attainment of specified objectives. Focus is on ability to perform tasks rather than group ranking.

Cumulative Percentage Distribution This refers to the distribution of scores obtained by arranging examinees from lowest to highest scoring, finding the examinee-to-group percentage, and multiplying this percentage by group rank. Thus person five in a group of ten would score 50.

Decision Point Test A decision point test is a computer adaptive test that maximizes decision accuracy by loading the test with items whose information index is highest at the decision points along the ability continuum.

Degrees of Freedom   Degrees of freedom are the number of units of analysis after loss due to statistical computation. With correlation, two degrees of freedom are lost to position the regression line. With chi square, d.f. loss equals rows plus columns minus one.

Demographic Questionnaire   This is an instrument used to elicit information about persons such as age, sex, place of birth, languages known, educational background, and so on. Kinds of information elicited depend on particular research questions or program needs.

Diagnostic Test   A diagnostic test is designed to provide information about the specific strengths and weaknesses of the test taker. It is usually designed to guide remedial instruction.

Difficulty Index   In classical measurement theory the difficulty index is the proportion, p, of respondents who scored correctly on an item. Thus, the higher the proportion, the easier the item is said to be.

Direct Test   A direct test is one that measures ability directly in an authentic context and format, as opposed to an indirect test that requires performance of a contrived task from which inference is drawn about the presence of the ability concerned.

Discrete-point Test   A discrete-point test is one that employs items measuring performance over a unitary set of linguistic structures or features. An example would be a multiple-choice test of article usage.

Discriminability   Discriminability is the capacity of an item to differentiate between those who have the knowledge or skill measured and those who do not. This capacity is measured in several ways, including item-total point biserial correlation.

Discriminant Validity   This is a kind of construct validity established with reference to a multitrait-multimethod validation matrix when convergent validity coefficients exceed adjacent heterotrait-monomethod and heterotrait-heteromethod correlation coefficients.

Distractor Tally   A distractor tally is a tally of the response frequencies for each of the available multiple-choice distractors. It is used to improve items by ascertaining whether distractors are functioning as intended.

Effective Range   The effective range is that portion of the possible range of scores where effective measurement occurs. With multiple choice items this begins immediately above the chance level. Thus, with a 100-item four-option test it begins with score 26.

Equated Forms   Equated forms are tests or forms of a test having scoring distributions adjusted or interpreted to coincide with the same scale. Methods of equating such as equipercentile or regression are used to permit performance comparisons across tests.

Equivalent Forms   Equivalent or alternate forms of a test are those whose scores exhibit equal means, variances, and covariances when the different forms are applied to the same examinee groups within an appropriate time interval.

Error Control Test   This is a variety of computer adaptive test that provides ability and associated error re-estimation after each item attempted. The decision to terminate the test is reached after measurement error has diminished to a pre-set acceptable level.

Eta Coefficient   An eta coefficient is commonly used to indicate the strength of relationship between two variables when the relationship is non-linear, whereas product-moment correlation is commonly used for linear relationships.

F max Test This is a statistical procedure for testing whether variances are significantly different. It requires dividing the larger variance by the smaller variance and checking the resulting F-value with its associated degrees of freedom in an ANOVA table.

Face Validity Face validity is a subjective impression, usually on the part of examinees, of the extent to which the test and its format fulfills the intended purpose of measurement. Some authors do not distinguish between face and content validity.

Factor Analysis Factor analysis refers to a variety of multivariate, correlational statistical procedures used to aggregate data into non-overlapping or minimally overlapping categories or factors. This allows reduction of test data into non-redundant categories.

Filler Item A filler item is an unscored item in a test or questionnaire that is used to disguise the purpose of the questionnaire in situations where knowledge of the purpose might invalidate responses.

Fisher z Fisher z is a normalization transformation used to convert correlation coefficients from an ordinal to an interval scale.

Fit Validity Fit validity is an estimate of item or person fit to the predictions of a latent trait model. As such, it serves as an indication of response validity for persons or items.

Formative Evaluation This is an evaluation which is ongoing and iterative during an instructional sequence. This kind of evaluation permits midstream adaptation and improvement of the program.

Frequency Distribution A frequency distribution is a sequential arrangement of obtained scores such that the horizontal axis reports the score and the vertical ordinate reports the frequency or number of times that score has occurred in the distribution.

Gain Scores Gain scores are obtained as the difference between a pretest and a posttest administration of the same or an equivalent test. As such gain scores are usually employed as a measure of achievement.

Growth Referenced Evaluation This is an instructional program evaluation technique relying on correlational and cross-sectional data to ascertain critical areas for program intervention in a manner that is comparative and iterative rather than absolute and fixed.

Halo Effect A halo effect is a tendency on the part of respondents to inflate positive evaluations by consistency and arbitrarily giving high ratings. This tendency is often overcome by wording some questions negatively so that rating direction must change.

Heterotrait-Heteromethod Validity This is a kind of discriminant construct validity established according to multitrait-multimethod validation procedure when convergent validity coefficients exceed in magnitude their associated heterotrait-heteromethod correlation coefficients.

Heterotrait-Monomethod Validity This is a kind of discriminant construct validity established according to multitrait-multimethod validation procedure when convergent validity coefficients exceed in magnitude their associated heterotrait-monomethod correlation coefficients.

Homoscedasticity This is a property of a bivariate distribution when the variance is the same (i.e., homogeneous) at all points along the regression line. It is also an assumption of analysis of covariance that all within-cell slopes are equal (i.e., homogeneous).

IQ-Equivalent Scores These are used to approximate an intelligence quotient scale where mental age is divided by chronological age and multiplied by 100. IQ-equivalent scores are obtained by multiplying 15 by a given z-score and adding 100 to the product.

Indirect Test An indirect test is one that fosters inference about one kind of behavior or performance through measurement of another related kind of performance. An example would be the measurement of vocabulary use through a test of vocabulary recognition.

Information Function The information function of an item is the same as the item variance, or the product of the proportion who got it correct and the proportion who got it wrong. The item information function can be used to shape the test information function or curve.

Integrative Test An integrative test is one that measures knowledge of a variety of language features, modes, or skills simultaneously. An example would be dictation, which could be used to measure listening comprehension, spelling, or general language proficiency.

Internal Consistency This refers to a group of methods for estimation of test reliability that depend on homogeneity of item variance as a reflection of consistency of scoring. Such methods include split half, Kuder-Richardson 20 and 21, and Cronbach's alpha.

Interrater Reliability Interrater reliabilty is a method of estimating the reliability of independent ratings. It consists of the correlation between different raters' ratings of the same objects or performances, adjusted by the Spearman-Brown Prophecy Formula.

Interval Scale An interval scale is more precise than a nominal or ordinal scale in that it permits not only quantification and ranking but assessment on a continuum having equal units of measurement. It differs from a ratio scale in its lack of a zero or origin.

Item Bank An item bank is a collection of test items administered and analyzed for use with an intended population. The bank also contains information about the items and links them to a common difficulty scale using latent trait measurement procedures.

Item Response Theory This is another term for latent trait theory. It refers to a family of probabilistic models for positioning person and item response parameters along a hypothesized continuum and testing goodness of fit to model predictions.

Kuder-Richardson Reliability This refers to two formulas (i.e., KR-20 and 21) used to estimate internal consistency reliability of a test. KR-20, like Cronbach's alpha, provides the same estimate as the mean of all possible split-half reliability estimations for the same test.

Kurtosis Kurtosis is a departure from normalcy in a distribution such that the distribution is either flatter than (i.e., platykurtic) or more peaked than (i.e., leptokurtic) the normal distribution.

Latent Trait Theory Latent trait or item response theory unlike classical theory consists of a family of probabilistic models locating person and item parameters of ability, difficulty, discriminability, and guessing on characteristic curves on a latent trait continuum.

Likert Scale This rating scale is used to determine comparative magnitude of some attitude or opinion in the respondent. Typically the scale has five points, ranging from Strongly Agree to Strongly Disagree, to show amount of agreement with a series of assertions.

Line of Best Fit The line of best fit is another term for the regression line used in regression analysis.

Linear Transformation A linear transformation takes place when a constant or set of constants is arithmetically applied to a distribution of scores in order to change the form of the distribution. Converson from a raw score to a percentage score is an example.

Link   A link is a group of items or persons calibrated for difficulty or ability according to a latent trait model and chosen for the purpose of equating tests or joining newly calibrated items to the same measurement scale used with an existing item bank.

Logit   A logit is a unit of measurement on an interval latent trait scale. It is derived by natural logarithmic transformation of proportion-correct/incorrect ratios, and scalar adjustment for test length and sample size.

Mean   The mean is the arithmetic average obtained by summing the scores and dividing by the total frequency or number of occurrences.

Median   The median is the centermost score in a distribution of scores arranged in sequence. In even-numbered distributions with no central score, the median is either the midpoint between the two centerbounding scores or a weighted point between them.

Mode   The mode of a distribution is the point at which scores occur most frequently (i.e., the highest point of the distribution curve). Some distributions are irregular, having more than one mode. Such distributions are called bimodal or polymodal.

Multi-Stage Test   A multi-stage test is one which bases selection of successive subtests to be attempted on performance with prior subtests already attempted. This kind of computer adaptive or tailored test minimizes the number of items needed for accurate decisions.

Multiple Correlation and Regression   These multivariate statistical procedures are used to combine overlapping relationships to form a non-redundant composite (correlation) and to predict a dependent variable with multiple independent variables (regression).

Multitrait-Multimethod Validation   This is a technique originated by Campbell and Fiske (1959) for the testing of construct validity through the examination of a correlation matrix of specified traits and methods.

Need-Press Interaction Analysis   This is a survey technique for evaluation of instructional programs. It involves eliciting student ratings of components of the programs with regard to importance (need) and emphasis (press). Components with inappropriate emphasis are identified.

Nominal Scale   A nominal scale permits frequency tallies of categorical data. It is used to quantify the number of cases, occurrences, or instances of objects or phenomena under specific classifications or categories.

Norm-Referenced Test   A norm-referenced test evaluates ability against a standard of mean or normative performance of a group. It usually implies standardization through prior administration to a large sample of examinees.

Normal Distribution   A normal distribution is a frequency distribution in which mean, mode, and median are equal, the shape is symmetrical around the mean, the tails are asymptotic, and the curve inflection points are plus and minus one standard deviation from the mean.

Normal Distribution Area Proportion   This is the proportion of a normal distribution accounted for at any given point along the z-score continuum. It is the proportion of the total area under the normal curve, which is delimited by a vertical line from the given z-score point.

Normalization Transformation   This transformation is used to standardize or normalize a distribution of scores as by z-score transformation. Also, sometimes logarithmic and trigonometric transformations are used to make deviant distributions conform to the normal distribution.

Objective Test An objective test is one that can be scored with reference to a scoring key and, therefore, does not require expert judgment in the scoring process. This is unlike a subjective test that depends on impression and opinion at the time of scoring.

Objectives-Referenced Test An objectives-referenced test is a test constructed with items or tasks constructed to match objectives without reference to a pre-established domain of objective-based items or tasks typical of a criterion-referenced test.

One Parameter Model This refers to a variety of latent trait measurement models, such as the Rasch Model, that operate with a single ability/difficulty scale for the calibration of persons and items and the estimation of fit to model predictions of response patterns.

Ordinal Scale An ordinal scale is one that permits merely a rank ordering of persons or other objects of assessment with regard to comparative standing in the group of those examined. Raw scores or ordinal rankings fall into this category.

Parallel Forms Parallel or random parallel forms are forms of a test that are constructed according to specifications in order to be similar in content and statistical characteristics. The correlation between such forms is one method used to estimate reliability.

Parameter A parameter is a quantitative characteristic of a population. It is signified by a Greek symbol. Because of the frequent inaccessibility of populations, a parameter is often unknown and only estimated by means of a statistic.

Part-Whole Overlap Part-whole overlap is a phenomenon that occurs when a component variable such as item scores are correlated with a composite variable like test scores. The inflation due to the presence of the component in the composite can be removed by correction.

Path Analysis Path analysis is a multiple regression procedure for comparing the explanatory efficacy of causal models. It assumes superiority of more parsimonious models requiring fewer explanatory paths to account for the same predictive relationships.

Percentage Score The percentage score is equal to the number of correct items divided by the total number of items on the test, times 100. It is also expressible as 100 times the obtained score divided by the total score possible.

Percentile Score or Rank This is found by adding the number of examinees scoring below a given examinee to one-half the number obtaining the same score, dividing this total by the total number of examinees, and multiplying by 100.

Person Separability This is another term for reliability or consistency of measurement. It occurs when person scores are widely dispersed on the scoring continuum so that it is unlikely that they would change rank order on repeated measurement.

Phi Coefficient A phi coefficient is a variation of product-moment correlation used to show the strength of relationship between, and the covarying of, two binary variables, such as scores for two test items scored as correct $= 1$ and incorrect $= 0$.

Point Biserial Correlation Point biserial correlation is the correlation between a binary and a continuous variable, such as between item scores and test scores. It is a variation of the usual Pearson product-moment correlation.

Population A population is a total aggregation of all persons or observations within a certain category. Usually the number is so great that it is not possible to examine them all, and instead estimates are made of their parameters based on a random sample.

Portfolio Evaluation   This is a technique for qualitative evaluation of instructional programs. It is characterized by teacher and administrator involvement in the regular maintaining of descriptive files recording ongoing programmatic teaching and learning experiences.

Possible Range   This is the range of scores possible on a test. For a test of 100 items, the possible range of raw scores would be from zero to 100.

Power Test   A power test is one that allows sufficient time for nearly all examinees to complete it, but which contains material of sufficient difficulty that it is not expected that a majority of examinees will get every item correct.

Predictive Validity   Predictive validity is an indication of how well a test predicts intended performance. A university admissions test is said to have predictive validity if its scores correlate highly with a performance criterion such as university grades.

Proficiency Test   A proficiency test measures general ability or skill, as opposed to an achievement test that measures the extent of learning of specific material presented in a particular course, textbook, or program of instruction.

Random Parallel Forms   Random parallel forms of a test use the same item specifications in constructing parallel content domains from which equivalent numbers of items are drawn at random to comprise tests that are presumed comparable in content, difficulty, and length.

Rasch Model   The Rasch Model is a family of one-parameter logistic latent trait measurement models used to calibrate item difficulty and person ability and give probabilistic estimates of performance fit to model predictions of person-to-item response behavior.

Ratio Scale   A ratio scale is an interval scale with the added feature that it has an origin or zero point at which none of the quality measured is present. Examples would be minutes, inches, or kilograms used to measure rate, height, or weight.

Raw Score   The raw score is the score obtained on a test before any adjustment, transformation, weighting, or rescaling is done. On an item-based test the raw score is usually equal to the sum of the correct items.

Regression Line   The regression line or line of best fit is the central line through a bivariate scatterplot that best shows the linear relationship between the two variables. The line is defined as $Y = a + bX$, and the constants a and b are the y-intercept and slope.

Reliability   Reliability refers to the consistency of the scores obtainable from a test. It is usually an estimate on a scale of zero to one of the likelihood that the test would rank testees in the same order from one administration to another proximate one.

Response Validity   Response validity is the extent to which examinee responses to a test or questionnaire can be said to reflect the intended purpose in measurement. Lack of adequate instructions, incentives, task familiarity, or courtesy could invalidate responses.

Sample   A sample is a subgroup of persons or observations drawn from a population for research purposes. The sampling procedure may be systematic, random, stratified, proportional, or a combination of these.

Scoring Matrix   A scoring matrix is a response grid used to organize and record the responses for all items in a test battery by every examinee considered.

Semantic Differential Semantic differential is a scale, often with seven points, for rating position on a continuum between opposing descriptors, such as rich-poor, good-bad, etc. These items are usually nonadditive, clustering in evaluative, activity, and potency domains.

Significance Statistical significance, or alpha, is the probability, p, of type I error of generalizing a statistic from a sample to its population. By convention, p is usually set to be less than 0.05 to permit rejection of a null hypothesis.

Skew Skew is a deviation from the normal distribution such that the pattern of scores is not symmetrical around the mean. Positive skew occurs with difficult tests having an extended distribution tail to the right; negative skew, easy tests, to the left.

Slope The slope is the rate of increment of the regression line. It is equal to the rise divided by the run, to the tangent of the angle of incline, or to the product of the correlation of X with Y and the ratio of the standard deviations of Y and X.

Spearman-Brown Prophecy Formula This is a formula used to adjust estimates of reliability to coincide with changes in the numbers of items or independent raters in a test. It may also be used to predict numbers of items or raters needed in order to achieve specified reliabilities.

Speed Test A speed test is one that limits time allowed for completion so that the majority of examinees would not be expected to finish it. The material contained in the test is usually so easy that, given enough time, most persons would respond correctly.

Split-Half Reliability This is a method for estimating internal consistency reliability. It involves dividing a test into two nearly equal parts, correlating the scores together for the two parts, and adjusting this coefficient using the Spearman-Brown Prophecy Formula.

Standard Error of Estimate The standard error of estimate is the standard deviation of the distribution of errors made in predicting values in variable Y from values in variable X. It equals the standard deviation of Y times the square root of one-minus-the-correlation-square.

Standard Error of Measurement This is the standard distribution of the errors of measurement in a scoring distribution. It is obtained as the standard deviation of test scores times the square root of the quantity, one minus the reliability coefficient.

Standardized Test A standardized test is one that has been administered to a large group of examinees from a target population, often more than 1000 persons, and has been analyzed and normed for use with other samples from that population.

Stanine Scores Stanines or standard nines comprise a nine-point interval scale with a mean of five and a standard deviation of 1.96, except at the ends of the distribution where there is a slight distortion due to the desire to maintain just nine points.

Statistic A statistic is a quantifiable characteristic of a sample, and it is most frequently used as an estimate of a population parameter. It is usually signified by a Latin symbol.

Step Ladder Test This is a kind of computer adaptive test that groups items at successive stages along the latent difficulty continuum. The score obtained on the test is the stage reached, as shown by the proportion of correct items at successive stages attempted.

Summative Evaluation Evaluation that comes at the conclusion of an educational program or instructional sequence.

T-Score The T-score or standard score, as distinct from the t-value obtained with the t-test, is from a distribution designed to have a mean of 50 and a standard deviation of 10. A T-score is equal to 10 times the respective z-score, plus 50.

t-Test This is a procedure for determining whether the difference between two means is statistically significant. It is also applied to test the difference between correlation coefficients and to measure goodness of fit to the Rasch Model.

Tailedness Tailedness refers to specificity of hypothesized outcomes. Some hypotheses are stated as allowing two directions of outcomes or "tails" (e.g., positive or negative, less than or greater than). More powerful hypotheses permit only one tail.

Test Tailoring Test tailoring is the process of designing tests for particular outcome decisions matching specific examinee characteristics. It includes shaping the test information function, constructing multi-stage tests, and using computer adaptive tests.

Test-Retest Reliability This is an estimate of the consistency of scores with a given test. It is obtained by testing the same persons with the same test at two different times within a reasonable time interval and correlating the scores from the two administrations.

Tetrachoric Correlation This is a correlation between two variables that are normally distributed and artificially dichotomized. If the variables are scored 1 and 0, then computation of a tetrachoric is the same as a phi coefficient and product-moment formulas also apply.

Three Parameter Model This is a latent trait measurement model that usually incorporates estimates of ability/difficulty, discriminability, and guessing. The guessing parameter is often called the lower asymptote parameter since it does not measure guessing only.

Translation Constant A translation constant is an arithmetic adjustment derived from a set of linking items or persons, used to place items from a newly analyzed test on the same latent trait scale with the same origin as that of items from a previous test or item bank.

True Score This is the actual score an examinee would be expected to obtain if no measurement error were present at the time of testing or scoring.

Truncation Truncation is a phenomenon that occurs when a portion of the range of the distribution of a variable has been eliminated or constrained. It usually results in artificially low coefficients of correlation, reliability, or validity.

Two Parameter Model A two parameter model is a latent trait measurement model that includes an additional measurement parameter beyond the ability/difficulty parameter of one parameter models. Usually this second parameter is an item discriminability parameter.

Validity Validity is the extent to which a test measures the ability or knowledge that it is purported to measure.

Variance Variance is a measure of dispersion around the mean. It is equal to the square of the standard deviation, and is obtained as the mean squared difference between observed scores and the mean.

Y-Intercept The Y-intercept is the point at which the regression line crosses the Y axis or ordinate. It is measured in units of Y.

z-Score The z-score or standard deviation score represents the number of standard deviations the raw score is located from the mean score. It is obtained by subtracting the mean score from the raw score and dividing the result by the standard deviation.